VIKING SOCIETY FOR NORTHERN RESEARCH
TEXT SERIES

GENERAL EDITORS

Anthony Faulkes and Richard Perkins

VOLUME XV

THOR THE WIND-RAISER
AND THE EYRARLAND IMAGE

The Eyrarland image (Þjms 10880).
(By kind permission of the photographer, Páll Stefánsson.)

# THOR THE WIND-RAISER
# AND THE EYRARLAND IMAGE

BY
RICHARD PERKINS

VIKING SOCIETY FOR NORTHERN RESEARCH
UNIVERSITY COLLEGE LONDON
2001

© Richard Perkins 2001

ISBN 0 903521 52 0

Printed by Short Run Press Limited, Exeter

The cover picture is of the amber figure from Feddet, Roholte parish, Sjælland, Denmark (= FI; DNM C24292; height: 4.6 cm.). (By permission of Nationalmuseet, Copenhagen.) Cf. also Figure 6.

TILL INGEGERD
$20\frac{14}{7}01$

## CONTENTS

LIST OF FIGURES ......................................................................... viii
PREFACE ....................................................................................... ix
CHAPTER ONE: Wind-power and wind-gods ................................ 1
CHAPTER TWO: An episode in *Rǫgnvalds þáttr ok Rauðs* .......... 27
CHAPTER THREE: Three beard-clutching figures ....................... 53
CHAPTER FOUR: The Eyrarland image ........................................ 82
CHAPTER FIVE: Conclusions. Contexts ..................................... 150
APPENDIX: *Rǫgnvalds þáttr ok Rauðs* and 'Rauðs þáttr ins ramma'  159
BIBLIOGRAPHY AND ABBREVIATIONS ................................. 165

# LIST OF FIGURES

The Eyrarland image .................................................... *Frontispiece*
1: Vignette from Olaus Magnus's *Historia* ................................. 12
2: AM 61, fol., f. 34ra, lines 22–37 ........................................... 37
3: Walrus-ivory figure from Lund, Skåne, Sweden ..................... 64
4: The Lund figure (reverse) ..................................................... 65
5: The Lund figure compared with Swedish Thor's hammer ....... 67
6: Amber figure from Feddet, Denmark .................................... 69
7: Bronze figure from Chernigov, Ukraine ................................. 71
8: Vėjopatis ............................................................................... 79
9: Pictures of the Eyrarland image from *Iduna* ......................... 84
10: The Eyrarland image (side view) ........................................... 86
11: The Eyrarland image (front view) .......................................... 87
12: Silver pendant from Foss, Iceland .......................................... 91
13: Rune-stone at Ledberg, Sweden ............................................. 98
14: The rune-stone at Ledberg (reverse) ....................................... 99
15: Bronze image from Rällinge, Sweden ................................... 100
16: Bronze image from Lindby, Skåne, Sweden .......................... 101
17: Thor's hammer from Eketorp, Sweden ................................. 110
18: *Þórshamar* ........................................................................ 110
19: Rune-stone from near Grästorp, Sweden ............................. 111
20: Runic rock at Norra Åby, Sweden ........................................ 112
21: Rune-stone at Stenkvista church, Sweden ............................ 113
22: Lead alloy mask from Ribe, Denmark .................................. 114
23: Thor's hammers from Hilda, Norway .................................. 116
24: Thor's hammer from Skåne, Sweden .................................... 120
25: Thor's hammer from Er(ik)storp, Sweden ............................ 120
26: Thor's hammer from Bredsätra, Öland, Sweden ................... 121
27: Thor's hammer from Mandemarke, Denmark ...................... 121
28: Pendant from Rauðnefsstaðir, Iceland .................................. 129
29: Whalebone figure from Baldursheimur, Iceland ................... 135
30: Séra Jón Prímus at his chess-board ....................................... 138
31: Thor's hammers from Vålse and Sejerby, Denmark .............. 142
32: Buddha from Helgö, Sweden ............................................... 145
33: Egyptian amulet, clasping *was*-sceptre ............................... 147
34: Egyptian amulet, lion-headed .............................................. 147
35: Egyptian amulet, archer ...................................................... 147

# PREFACE

The immediate stimulus for the present study which concerns amongst other things the Eyrarland image was an article by the distinguished Icelandic archaeologist Kristján Eldjárn. In the memorial volume for Gabriel Turville-Petre of 1981, Kristján put forward an interpretation of the Eyrarland image which he expressly intended to provoke discussion and reassessment. His arguments were tentatively presented, with learning and good humour. They certainly had a provocative and catalytic effect on me and I counter them in my Chapter 4. Although, then, as will be seen, I disagree with various of Kristján's arguments in their essentials, I owe him a special debt of gratitude for drawing attention to problems connected with the Eyrarland image.

The work of three British scholars has had particular influence on this book. Not only did Gabriel Turville-Petre, whom I have just mentioned, give me my first scholarly introduction to Norse mythology, but, as will be seen, I draw extensively on his *Myth and religion of the North*, first published in 1964. This book remains one of the most humane and balanced treatments of the subject perhaps in any language. In the writings of Hilda Ellis Davidson, I have found a number of thought-provoking observations about Thor suggestive of various of the conclusions I arrive at myself. Some of the ideas I put forward in this monograph will scarcely come as much surprise to her. Thirdly, a work by a former member of University College London has been of special interest to me: George Stephens's *Thunor the Thunderer, carved on a Scandinavian font of about the year 1000* of 1878 is a decidedly idiosyncratic work by present-day standards. I am afraid that I am as little able to accept the main thesis of this work as I am that of Kristján Eldjárn's article. In it, however, Stephens makes a number of valuable observations on the iconography of Thor which certainly deserve more attention than they have received over the years. I became aware of Stephens's arguments at a relatively late stage in my research for this volume, but found them corroborative and reassuring when I did.

In this study, I necessarily take an interdisciplinary approach. In particular, I stray from my home ground of philology and allied subjects into the field of archaeology where I tread far less confidently. In an article of 1900 cited in my bibliography, the German classical philologist Hermann Usener wrote 'ich fühle mich nur als Gast unter den

Archäologen', and I feel very much the same in the present context. Archaeologists will doubtless detect much which reveals amateurism and ignorance in my approach. Whatever shortcomings exist in this respect, however, they are not for want of generous help from archaeologist colleagues and those in allied fields. Readers will readily discern my indebtedness to the published catalogues of Viking-Age and Norse antiquities of James Graham-Campbell (1980) and Else Roesdahl (1992), both of whom have also aided me in other ways than through their writings. I have received much kind co-operation from colleagues at museums in Scandinavia. At Statens Historiska Museum in Stockholm, Elsie Lindström was the epitome of efficiency and helpfulness. Claes Wahlöö and Maria Cinthio at Kulturen in Lund showed and discussed with me the walrus-ivory figure in that collection which is one of the subjects of my third chapter. In Västerås, Krister Ström shared his specialist knowledge of Thor's hammers with me. Sigrid Kaland gave me information on Thor's hammers in Historisk Museum in Bergen. Elisabeth Munksgaard and Helga Schütze provided me prompt answers to a number of queries about objects in Nationalmuseet in Copenhagen.

But I have also had much help from scholars other than archaeologists. Rory McTurk gave me pertinent bibliographical references, Peter Foote read and criticised the monograph in draft and Jeffrey Cosser assisted me in various ways, not least by translating material from Russian. I also had help with Russian from Gavin Orton, and David Dixon allowed me to benefit from his huge expertise in Egyptological matters. I received invaluable lexicographical information from Guðrún Kvaran and Gunnlaugur Ingólfsson of Orðabók Háskólans in Reykjavík and from Christopher Sanders of the Arnamagnæan Dictionary in Copenhagen. Of librarian colleagues who have been unfailingly helpful I should particularly mention John Townsend, Bess Ryder and Anna-Lisa Murrell in London, Ólöf Benediktsdóttir in Reykjavík and Olle Andersson in Lund. Birutė Butkevičienė, Director of Vilnius University Library kindly arranged for me to receive the picture I have as my Figure 8. Marit Åhlén and Thorgunn Snædal at Runverket in Stockholm discussed runological matters with me and not least the runic rock at Åby in Södermanland which I regard as significant for my arguments in Chapter 4. Desmond Slay kindly read a proof and made suggestions for improvements.

## Preface

There are five Icelandic colleagues to whom I am especially indebted: Þór Magnússon, formerly Þjóðminjavörður, allowed me to inspect the object in his keeping which I believe to represent his namesake and gave me information about it which I would not have discovered by myself. Ólafur Halldórsson provided me with unpublished material and much other information on *Óláfs saga Tryggvasonar in mesta* which contains a passage of key significance for the present study and on which he is the expert. Helgi Guðmundsson made suggestions for lines of investigation which proved very fruitful. Guðrún Sveinbjarnardóttir helped me in several different ways, not least to bridge the gap between London and Reykjavík. And Stefán Karlsson showed me exceptional hospitality while I was in Iceland researching this study.

I should here also record my gratitude for grants to the Dean's Travel Fund of the Faculty of Arts and Humanities of University College London which helped to cover the costs of visits to Scandinavia, including Iceland, to research the present study.

Lastly I wish particularly to thank my co-editor of the Viking Society's Text Series, Anthony Faulkes. The publication of this volume owes much to his positive approach, technical skills, patience and care. I have been fortunate in having him as a collaborator.

To all these colleagues, then, and to others whom I must regrettably leave unmentioned, I extend my warmest thanks for time and trouble taken and for good offices. The shortcomings and imperfections which doubtless remain in this book after help and assistance generously given are, of course, entirely my own responsibility.

Richard Perkins<br>
Department of Scandinavian Studies<br>
University College London<br>
November, 2001

CHAPTER ONE

## WIND-POWER AND WIND-GODS

> Austmenn... kváðu seint mundu at róa til Nóregs.
> *BANDAMANNA SAGA*
>
> Remorum ductus velorum vincitur usu.
> *SAXONIS GESTA DANORUM*
>
> 'Thor,' inquiunt, '... ventos... gubernat.'
> ADAM OF BREMEN

THE EXPANSION of the Scandinavian peoples during the Viking Age is striking more for its range than for the permanent effect it had on World History. We find, for example, the Norse at L'Anse aux Meadows in northern Newfoundland and they doubtless got further down the Atlantic coasts of North America. In the east, a number of sources written in Arabic tell us how the Rus invaded the town of Barda in Azerbaijan in c. 943; according to one source they sometimes even travelled to the capital of the Caliphate itself, Baghdad, and then with the help of camel transport (see Birkeland, 1954, 54–58; 11). And we find the Norse, perhaps rather after the end of the Viking Age, probably as far north as Spitsbergen and, if not there, on Jan Mayen; we find them far up the west coast of Greenland (see *KL*, s.v. *Opdagelsesrejser* and references). And as early as the ninth century Vikings are attacking towns along the North African littoral, for example, Nakur (in present-day Morocco) and Alexandria in Egypt (see, for example, Birkeland, 1954, 46). But it is, of course, a fact that the permanent impression made by Viking-Age Scandinavians over the huge area of their activity is not so impressive. It is really only in the Faroes and Iceland of the places colonised during the Viking Age that medieval Norse culture can be said to have endured in continuity down to the present day. Elsewhere the Scandinavians withdrew, were driven out, were exterminated or, little by little, allowed their Scandinavian culture to be absorbed into another one. One imagines, for example, that the inhabitants of L'Anse aux Meadows simply abandoned their settlement and returned, presumably to Greenland.

The Rus were driven out of Barda in disease-ridden disarray by a local potentate. In Greenland itself, the Norse colonies died out, their inhabitants exterminated probably by a combination of disease and malnutrition, and perhaps attacks by the Eskimos. In Russia, France and England, Norse culture and language gave way to others, more local, or larger or superior. This, of course, is not to belittle the part played by Scandinavians in, to take some rather random examples, the establishment of coastal towns in Ireland, the foundation of the duchy of Normandy and perhaps even of the principality of Kiev. And we must remember in this context that the Norse of the Viking Age were more adaptable than many other peoples. But in terms of broader, permanent, long-term effects, the Viking-Age expansion stands in stark contrast to the age of Islamic conquests in the seventh and eighth centuries, which led, in time, to the spread of the Arabic language and Islam to large parts of Asia and Africa. And it stands, of course, in even starker contrast to the sea-borne expansion of the European nations (most notably the English, Spanish, Portuguese, Dutch and French) beginning around 1500, which led to widespread and permanent European colonisation and the dissemination of European culture and Christianity in vast areas all over the world. But the fact remains that the Vikings and the Norse had an extraordinary genius for 'getting places'. They 'travelled widely' (cf., for example, the suggestive title of Lundström's book of 1981, *De kommo vida . . .*, and his remarks on pp. 11–12 with respect to Gotland Vikings). Before the beginning of the modern age, few peoples can have moved with such relative facility throughout so wide and varied an area. Given this fact, then, it will not be inappropriate in the present context to attempt to identify the principal locomotive forces which the Norse exploited or were subject to in their movement throughout this area. It need hardly be stressed, of course, that one of their main means of travel was over water, by ship or boat. And again, it need scarcely be stressed that we are considering an age before the invention of the steam-engine, the internal-combustion engine, the electric motor, the nuclear engine, the rocket and the like. Perhaps rather roughly and amateurishly, I would identify and itemise the principal physical forces which provided locomotion for the medieval Norse (as well as, of course, for many other peoples before the beginning of the modern age) as follows:

(1) currents;
(2) gravity (of the Earth, Moon, Sun);
(3) centrifugal force;
(4) animal muscle-power (either human or non-human);
(5) wind (for sailing).[1]

This list may be elaborated on a little. The first three items are relatively minor. Currents at sea can certainly move ships and, to take another random example, the Norse would of course have benefited (whether unwittingly or otherwise) from the North Atlantic Drift at some time or other to aid their movements. The gravity of the Earth, for example, causes the waters of rivers to flow to the sea and to carry vessels with them; for example, the Rus merchants mentioned by Constantine Porphyrogenitus in ch. 9 of his *De administrando imperio* (*DAI*) would, of course, have been happy to let the flowing waters of the River Dnieper carry their *monoxyla* from Kiev down towards the Black Sea.[2] And a medieval Icelandic *sigamaður*, perhaps somewhat more nervously, might well have relied on the force of gravity, counteracted, of course, by checks and balances above him, to aid his descent down some sheer cliff-side to collect the eggs or feathers of sea-birds or to catch the birds themselves. And the gravitational forces of the Sun, Moon and also centrifugal force can cause or affect tides. Seafarers often exploit tides, where they exist, in their movements; and some scholars have pointed to the tactical advantages the shallow-drafted Viking ships could derive from tides to make speedy retreat after raids, not least around the coasts of Britain where tides are so pronounced

---

[1] The wind was, of course, normally exploited in the Viking Age to propel sailing-vessels *over water*. But the suggestion made in *RPC* (64) that it might sometimes have been used to assist the movement of wheeled vehicles *over land* is perhaps not quite as fantastic as it may at first sight seem; on this, cf. Obolensky, 1974, 243–244; *ER*, 115. In addition, it would doubtless have been used to aid the movement of sledges (and the like) *over ice* (cf. the ice-boats of more recent times). When *wind-mills* were introduced into Scandinavia, probably in the thirteenth century, the wind would of course have been used to drive those. And the wind may, of course, assist walkers, swimmers, skaters, etc. in their progress.

[2] They might also have been happy that one of the commodities they carried, slaves, would have been, as *ER* (119), puts it, 'self-propelling' (cf. item 4 in the list above) and thus well suited for negotiating the Dnieper Rapids.

(cf., for example, Almgren, 1963). But it is items 4 and 5 on the list above which have particular importance as locomotive forces in the context of Norse movement and travel. Animal muscle-power was of prime importance in this context. The *sigamaður* we have just left suspended on a cliff-side in Iceland will soon be hoping, again perhaps not without a certain nervousness, that his comrades above him will soon exert an animal muscle-power greater than that of gravity and pull him back up to safety at the top of the cliff. Altogether they will then again employ animal muscle-power in *walking* back to the *byggð* with their gains. And generally, of course, the use of muscle-power in walking was, and still is, the most common form of locomotion amongst humans. The Norse employed it in this activity no less, and perhaps considerably more, than other peoples, as, to take a third random example, a reading of *Sverris saga* will make clear. The medieval Norse were, of course, as ready to exploit non-human muscle-power as a means of locomotion as any other people. It is well known, for example, that the horse was often employed as a means of transport in medieval Iceland (where the terrain is often especially suited to the movement of that animal); medieval Icelanders travelled on horseback relatively quickly and efficiently throughout their country. And if we are to believe the source in Arabic mentioned above (Birkeland, 1954, 11), which tells how the Rus travelled from the southern end of the Caspian to Baghdad using camels, then we realise how exploitatively adaptable in matters of transport the Norse might be. In connection with the use of human muscle-power for travel over water, mention must, of course, be made of rowing, an activity of particular importance to the Vikings and the Norse in general. Indeed, it was the co-ordination of human muscle-power of often large numbers of oarsmen on rowed ships which played such an important part in the Viking-Age expansion of the Norse peoples. For example, it was the use of the oar which took Scandinavians of the Viking Age up the rivers of eastern Europe and thus opened up routes through Russia between the Baltic on the one hand and the Black Sea and the Caspian on the other; it was the use of the oar which enabled them to attack such inland towns as Paris and Seville; it was often the use of the oar which seems to have facilitated quick retreat by Vikings making raids on the coasts of the British Isles, western Europe and elsewhere; and it was the use of rowed ships which allowed the Vikings to establish bases and trading posts in places inaccessible to less manœuvrable vessels. Indeed, it is quite possible that the very words *víkingr* and *Rus* have their origins in the activity of rowing (see Daggfeldt, 1983, and Holm, 1992, 120–121; cf. also, for example, Ekbo, 1986). Much could be said on the subject of the use of rowing by the Norse and I have made some remarks on the matter elsewhere (see Perkins, 1984–1985, particularly pp. 155–156 and references); its significance in this context cannot be overestimated. But with this said we turn now to item 5 on the list above. It is, amongst other things, to the wind as a locomotive force that special attention will be given in this study.

In considering the wind as a locomotive force in the Norse context, an episode found in the Icelandic *Bandamanna saga* (ch. 11; *ÍF*, VII, 358) is relevant. Oddr Ófeigsson is waiting wind-bound in Þorgeirsfjörður (just to the east of the mouth of Eyjafjörður in northern Iceland) to sail abroad to buy materials to brew beer for his wedding-feast. Also waiting in the same place are some Norwegian merchants. Oddr climbs a high mountain and thinks that he sees that the wind conditions out at sea are more favourable. He returns to his *knǫrr* and has his men row it out of the fjord towards the open ocean. When the Norwegians see this, Oddr becomes the butt of their derision: *Austmenn spotta þá ok kváðu seint mundu at róa til Nóregs*. Fictional though this story doubtless is, the Norwegians' derisive words (and this sort of taunt was scarcely the invention of the author of *Bandamanna saga*), contain an essential truth. I have stressed just above and elsewhere the special significance of rowing to the Norse. But as the Norwegians suggest, one would hardly row from Iceland to Norway. And it goes without saying that the converse is also true. Indeed it is reasonable to say that the sail and wind-power were the *sine qua non* of 'the Norse Atlantic saga'. It may have been possible to row a good part of the distance from, say, Sweden to the opposite shore of the Baltic (although even there the sail would normally have been used). But in the Viking-Age movement westwards across the Atlantic (to the Faroes, Iceland, Greenland and North America) the use of the sail was indispensable. Indeed without the sail, it is unlikely that, for example, Iceland would have been colonised by the Norse in the Viking Age.[3] And it would

---

[3] On the utilisation of wind for the Norse crossing the North Atlantic, cf. Schnall, 1975, 167–180 and *passim*.

also have been used wherever possible in numerous other contexts. A favourable wind could confer enormous advantages on its beneficiary, as the exaggerated story of Oddr Ófeigsson in *Bandamanna saga* just mentioned makes clear. Oddr seems to have been generally lucky with the wind and this luck contributes to his success in fishing and trade (see e.g. *ÍF*, VII, 297). In the episode in question, Oddr has arrived in Þorgeirsfjörður with a fair wind, probably from Miðfjörður. He is, as noted, weather-bound there, but only temporarily. As soon as he has had his *knǫrr* rowed out of the bay, he straightway gets a favourable wind (*byrr hagstæðr*) and is transported direct, not to Norway, but to Orkney without once having to reduce sail. There he buys his malt and corn and stays for a time; then he puts out to sea again, again gets a following wind, this time an *austanveðr*, a wind from the east. This bears him back to Iceland to Þorgeirsfjörður where he perhaps gains some amusement from finding the Norwegian merchants still weather-bound; and then he is wafted back west to Miðfjörður, his home and precisely the place he wants to be. The round trip has taken a mere seven weeks. We are told elsewhere in Old Norse literature how cheerful sailors were when they got a favourable wind (cf. Note 5 below). And we sometimes hear of considerable risks being taken to draw advantage from a favourable wind (cf., for example, *ÍF*, IX, 103).

Always to have a following wind was, then, as it were, to have a tiger in one's tank.[4] But the story told in *Bandamanna saga* is entirely

---

[4] In this connection we may note that various figures in the Old Norse world are represented in the literary sources as *always* having good fortune with the wind. Reference has been made to Oddr Ófeigsson in *Bandamanna saga* who seems to have been extraordinary fortunate with the wind. It is, however, nowhere suggested that he owed this to supernatural forces; nor is the adjective *byrsæll* ever used of him (although the word *farsæll* is). But other sources do mention *byrsælir menn* and imply a connection between them and sorcery or supernatural powers. The Hrafnistumenn, for example, always got a fair wind when they raised their sails in a calm; this, it is implied, was because of some special *list* or *íþrótt* which they practised, or some *ættargipt* with which they were endowed (see *Gríms saga loðinkinna*, ch. 2 (*FN*, II, 194); *Ǫrvar-Odds saga*, 1888, 18, 123). In *Hkr*, I, 325 (cf. Appendix), we are told of Rauðr inn rammi of Goðey that he owned a splendid ship and that he *hafði jafnan byr, hvert er hann vildi sigla, ok var þat af fjǫlkynngi hans*. And in *ÓT* (II, 128) it is recounted how, when on this ship, Rauðr *lét . . . vinda á segl sitt*. Of Óláfr Tryggvason, Oddr Snorrason (*ÓTOdd*, 150; cf. 151) tells us

unrealistic, verging on the ridiculous. And there was, of course, another side to the coin. Reliance on the wind for one's means of locomotion also has its disadvantages and this not least so in the Norse context. Now the question of the degree to which Scandinavian ships of the Viking Age and the late Middle Ages could cope with contrary winds is a difficult one to answer. Nor is it one which can be dealt with in detail here. We may, however, accept Falk's statement that Scandinavian ships of the Middle Ages were inferior to those of modern times by virtue of their much greater dependence on a favourable wind (cf., for example, *AS*, 19). If contrary winds were encountered, a ship would have to remain in harbour; or if it was at sea, the sail would have to be lowered, a favourable wind awaited and the ship often allowed to drift (cf. *VAch*, 248; note the reference to Oddr not having to lower his sail between Þorgeirsfjörður and Orkney). And another factor to notice in this context is, of course, the enigmatic nature of the wind. In the real world, there is a reason for everything; nothing is random. In the course of the last two or three thousand years or so, and more particularly since the Renaissance, man has come to understand more and more the true causes of the universe's phenomena and the way they work. But in the Middle Ages, the real causes for what we call 'wind' were as yet undiscovered and the phenomenon itself highly unpredictable. Indeed, of the five locomotive forces enumerated above (p. 3), it is the wind which must have seemed the most mysterious and the most capricious. Currents and tides were phenomena which, while their causes may have been unknown, were at least relatively predictable. There must have been few adult human beings who have not in the course of their lives come to terms with the force of the Earth's gravity and its effects. (It is precisely the absence of this force which modern spacemen who escape from its influence find so strange.) And animal muscle-power, whether human or otherwise, is very often not only predictable and immediate, but also reliable and manipulable, not least when subject to external incentives, threats and persuasion, sticks and carrots, whether real or metaphorical. For example, most healthy human beings can count on their own

---

that *hann var byrsælli en aðrir menn ok sigldi þat á einum degi er aðrir sigldu þrjá*. Óláfr must have owed his special gift in this respect to divine favour. And when he and the heathen Rauðr inn rammi came into conflict, it was, of course, Óláfr's Christian 'wind-power' which prevailed. Cf. also *Bósa saga*, 38.

muscle-power to walk and often also even to swim; or one might rely, for example, on a docile slave to fetch and carry or a placid horse to transport one over short distances; or one might depend on a crew of rowers, half in fear of pursuit and half in hope of a share of the booty, to pull in unison on the oars of a Viking ship which had just raided some hostile coast. But by contrast, the wind was extremely unreliable. Indeed, even in the modern age of advanced technology its movements and strengths are relatively unpredictable. It is true, of course, that the Norse would have made general observations about prevailing winds in particular places. It is also true that sooner or later a wind of desired direction and strength would blow at any place on the waters travelled by the Norse. But it might be a question of waiting days, weeks or perhaps even months for this to happen. In the mean time, those dependent on the wind for movement would have to reconcile themselves to inconvenience or hardship. We may take, for instance, the converse situation to that of Oddr, the plight of the Norwegian merchants whom Oddr left weather-bound in Þorgeirsfjörður. They would have spent a very frustrating several weeks there enduring a contrary wind. Oddr's breezing in from Orkney on that very same wind would have done nothing to improve their mood. And in general, the business of relying on the wind as a locomotive force must have been the same testing experience for medieval Norsemen as for others. It would have meant long periods of tedious, time-wasting and unproductive inactivity in the place in question, kicking one's heels, watching the weather-vane. If one owned a ship or had a share in one, the delay would doubtless have entailed material loss. For crew and passengers, it would have meant inconvenience and discomfort. If the difficult crossing of the North Atlantic (or even the North Sea or Baltic) were in prospect, a certain nervous apprehensiveness might well have hung over the ship's company. Tempers might have frayed, quarrels broken out, enmities conceived. And these would have been only the beginning of problems caused by contrary winds. Once at sea, one might, for example, be driven back to the place one came from (*at verða aptrreka*). Or one's ship might be becalmed in mid-ocean with the attendant afflictions, hunger, thirst, exposure, the general squalor. Finally, of course, the wrong sort of wind could lead to a vessel being wrecked or foundering with all that that entailed: at best loss of property, immense discomfort and hardship; at worst, injury and loss of life.

## Wind-power and wind-gods

Around the coasts of Viking-Age Scandinavia, on the North Atlantic, on the Baltic and on the North Sea, there were to be found ships' crews and companies waiting for a favourable wind to allow them to further their voyages and other activities at sea. Two manifestations of this necessity of waiting and watching for a wind may be briefly mentioned here. The first, already suggested, is the obvious presence on many medieval Scandinavian ships of weather-vanes, some of artistically very elaborate design. Several of these have been preserved. The one from Källunge, Gotland is a well-known example; cf. p. 91 below. And they are also found represented on ornaments (*VH*, 391), toy ships (*VArt*, 80–81), in pictures (*VAch*, 233) and referred to in literary sources. (See further on weather-vanes: *AS*, 42, 59; *KL*, s.v. *Vindfløj*; *VArt*, 79–80; Blindheim, 1982; *VH*, items 3 and 417; and references in all these places.) The second manifestation is the existence of set alliterative phrases in Icelandic and the medieval Scandinavian languages referring to a (favourable) wind (*byrr*) and the business of waiting for it. C–V (91) notes *blásandi byrr* (cf. p. 162 below for an example), *blíðr byrr* and *beggja skauta byrr* as 'allit. naut. phrases'. The expression *at bíða byrjar*, 'to wait for a fair wind', is found in Old Icelandic on a number of occasions. Random examples have been noted in the following places: *ÍF*, IV, 137; XIII, 278; XXVIII, 252; XXXIV, 235; *ÓT*, I, 145; *ÓH*, 49, 360, 362, 451; *Jónsbók*, 1970, 240. And the expression is paralleled in Old Norwegian, Old Swedish and Old Gutnish, for example, in *Konungs skuggsjá* (1920, 89), in the Law of Uppland (cf. Wessén, 1959, 22) and in *Guta lag och Guta saga* (1905–1907, I, 69); cf. also Söderwall, 1884–1918, I, 167 and references. The incidence of this expression in places as far apart as Iceland and Gotland suggests that it was used throughout Scandinavia. There was probably also an alliterative expression *at bíða* (*vind*)*býsna*, 'to wait for the culmination of a storm (i.e. until better weather conditions are in prospect)' (cf. *ÍF*, XXVI, 139 and references). Cf. also Fritzner, I, 222–223; p. 19 below.

The wind, then, was one of the most powerful forces known to man in the pre-modern period. A favourable wind was a highly desirable asset which could confer enormous advantages; a contrary wind, on the other hand, could bring with it manifold problems and adversities. At the same time, the wind was a capricious, incomprehensible, enigmatic phenomenon, its true causes virtually unknown and mysterious to the medieval Norsemen (as to many others). *Hávamál* (strophe 74; *Edda*, 28) reminds us of the fickleness of the wind: *fiolð um viðrir / á fimm dǫgum, / enn meira á mánaði*. Now in his *Heaven's breath* (1984, 114), Lyall Watson quotes Sir James Frazer as saying: 'Of all natural phenomena, there are, perhaps, none which civilised man feels himself more powerless to influence than the wind.' 'And yet,' Watson adds, 'we keep trying.' And in another place, Frazer (1963, 105) says: 'the savage thinks he can make the wind to blow or to be still.' Now the two statements by Frazer just cited are not, or course, necessarily mutually contradictory. And we may consider the second of them. A characteristic of *Homo sapiens*, whether primitive or civilised, is, it is probably fair to say, his strong tendency to attempt to influence his surroundings by whatever means he thinks possible. And if man cannot genuinely manipulate the world and natural phenomena by what might be regarded as normal means, he will have recourse to less rational approaches. He will turn to sorcery and magic; he will appeal to the supernatural; he will invoke the aid of his deities, whether greater or lesser gods, whether the Christian God or his saints. To what degree such expedients were clearly distinguished from more rational methods in the minds of those who adopted them is, of course, difficult to assess. In many cases, there was doubtless little or no distinction. And there was, of course, frequently an element of deceit in the minds of those who pretended to influence natural phenomena (not least wind and weather) by supernatural means. Be these things as they may, the desire to control in particular the wind and in general the weather by supernatural means led to the development of a whole branch of magic concerned with meteorology. The various forms of wind-magic may be classified as follows (cf. *HWDA*, s.v *Wind*):

(1) Prophylactic wind-magic.
(2) Positive wind-magic:
    (a) wind-magic for one's own advantage;
    (b) wind-magic to another's detriment.

Thus wind-magic might be resorted to, for example, to still a storm; or to produce a favourable wind for one's own sailing-vessel; or to raise a violent and destructive wind to cause loss to one's enemy. (Wind-magic of this last category seems to have been particularly common in the Iceland of past centuries; cf. the Icelandic *gerningaveður*.) In the present context any survey of wind-magic as a whole is, of course, not possible; for useful discussions of various aspects of it, the reader is referred to Frazer 1911, I, 244–331; 1963, 79–109; *HWDA*, s.v. *Wind*; *KL*, s.v. *Vindmagi*; Watson, 1984, *passim*. And it is really only to the second of the categories just mentioned (i.e. (2)(a)) that attention is given in the present contribution. Some examples of this form of wind-magic from various places in the world (but not least Scandinavia) will be given in what immediately follows.

It was a common custom of seamen when their ship was becalmed to attempt to raise a wind by whistling, a mild form of mimetic magic (cf. Frazer, 1911, I, 323 (Estonia); Cameron, 1903, 301 (Caithness); Solheim, 1940, 62 (Norway); Norlén, 1972, 69 (Sweden); Watson, 1984, 261–262; *Nihongi*, 1956, I, 106 (Japan); on mimetic magic in general, cf. also pp. 57–58 below). Mimetic magic was also involved in the use of a bull-roarer which was whirled around on the end of a cord producing a roaring sound and thus summoning the wind (Watson, 1984, 261). An elaborate procedure for wind-magic was found amongst the Haida Indians of the Queen Charlotte Islands of Canada (see Frazer, 1911, I, 320):

> When a Haida Indian wishes to obtain a fair wind, he fasts, shoots a raven, singes it in the fire, and then going to the edge of the sea sweeps it over the surface of the water four times in the direction in which he wishes the wind to blow. He then throws the raven behind him, but afterwards picks it up and sets it in a sitting posture at the foot of a spruce-tree, facing towards the required wind. Propping its beak open with a stick, he requests a fair wind for a certain number of days; then going away he lies covered up in his mantle till another Indian asks him for how many days he has desired the wind, which question he answers.

In another place, Frazer (1963, 106) writes that a 'way of making wind which is practised in New Guinea is to strike a "wind-stone" lightly with a stick; to strike it hard would bring on a hurricane'. Incantations and amulets of various kinds were, of course, often used in wind-magic. A 'wind-amulet' which seems to have been particularly used in Scandinavia as well as in the northern parts of the British Isles is referred to by Frazer (1963, 107), Granlund (*KL*, s.v. *Vindmagi*) and Watson (1984, 118–119). This consisted of a thread or cord or like object in which three knots were tied. The first of these three knots should be untied for a light wind, the second for a strong one; but the third should never be undone as this would produce a violent storm. There is an account of such objects (sold by Lapps) with a vignette in

Olaus Magnus's *Historia de gentibus septentrionalibus* (OM, 159; Figure 1) and they seem to have been found in Scotland down to the present century. And in recent folk-practice in Sweden and Swedish-speaking Finland, one attempted to call up a favourable wind (for sailing-vessels or perhaps wind-mills; cf. Note 1 above) by some such invocation as *Blås (på), Kajsa!* and by making an offering, for example, by throwing a coin over the top of the mast. The name *Kajsa*, Norlén (1972) has convincingly argued, must go back to a form of the name of St Katherine of Alexandria who was regarded as having special connections both with the weather and with seamen (cf. also Note 9 in Chapter 2 below). The following points may be stressed in the present context. It was, of course, before the advent of motorised vessels that positive wind-magic was particularly common amongst sea-faring peoples (cf. *HWDA*, IX, col. 645). As has been suggested, the Vikings were not only great exploiters of the wind but, because of the not entirely perfect nature of their sailing techniques, were very dependent on it for their movements by sailing-vessel. Wind-magic may probably be said to be more common amongst pagan peoples than, say, Christians, and the Scandinavians of the larger part of the Viking Age were pagans. From this we may say that the practice of wind-magic was probably more common in Viking-Age Scandinavia than in most other societies or cultures.

Figure 1: Buying knots for a fair wind. (From Olaus Magnus, *Historia de gentibus septentrionalibus*, 1555, book 3, ch. 16.)

I would suggest, then, that in the Old Norse world, it was believed that one could get a fair wind by magical or supernatural means. One might be able to buy one from magicians or from Lapps. One could get it by the use of amulets or incantations or a combination of both. One might be endowed with some special quality which always gave one good luck with the weather and a fair wind (cf. Note 4 above). And one could get it by the invocation of supernatural beings, heathen or Christian, God himself or pagan gods, minor demons or saints. It is this last expedient which will be given special attention in the present context. And here a passage from the Icelandic *Hallfreðar saga* (probably composed in the early thirteenth century) is of relevance.[5]

The story of how Hallfreðr Óttarsson was converted to Christianity by Óláfr Tryggvason in Trondheim is well known. And the account in *Hallfreðar saga* of how Hallfreðr arrives in Norway prior to his conversion is of special interest for present purposes. It may be quoted from the Möðruvallabók text of the saga (from *ÍF*, VIII, 151–152, with one change of punctuation), but with variants or additions (in square brackets) from the version of the saga in *Óláfs saga Tryggvasonar in mesta* (cf. *ÓT*, I, 347; *Hallfr*, 37–38):

> Ok eitt sumar, er hann (viz. Hallfreðr) kom af Íslandi, þá lágu þeir við Agðanes.[6] Þar hitta þeir menn at máli ok spurðu tíðenda. Þeim var sagt, at hǫfðingjaskipti var orðit í Nóregi; var Hákon jarl dauðr, en Óláfr Tryggvason kominn í staðinn með nýjum sið ok boðorðum. Þá urðu skiparar [skipverjar allir] á þat sáttir, at slá í heit [til þess at þeim gæfi byr

---

[5] A related account of the story of Hallfreðr's conversion (although of no particular relevance in the present context) is found in *ÓTOdd*, 122–126; *Hkr*, I, 328–333; *Kristni saga*, 1892–1896, 139. Hallfreðr is found at Agðanes on an entirely different occasion, in *Gunnlaugs saga ormstungu*, ch. 10 (*ÍF*, III, 84–85), in the time of Eiríkr jarl. On that occasion Hallfreðr transports Gunnlaugr to Iceland. They immediately get a favourable wind, *váru vel kátir*, and Gunnlaugr declaims a verse which mentions the wind. The author of *Gunnlaugs saga* probably knew *Hallfreðar saga*.

[6] Agðanes (modern Norwegian *Agdenes*) lies on the south side of the mouth of Trondheimsfjorden, about 40 km. as the crow flies from Trondheim. It was an important harbour in the medieval period. Because of difficult currents in the fjord, passengers and pilgrims often disembarked at Agdenes and continued overland to Trondheim. It seems to have had 'direct' connections with Iceland (cf. *ÍF*, IX, 265) and must have been a place through which many Icelanders passed. It is frequently mentioned in Kings' Sagas. Cf. *KL*, s.v. *Hamn. Norge* and references; Perkins, 1999, 178–182.

at sigla brottu af Nóregi nǫkkur til heiðinna landa], ok skyldi gefa Frey fé mikit [ok þriggja sálda ǫl], ef þeim gæfi til Svíðjóðar, en Þór eða Óðni, ef til Íslands kœmi.[7] En ef þeim gæfi eigi í brott, þá skyldi konungr ráða. Þeim gaf aldri í brott, ok urðu at sigla inn til Þrándheims.

Subsequently Hallfreðr meets Óláfr Tryggvason and the king stands sponsor to him at his baptism. Now the moral of this story is clear. It is, of course, essentially of Christian authorship and, in Christian eyes, it is the Christian God who controls the winds. The heathen Icelanders pray to pagan gods to give them a wind to escape from a Norway under the sway of the Christian Óláfr. But no such wind comes and the Icelanders are forced to go to Trondheim and be baptised there. The Christian god is mightier in his control of the winds. And this, of course, is not the only place in Norse literature where we find the Christian God or his saints controlling wind and weather. A few other examples may be given:

(a) In ch. 57 of *Orkneyinga saga* (*ÍF*, XXXIV, 123), Bishop Vilhjálmr finds himself weatherbound in Shetland on his way back from Norway. Winter comes and there are storms and contrary winds. Then the captain of the ship proposes that the bishop make a promise to God that if they get a fair wind, he will no longer oppose the translation of the holy relics of Jarl Magnús. The bishop agrees and as soon as he has made his vow, the weather changes and they get such a favourable wind that Vilhjálmr is able to sing mass at home in Orkney the very next Sunday.

(b) The following is a paraphrase of one of the miracles connected with St Þorlákr (see *Byskupa sǫgur*, 1938–1978, 236, 323): 'Another happening was that certain men were sailing out along a fjord with a following wind. But they met another ship sailing in along the fjord in the opposite direction. As they passed, they asked the men sailing inwards how it was that they were sailing against the wind. The others said that they had urgent need of a speedy voyage and had prayed to Bishop Þorlákr for a fair wind (*hǫfðu heitit á Þorlák byskup til byrjar*).

---

[7] We note the links suggested here between Thor and Odin and Iceland, and Frey and Sweden (*Svíþjóð*). Frey was certainly thought of as a god particularly connected with the Swedes and this doubtless reflects actual belief (*MRN*, 165–175; note, for example, the reference in *Flat*² (IV, 11) to *Freyr Svíagoð*). And the cult of Thor was particularly strong in Iceland (see *MRN*, 86–87). On the other hand, there is very little evidence for worship of Odin in Iceland (see *MRN*, 64–70; *VAch*, 391).

They parted and both ships reached the different harbours they wanted to by the evening.'

(c) Third in this context, attention may be drawn to a prayer to the Christian God in skaldic *dróttkvætt* for a favourable wind. In a chapter of *Sverris saga* found only in the version in AM 327, 4to, we are told how Magnús Erlingsson with his fleet are becalmed for a week at Unnardys (probably modern Hummardus, near Farsund, not far from the southern tip of Norway; cf. *NO*, 469). With the king is an Icelandic skald called Máni and he addresses this verse to the Deity (*Sverris saga*, 1920, 90):

> Byr gef brátt, inn ǫrvi,
> Bjǫrgynjar til mǫrgum
> —þess biðjum vér—þjóðum,
> þungstóls konungr sólar.
> Angrar oss, þats lengi
> útnyrðingr heldr fyrðum
> vindr's til seinn at sundi
> sunnrœnn, í dys Unnar.

(Prose word-order and translation: *Gef brátt, inn ǫrvi konungr sólar þungstóls, byr mǫrgum þjóðum til Bjǫrgynjar. Þess biðjum vér. Oss angrar, þats útnyrðingr heldr fyrðum lengi í Unnardys. Sunnrœnn vindr's til seinn at sundi.* 'Give the great host soon, O generous King of heaven (*sólar þungstóls*), a fair wind to Bergen. This we pray Thee. It vexes us that a north-west wind delays men at Unnardys. A southerly wind is too slow in coming over the ocean.')

(d) In the story of Óláfr Tryggvason's dealings with Rauðr inn rammi in *Heimskringla* (cf. Appendix), the wind produced by the heathen Rauðr is overcome by the greater power of Christianity (cf. also Note 4 above).

In the outlook of Christians, then, and not least Christian seafarers of the Scandinavian North, it was, of course, the Christian God, the Virgin Mary and His saints who were thought of as controlling wind and weather. Such saints as were invoked might be local ones, for example, St Óláfr or St Þorlákr or St Eric of Sweden; or they might be non-Scandinavian, for example, St Peter, St Nicholas of Myra or St Katherine of Alexandria (see above; *KL*, s.v. *Vær og vind*; Norlén, 1972, 75–79). But we may now turn to the three heathen gods specifically mentioned by name in the passage in *Hallfreðar saga*,

Frey, Odin and Thor. What evidence is there, we may ask, that they were regarded as deities on whom one might sanguinely call for a favourable wind? To what extent were they wind-gods?

The proposition that Odin may have been regarded as a god who had control over the wind finds support in various sources. In verse 154 of *Hávamál* (*Edda*, 43), Odin himself appears to boast:

> Þat kann ec iþ níunda,   ef mic nauðr um stendr,
>     at biarga fari míno á floti:
> vind ec kyrri   vági á
>     oc svæfic allan sæ.

In verse 3 of *Hyndluljóð* (*Edda*, 288), the various benefits Odin can bestow on mankind are enumerated. Not only can he give victory, wealth, eloquence, the gift of poetry and manliness to those he wishes but, we are also told, *byri* (plural) *gefr hann brǫgnum*, 'he gives favourable winds to men'. It is true that Snorri Sturluson knew *Hávamál* and *Hyndluljóð* in some form or other but there is no reason to suppose that he was particularly influenced by them when he wrote of Odin in ch. 7 of *Ynglinga saga* (*ÍF*, XXVI, 18): *Þat kunni hann enn at gera með orðum einum at sløkkva eld ok kyrra sjá ok snúa vindum hverja leið, er hann vildi*. (Snorri then goes on to say that Odin also owned the ship Skíðblaðnir; cf., however, the next paragraph below.) We also note that one of the names for Odin, *Viðrir*, probably refers to his role as a god who controls wind and weather (*veðr*) (cf. *ÍO*, 1131). But of most interest in this context is the well-known story of King Víkarr's death in ch. 7 of *Gautreks saga* (*FN*, IV, 28–31) King Víkarr is engaged on an expedition to Hordaland with his fleet:

> Hann lá í hólmum nokkurum lengi ok fekk andviðri mikit. Þeir felldu spán til byrjar, ok fell svá, at Óðinn vildi þiggja mann at hlutfalli at hanga ór hernum. Þá var skipt liðinu til hlutfalla, ok kom upp hlutr Víkars konungs.

This outcome causes great consternation in Víkarr's army but eventually, by trickery, Víkarr is indeed consecrated to Odin, pierced with a spear and hanged by Starkaðr. This suggests that human sacrifice was made to Odin, and then by hanging, in the hope of getting a favourable wind (cf., for example, *MRN*, 44–46, 206–207 for commentary).[8]

---

[8] The story is referred to briefly by Saxo in his sixth book (153). Saxo says of the fleet: *Cumque quodam in loco diutina tempestatum sævitia vexarentur, ita ventis navigationem frustrantibus, ut maiorem anni partem quieti tribuerunt,*

Factors which suggest that Frey was a god who could control the wind are less convincing but not negligible. While, as noted, Snorri attributes ownership of the ship Skíðblaðnir to Odin in *Ynglinga saga*, it was doubtless more usual to attribute it to Frey, as Snorri himself does in both *Gylfaginning* (*SnE*, 47–48) and *Skáldskaparmál* (*SnE*, 123); and that it was rather Frey who was thought of as owning Skíðblaðnir is borne out by verse 43 of *Grímnismál* (*Edda*, 66). Of Skíðblaðnir, Snorri says that it had a favourable wind as soon as the sail was hoisted (and that it could be folded up and kept in one's pouch; *SnE*, 123: *Skíðblaðnir hafði byr, þegar er segl kom á lopt, hvert er fara skyldi, en mátti vefja saman sem dúk ok hafa í pung sér, ef þat vildi*). In an episode in the version of *Óláfs saga Tryggvasonar in mesta* represented by AM 62, fol. and Flateyjarbók (*ÓT*, III, 2; cf. p. 28 below), we are told how, in a race to reach a temple of Frey, Óláfr Tryggvason outsails some Frey-worshipping Tronds: *Kepptu hvárirtveggju at sigla sem mest. Fór þá sem optast, at gipta konungsins* [cf. Note 4 above] *mátti meira en fjǫlkynngi Freys ok illr átrúnaðr þeira er honum þjónuðu, ok þat bar svá til at, sem inn bezti vildi, at skip konungsins gekk miklu meira, ok því kom hann fyrr til hofsins*. Frey was a god very close to his father Njǫrðr and was in many ways an aspect of him (see *MRN*, 156–179; both Frey and Freyja were the result of an incestuous union between Njǫrðr and his sister). Njǫrðr was, of course, particularly connected with ships and the sea. It would not be surprising, then, if he should be thought of as having control of the winds. And Snorri (*SnE*, 30) specifically says of him: *Hann býr á himni, þar sem heitir Nóatún; hann rœðr fyrir gǫngu vinds ok stillir sjá ok eld; á hann skal heita til sæfara ok til veiða*.

We might conceivably have heard more about Frey as a controller of the winds if our written sources for pagan Norse religion were from

---

*deos humano sanguine propitiandos duxerunt* ('And when, in a certain place, they were troubled by a lengthy period of violent storms and the winds impeded their voyage to such an extent that they had to spend the greater part of the year in inactivity, then they decided that the gods must be placated by a sacrifice of human blood'). And he continues: *Itaque coniectis in urnam sortibus, regiæ necis victimam deposci contigit* ('And when lots were cast in an urn, it turned out that the death of a royal victim was required'). We may infer that Odin, who wished to bring about Víkarr's death, is behind the unfavourable winds and also, presumably, the outcome of the sortilege.

Sweden, the area where he was predominantly worshipped (cf. Note 7 above), rather than from Iceland.

We turn now to evidence that Thor was regarded as a god who had control over the wind. This is, as might be expected, rather more extensive than that relevant to Odin and Frey. Special attention may first be given to the witness of three particular texts:

(1) In the comparatively late *Flóamanna saga* (*ÍF*, XIII, 274–282), it is told how the hero of the saga, Þorgils Þórðarson, has embraced Christianity at the time of the conversion of Iceland, but is persecuted by Thor, the former object of his faith. Þorgils decides to emigrate to Greenland. While waiting for a favourable wind (the expression used is *at bíða byrjar*; cf. p. 9 above), he is again visited by Thor in a dream and the god threatens him with a stormy passage. Þorgils is undeterred and sets sail with a favourable wind. As soon as they are out of sight of land, however, this wind drops and the ship is becalmed. Food and water begin to run short and the ship's company suffer great hardship. Autumn sets in. Then (*ÍF*, XIII, 280; longer text):

> Mæltu sumir menn, at þeir mundu blóta Þór til byrjar [the shorter text has 'skyldi heita á Þór'], kváðu betr þá farit hafa ráð manna, er þeir blótuðu hann, ok kváðu ráð at fella þangat hugi sína. Þorgils segir: 'Ef ek verð varr við þat, at nökkurr maðr blótar ok gerist guðníðingr, þá skal ek þat harðliga hefna.' En við þessi orð hans treystist engi at kalla á Þór.

And when Þorgils discovers that he has an old ox on board which he once, presumably before his conversion, dedicated to Thor, he has it thrown overboard, despite the protestations of those of the ship's company who are still avowedly pagan and who object to the way 'their Thor' ('*Þórr várr*' in direct speech) is being insulted. After some three months of hardship at sea, the ship is wrecked on the desert coast of Greenland, through, one infers, the agency of Thor. It is some time before Þorgils finally frees himself from the god's harassments.

This episode in *Flóamanna saga* has twofold interest. Although Þorgils Þórðarson is, in all probability, a historical character, the story told about him here is, of course, fictional. There is no reason to believe that the historical Þorgils ever went to Greenland. On the other hand, there is equally no reason why the narrative of the saga should not give a fairly realistic picture of what might have happened on board an Icelandic ship becalmed in the North Atlantic around AD 1000. The privations of such a situation would, as already suggested, be severe. While hunger would be a heavy affliction, the thirst would probably be worse. There would probably have been squalid conditions on board, possibly sickness and perhaps extremes of temperature. It would not be surprising, then, if under such conditions, men resorted to their deities, whether Christian or heathen, for succour and relief, not least in the form of a favourable wind to get them to land. And in such circumstances, the newly-converted might well have been tempted to revert to their former beliefs, to turn apostate, perhaps even thinking the sea to be more the province of the old heathen gods than of the new Christian one. And those who had been unwillingly baptised but were still heathen at heart might have had no scruples in having recourse to the heathen gods. And that they should supplicate particularly Thor is not surprising either; Thor was, of course, the god most worshipped by the Icelanders (cf. Note 7 above). Second, a detail in the passage may be considered, the alliterative phrase *blóta Þór til byrjar*. It is true that the author of *Flóamanna saga* seems to have a distinct predilection for alliteration; this, for example, he indulges in the direct speech he attributes to Þorgils in the passage quoted above. But also, of course, he occasionally uses established alliterative expressions, including, as noted, the expression *bíða byrjar* (*ÍF*, XIII, 278); this expression, as observed (p. 9 above), is an example of alliterative terminology relating to the wind which is attested widely in the Scandinavian dialects. The verb *at blóta* is usually used in Old Norse with the name of the god for whom any sacrifice is intended in the accusative; there is an example in the passage from *Flóamanna saga* just cited (cf., for example, *LP*, 55; *VAch*, 400–401). And the words *blóta til byrjar* (i.e. with *til* + the thing solicited in the genitive) are, of course paralleled by such phrases as *at blóta til árs, friðar, sigrs* (cf. C–V, 70 for citations). Expressions like these must surely go back to the heathen period. It seems probable, then, that in the alliterative words *blóta Þór til byrjar* we have a genuine piece of pagan terminology relating to the business of getting a favourable wind by making sacrifice to the god. It can be compared with those already discussed above. It was perhaps remembered over the years particularly because of its alliterative form. (And it may have been replaced in the Christian period in Iceland by some such equally alliterative phrase as *at heita á byskup til byrjar* or perhaps an even more alliterative *at biðja byskup byrjar*; cf. *Byskupa sǫgur*, 1938–1978, 236, 343; Máni skáld's verse quoted on p. 15 above.)

(2) *Flóamanna saga* is, as noted, a relatively late source probably from the end of the thirteenth century or the first decades of the

fourteenth. We turn now to a substantially earlier work and one of entirely different provenance, Dudo of St Quentin's history of the early dukes of Normandy, *De moribus et actis primorum Normanniæ ducum*, probably completed in the first two decades of the eleventh century. In ch. 2 of his first book, Dudo (1865, 129–130) gives a vivid account of the way the Norman Vikings made human sacrifice to Thor in order to secure a successful outcome for their undertakings:

> Cæterum, in expletione suarum expulsionum atque exituum, sacrificabant olim venerantes Thur, Deum suum. Cui non aliquod pecudum, neque pecorum, nec Liberi Patris, nec Cereris litantes donum, sed sanguinem mactabant humanum, holocaustorum omnium putantes pretiosissimum; eo quod, sacerdote sortilego prædestinante, jugo boum una vice diriter icebantur in capite; collisoque unicuique singulari ictu sorte electo cerebro, sternebatur in tellure, perquirebaturque levorsum fibra cordis, scilicet vena. Cujus exhausto sanguine, ex more suo, sua suorumque capita linientes, librabant celeriter navium carbasa ventis, illosque (*v.l.* deosque) tali negotio putantes placare, velociter navium insurgebant remis.

This may be translated tentatively as follows:[9]

> Moreover, as the last act on expulsion and departure (?), they used formerly to make sacrifices in veneration of their god Thor. To him they offered neither gifts of sheep nor cattle (?), nor of Father Liber (i.e. 'wine'), nor of Ceres (i.e. 'corn' or 'bread'), but they used to sacrifice the blood of human victims, thinking that to be the most valuable of all offerings. The procedure was this: When a divinatory priest had decided how things should be, the victims were struck viciously on the head with a single blow from an ox-yoke. And then, when the brain of each and every victim, selected by lot, had been crushed by a separate blow, he was spread out on the ground and the fibre (*fibra*) of the heart, that is to say the vein (*vena*), was carefully examined on the left-hand side (*levorsum*). After that, and in accordance with their custom, they would smear their own and their comrades' heads with the drained blood and promptly spread the sails of their ships to the winds, thinking to placate them (i.e. 'the winds'; or, accepting the reading *deosque*, 'the gods') by such actions. Then they would rapidly ply the oars of their ships.

There are, of course, various obscurities here. One issue is which of the two readings *illosque* or *deosque* to accept. Although the latter is preferred by Steenstrup (1925, 20) and by Albrectsen (translation,

---

[9] I am grateful to David and Ian McDougall, Robert Ireland and Peter Foote for their help in making this translation. Any shortcomings in it are, of course, my responsibility. Cf. Dudo, 1998, 15–16.

1979, 24), it appears, as far as can be seen from Lair's edition, in one manuscript only; and Lair himself has *illosque* in his main text. But whichever reading is the more original probably makes little difference to the point being made here. This is that the account can safely be interpreted as demonstrating that human sacrifice was offered to Thor in expectation of assuring favourable winds at sea (so e.g. in *RGA¹*, IV, 323; *NG*, I, 441; Schomerus, 1936, 109; *MRN*, 94). And as van Houts (1984, 110) remarks, there is no reason why Dudo should not have been in possession of reliable information about heathen Scandinavian customs. Grandchildren of the first permanent settlers of Normandy would have been alive when he was writing. And the information he received from such people could be corroborated by knowledge of the customs of heathen Scandinavians of his own time, of whom, of course, substantial numbers must still have existed. Mogk (1909, 618–622) has produced evidence that the Germanic peoples of earlier times made human sacrifice to wind- and sea-spirits in order to ensure favourable weather conditions. Such offerings, Mogk suggests, were later transferred to Thor. Just, then, as we get an account of human sacrifice to Odin for a favourable wind in Scandinavian sources of two or three centuries later (*Gautreks saga*; Saxo; see above), so here we have a source from Normandy of around the year 1000 that suggests human sacrifice was made to Thor with similar aims.[10]

(3) So much for Dudo of St Quentin. But probably the most important testimony we have in the present context comes from a source completed in the 1070s, some sixty or seventy years after Dudo's work. In the fourth book of his *Gesta Hammaburgensis ecclesiae pontificum*, Adam of Bremen (468–471) touches on the heathendom of the Swedes (*Sueones*). He first describes their temple at Uppsala with its effigies of Thor, Wodan and Fricco. He then goes on to talk of the significance of the three gods. And of the first of them, Thor, Adam writes: '*Thor,*' *inquiunt* [the subject of this verb is probably to be understood as Sueones], '*presidet in aere, qui tonitrus et fulmina, ventos ymbresque, serena et fruges gubernat.*' This much-cited statement has normally

---

[10] In connection with this passage from Dudo and the story of the sacrifice of Víkarr to Odin, we note ch. 18 of *Ljósvetninga saga* (*ÍF*, X, 93–95), where we hear of a ship's long wait for wind off Hrísey in Eyjafjörður. When the putative culprit for this lack of wind is exposed by sortilege, the rest of the people on the ship want to kill him.

been accepted at face value; we have no real reason to doubt it. For present purposes, however, in using it as evidence for the Swedes' belief in Thor's control over the wind, it might be appropriate to show very briefly by a few examples from external evidence its validity with respect to belief in the god's control over the other five phenomena Adam mentions. Thus:

> (a) *tonitrus*, 'thunder'. There is, of course, ample evidence from sources other than Adam that Thor was connected with thunder. For example, the very name *Thor* (*Þórr*) is cognate with Germanic words for thunder, including, of course, English *thunder*; it is also etymologically related to the the Latin word for thunder, *tonitrus*, used by Adam himself (cf. Latin *tonare*, 'to thunder'); cf. *ÍO*, 1186. Various kennings and *heiti* for Thor would seem to refer to him as a controller of thunder (see Ljungberg, 1947, 212–214). Cf. *KL*, s.v. *Torden*.
> 
> (b) *fulmina*, 'lightning; thunderbolts'. While it not inconceivable that Adam had some inkling of the relationship of the word *Thor* (*Þórr*) to words for 'thunder' in German or other Germanic languages (see (a) above), he can scarcely have known anything of the name given in Icelandic sources to Thor's hammer, *Mjǫllnir*, and even less of its etymology. One etymology of *Mjǫllnir* connects it with Icelandic *mala*, 'to grind', and *mølva*, 'to crush'. But others relate it to Russian *molniia* and Welsh *mellt*, both of which words mean 'lightning', and this etymology seems particularly attractive (see *AEW*, 390; *MRN*, 81; cf., however, *ÍO*, 627). At all events, in the eighth book of Saxo Grammaticus's *Gesta Danorum*, we are told how, in a fight between Thor and the giant Geruthus, the giant's women are smashed by Thor's thunderbolts (*fulmina*) (Saxo, 242; cf. *MRN*, 80). Cf. further on Thor and *fulmina*, *KL*, s.v. *Torvigg* and references.
> 
> (c) *ymbres*, 'showers, rain'. As late as the seventeenth century, Thor was being held responsible for rain in Småland in Sweden (see Montelius, 1900, 294 and references). And the Finnish god Ukko, who is very much to be regarded as a 'loan' from pagan Scandinavian religion, was often invoked when rain was needed (see, for example, *NK*, XXVI, 126; Ljungberg, 1947, 56–57; *MRN*, 98; *KL*, s.v. *Ukko*). Cf. also again *KL*, s.v. *Torden*.
> 
> (d) *serena*, probably strictly 'cloudless skies', but usually understood as 'fine weather; sunshine'. While I cannot point to any evidence to suggest that Thor was thought of as having control specifically of the clouds, Bronze-Age petroglyphs from Scandinavia often show a figure, identified with Thor because of such attributes as hammer or axe, carrying a 'sun-disc'. This, with other evidence, suggests that he was already regarded as a sun-god at this early stage (cf. *RGA*[1], IV, 323–324; Ljungberg, 1947, 91–111 and references).
> 
> (e) *fruges*, 'produce of the earth; crops'. There is ample evidence external to Adam's *Gesta* that Thor was thought of as a god who brought fertility

to crops. The proposition is suggested, to take a quite random piece of evidence, by the occurrence of such place-names as *Torsåker* in Sweden and *Torsager* in Denmark, both of which may be interpreted as 'Thor's Cornfield'; cf. *NK*, XXVI, 125; *AR*, II, 120; *MRN*, 93. Also, more generally, *NK*, XXVI, 129.

These are sample pieces of evidence which bear out Adam's statement concerning the Swedes' belief in Thor as governing lightning, rain, sunshine and crops. They show that Adam is giving us more than a set of commonplaces, more than the kind of information a medieval Christian writer might conventionally offer concerning any pagan sky-god. And if Adam is correct in what he says about the Swedes' statement concerning Thor's control of the five phenomena in question, then it is not unreasonable to conclude that he may well be right in what he says about the sixth, the wind. We should note the explicit nature of Adam's evidence on this matter. In what is after all a work more or less of fact (rather than fiction), it is specifically stated that the Swedes believed that Thor had control of the wind. The present tense of *inquiunt* should be noted. Here, then, we have a particularly direct and unambiguous statement about pagan Scandinavian belief in Thor's powers over the wind.

Here, then, in *Flóamanna saga*, Dudo and Adam of Bremen, are three specific items of evidence which suggest that Thor was thought of as in some way having power of command over the wind. These, as noted, come from sources of rather different provenance. Taken together, however, they have decisive weight. And that Thor was thought of as controlling the wind can also be concluded, or perhaps rather inferred, from a number of other sources and not least Icelandic ones. A few perhaps somewhat random examples may be given:

In at least one of the two skaldic verses attributed to the poetess Steinunn, Thor is credited with having destroyed the ship of Þangbrandr, a man known from the prose of the works in which the verses are preserved as one of the first Christian missionaries in Iceland (see *Skj*, A, I, 135–136; B, I, 127–128; Turville-Petre, 1976, 65–67; *MRN*, 89–90). This the god was presumably thought of as having done by producing stormy weather, directed against the agent of his arch-enemy, Christ.

The Hauksbók redaction of *Landnámabók* (*ÍF*, I, 53, 55) tells of Kollr who encounters a storm off north-western Iceland. He appeals to Thor for help but is subsequently shipwrecked. His foster-brother

Ørlygr Hrappsson in another ship, however, calls on 'Bishop Patrekr' and comes safely ashore in Patreksfjörður. The story has, of course, a Christian bias, but is doubtless realistic in representing heathens as invoking the aid of Thor (albeit in vain in this instance) when in difficulties at sea.

The account given of Helgi magri Eyvindarson in *Landnámabók* (*ÍF*, I, 250) is of interest in this context. We are told of Helgi that he believed in Christ but had recourse to Thor when on journeys by sea and in difficult situations: *Helgi var blandinn mjǫk í trú; hann trúði á Krist, en hét á Þór til sjófara ok harðræða*. Helgi presumably believed that Thor had some influence over the forces of nature so important to seafarers. (When *SnE* (cf. p. 17 above) says of Njǫrðr that *á hann skal heita til sæfara ok til veiða*, the implied reason is that he controls the movements of the wind, moderates the sea, etc.) And when Helgi approached Iceland in his ship as prospective *landnámsmaðr*, he sought advice from Thor as to where he should settle (*gekk hann til frétta við Þór, hvar land skyldi taka*; cf. *KL*, s.v. *Frett I* and references). Thor (or his oracle) directed (*vísaði*) Helgi to the north of Iceland and he settled in Eyjafjörður at Kristnes.

In *Landnámabók* and elsewhere there are, of course, a number of accounts of how intending colonisers of Iceland threw their high-seat pillars (*ǫndvegissúlur*) overboard on approaching the island for the first time and settled where the pillars drifted ashore (see Strömbäck, 1970, 136–142 for a full list of references). One of these is of particular interest in the present context. In ch. 4 of *Eyrbyggja saga* (*ÍF*, IV, 7–8; cf. *ÍF*, I, 124–126), we are told how Þórólfr Mostrarskegg, a particularly fervent devotee of the god, is sailing to Iceland with a favourable wind. He gets becalmed, in Faxaflói we may infer, and here Þórólfr makes the vow that he will settle where his *ǫndvegissúlur* (on one of which the image of Thor is carved) drift ashore. The pillars go overboard and are driven by the elements, and rather faster than might be expected (*eigi vánum seinna*), around Snæfellsnes and into Breiðafjörður. At the same time a sea breeze (*hafgula*) springs up and drives Þórólfr's ship in the same direction. He subsequently finds the pillars washed ashore on a headland. Here he settles and calls the place Þórsnes. It was presumably wind, wave and current controlled by Thor which was thought of as driving Þórólfr's pillars, and after them his ship, to Þórsnes. But we also note the words of the saga, *Þórr var á land kominn með súlurnar*, with their implication that the god was more or less identified with the pillars or that the god himself was in them (cf. Turville-Petre, 1962, 247; *MRN*, 87). In other allusions to this custom, Thor is not specifically mentioned. Even so, some have seen a general connection between the practice and the cult of Thor (e.g. Meyer, 1891, 212; cf., however, Strömbäck, 1970, 136, note 1).

One colonist, Kráku-Hreiðarr Ófeigsson (*ÍF*, I, 232–233) declares (perhaps significantly, at the mast of his ship) that rather than throw his high-seat pillars overboard, he will invoke the guidance of Thor direct to show him a place to settle and says he will fight for the land if it is already settled (*kvezk heldr mundu heita á Þór, at hann vísaði honum til landa, ok kvezk þar mundu berjask til landa, ef áðr væri numit*). He subsequently makes a difficult landing at Borgarsandur in Skagafjörður. The following spring, Eiríkr Hróaldsson persuades Hreiðarr not to fight a certain Sæmundr for his *landnám* adjacent to Borgarsandur, but says that he will give him *tungan ǫll niðr frá Skálamyri, kvað þangat Þór hafa vísat honum ok þar stafn á horft, þá er hann sigldi upp á Borgarsand*.

A story related to some of the above is told in *Landnámabók* (see *ÍF*, I, 163–164) of Þórólfr Mostrarskegg's son Hallsteinn who settled in Þorskafjörður. He sacrifices to Thor to send him some high-seat pillars.[11] After this, a huge tree is washed ashore and is used for making pillars for almost all the farms in the neighbourhood.

Finally, a well-known story in ch. 8 of *Eiríks saga rauða* (*ÍF*, IV, 425) has interest in this context. Þorfinnr karlsefni and his followers have run short of food on their expedition to Vínland. They call on their Christian God for help but to no avail. One of the party, Þórhallr veiðimaðr, apparently still a committed heathen, disappears and is subsequently found lying on a cliff-top staring upwards and chanting something (*hann horfði í lopt upp, ok gapði hann bæði augum ok munni ok nǫsum ok klóraði sér ok klýpði sik ok þulði nǫkkut*). Soon after, a whale of unknown species drifts ashore and they cook and eat its meat,

---

[11] The Hauksbók redaction adds the detail (*ÍF*, I, 164, note 1) that he *gaf þar til son sinn*. This could possibly imply human sacrifice (cf. the accounts of Dudo and *Gautreks saga* quoted above) but more probably means that Hallsteinn dedicated his son to Thor to become his devotee (cf. *ÍF*, IV, 12–13; Briem, 1945, 170, note 2).

but are ill as a result. Þórhallr then boasts that he has got his reward for the poetry (*skáldskapr*) he has composed in honour of his patron Thor (whom he familiarly refers to as *hinn rauðskeggjaði*), and we may infer that it was this poetry he was declaiming on the cliff. His companions now realise who has sent the whale and throw its meat away. We are left to draw the conclusion that it was by his control of current, wind and wave that Thor was thought of as able to send the whale to the starving company.[12]

---

[12] For further discussion of the relevant passage in *Eiríks saga rauða* with perhaps a slightly different or more specific interpretation than that given here, see Perkins, 2000.

CHAPTER TWO
# AN EPISODE IN *RǪGNVALDS ÞÁTTR OK RAUÐS*

> Blés Þórr . . . í kampana ok þeytti skegg-
> raustina. Kom þá þegar andviðri móti konungi.
> *ÓLÁFS SAGA TRYGGVASONAR IN MESTA*

WE HAVE SEEN in the previous chapter how desirable a favourable wind was to the medieval Norse and how the god Thor was believed by some to be able to control the winds in general and to produce favourable winds in particular. These questions now arise: How was Thor thought of as producing winds and breezes? Did he simply have wind and weather at his command? Or did he do it in some other way? In attempting to give some answers to these questions, attention may be drawn to a passage in an Icelandic work normally known as *Rǫgnvalds þáttr ok Rauðs* (abbreviated *RR*). And because *RR* has not received much scholarly attention, it will not be out of place to offer first some basic information about its preservation, content, sources, dating, and other aspects. This, it should be stressed, is done without an exhaustive study having been made and with heavy reliance on the work of Strömbäck (1940) and Ólafur Halldórsson (see Bibliography).

## (A) Manuscripts of *RR*

*RR* is preserved in two major redactions in eight different manuscripts with independent value as follows:

(1) It exists as a separate, continuous entity (referred to here as *RR557*) only in the manuscript AM 557, 4to which preserves a dozen items or so (some defective) including *Gunnlaugs saga ormstungu*, *Hallfreðar saga*, *Eiríks saga rauða* (which immediately precedes *RR557*) and *Dámusta saga* (which immediately follows *RR557*). AM 557, 4to was probably written in the period 1420–1450 by Ólafur Loftsson whose work as a scribe is far from unimpeachable (cf. Stefán Karlsson, 1970, 137–138).

(2) *RR* is incorporated as four separate passages in *Óláfs saga Tryggvasonar in mesta* (*ÓT*). (On *ÓT* in general, see *KL*, s.v. *Óláfs saga Tryggvasonar*; Ólafur Halldórsson, 1990; *MS*, 448–449; *ÓT*, III,

xv–cccl; and references in these places.) This redaction is referred to as *RRÓT*. The most significant manuscripts of *ÓT* are: AM 61, fol.; AM 53, fol.; AM 54, fol.; Perg. fol. nr 1 (Bergsbók); Papp. fol. nr 22 (Húsafellsbók); and, representing a different, later version, AM 62, fol. and Gl. kgl. sml. 1005, fol. (Flateyjarbók). *RRÓT* appears in six of these seven manuscripts (although only part of it in the defective AM 53, fol.). It is not found in AM 54, fol. in its present form. It is, however, also found in AM 325 IX 1 b, 4to.

Further on manuscripts, editions, translations etc. of *RR*, see the Appendix. In what follows Ólafur Halldórsson's editions, *RRÓT* and *RR557*, will be referred to. (*RRÓT* is based on AM 61, fol. and gives variants from all independent manuscripts other than Húsafellsbók; variants from this last-mentioned manuscript are given in *ÓT*, III, ccxviii–ccxxi.)

**(B) Redactions of *RR***

There is, to my knowledge, as yet no exhaustive study of the differences between the two main redactions of *RR* (cf., however, Strömbäck, 1940, 15–18). Attention may, then, on a tentative basis and briefly, be drawn to the main differences between the two redactions (i.e. that represented by *RR557* on the one hand and by *RRÓT* on the other) under four headings as follows:

(a) *Independence*. As suggested, *RR557* may, for practical purposes, be regarded as an independent entity, totally unrelated in content to the material which precedes and follows it in its single manuscript; *RRÓT*, on the other hand and as noted, exists only as four separate passages integrated into *ÓT*. It seems entirely probable that the situation represented by *RR557* is the more original, i.e. that *RR* existed as an independent whole and has subsequently been incorporated into *ÓT*. That the converse has happened, that the redaction represented by *RR557* has been put together from originally separate passages extracted from *ÓT*, seems altogether unlikely (cf. Strömbäck, 1940, 17).

(b) *Volume*. In Ólafur Halldórsson's edition (*ÓT*, III, 95–102), *RR557* may be said on a rough calculation to take up about 242 lines; by a similar rough calculation, *RRÓT* may be said to take up some 346 lines in Ólafur's edition of *ÓT*. Approximate though these figures may be, it will be seen that *RRÓT* is substantially longer than *RR557*, indeed, more than a third as long again. Three theoretical possibilities exist: (i) that *RR557* represents a shortening of *RR* in its original form; (ii) that *RRÓT* represents a lengthening of *RR* in its original form; (iii) that both (i) and (ii) obtain. Without having undertaken a detailed investigation of the matter, I would be reluctant to dismiss any of these three possibilities. The difference in volume is not least pronounced in the account of Óláfr Tryggvason's visit to Rauðr on his island which is of special interest to us (see below) and which, roughly calculated, takes up 57 lines in Ólafur Halldórsson's edition of *RR557* (i.e. 100/12–101/35) but 88 lines in Ólafur's edition of *RRÓT* (i.e. 328/9–332/17).

(c) *Content*. Strömbäck (1940, 16–17) mentions certain differences of detail in the content of the two versions (e.g. in *RR557*, Sigríðr seeks out Óláfr Tryggvason in Garðaríki, in *RRÓT* in England). A few of these differences are noted in the plot-summary of *RR* given below.

(d) *Style*. Strömbäck (1940, 16, 17) stated that the version of *RR* in *Fms* and Flateyjarbók (i.e. *RRÓT*) is characterised by 'rhetorical ornamentation' and that this feature is absent from the version of *RR* in AM 557, 4to; also that the redaction in AM 557, 4to gives the impression of being 'somewhat more archaic' than the other version. One cannot be absolutely certain what features Strömbäck is referring to here; but it seems quite possible that the 'rhetorical ornamentation' he discerns in *RRÓT* may include, for example, the element of alliteration found in the passage, *RRÓT*, 329/14–330/19. It also seems possible, however, that the features in question are secondary and were introduced by the redactor who interpolated the *þáttr* into *ÓT*.

**(C) Summary of *RR***

A resumé of *RR* may be offered (see Harris, 1980, 168–169 for another). Because the text of *RRÓT* is of greater interest in the present argument, the resumé here is based on this version (as represented by AM 61, fol.) rather than on *RR557*.

[Cf. *RRÓT*, 313/8–322/21; *RR557*, 95/25–99/22] Þórólfr skjálgr Qgmundarson, father of Erlingr, is a powerful man of Jaðarr. (*RR557* does not give Þórólfr a nickname or say that his father is Qgmundr; towards the end of its text, however, it refers to him as Þórólfr Skjálgsson (*RR557*, 102/4–5).) He is responsible, it is implied, for plotting the murder of Loðinn on the latter's farm at Ærvík in Staðr. Þórólfr takes Loðinn's widow as his concubine, appropriates his estate and reduces one of his two young sons, Rǫgnvaldr, to servitude. Rǫgnvaldr grows to be a fine man and becomes Þórólfr's overseer. He asks Þórólfr to find him a wife and is married to a woman called Sigríðr.

By Sigríðr, Rǫgnvaldr has a son called Gunnarr whom Þórólfr treats more or less as his own child. One summer, Þórólfr plans a raiding expedition and commands Rǫgnvaldr to build a splendid drinking hall while he is away. Rǫgnvaldr complies and employs the services of two Wendish craftsmen for the task.[1] Rǫgnvaldr also has large heaps of firewood gathered near the hall. On his return, Þórólfr is pleased with the new hall and seems to accept an explanation from Rǫgnvaldr for the presence of the firewood. He then makes preparations for a great feast. At this feast, Gunnarr sits at Þórólfr's side in the high-seat, dressed in a red tunic. Rǫgnvaldr and the two Wends get the company drunk on particularly strong drink. They then set fire to the hall and the piles of firewood around it, burning all the people in it, including Þórólfr. Rǫgnvaldr then makes his escape by sea, together with Sigríðr, a sleeping Gunnarr and the two Wends. Out on the fjord, Gunnarr awakes, sees the burning hall and rebukes Rǫgnvaldr harshly for the crime against Þórólfr. Rǫgnvaldr silences him and the company sails northwards. They are shipwrecked off Staðr, the Wends perish, but Rǫgnvaldr, with his family, survives and is able to return to Ærvík and establish himself there on his father's estate. One day, Rǫgnvaldr sets Gunnarr adrift in a small boat, with the purpose, it seems, of disposing of a witness to the burning of Þórólfr. The boat is driven northwards to an island located off Hálogaland. Here the boy is found and adopted by the chief man of the island (nameless in the interpolated version, but called Kati in *RR557*).[2] This man is a devotee of Thor (*RRÓT*, 319/15–16: *Fyrir eyju þeiri er bátrinn var at kominn réð einn blótmaðr.*

---

[1] Harris (1980, 178) suggests that the role of Wends in this context is unlikely to reflect reality. We might, however, note that this nation was close to medieval Scandinavia and members of it seem to have settled in the southern Danish islands (see *KL*, s.v. *Vender*). The proposition that some of them found their way further north is, therefore, not as improbable as it may at first sight seem. And itinerant carpenters and other craftsmen would, of course, have been familiar figures in medieval Scandinavia (cf., for example, Trotzig, 1995, 22, where it is suggested that the chest of Viking-Age tools from Mästermyr in Gotland belonged to such a person).

[2] Strömbäck (1940, 17) thought that the name of Gunnarr's/Rauðr's foster-father in AM 557, 4to (cf. *RR557*, 98/11) might be read as *Káti* but could perhaps also be read as *Kári* (cf. pp. 48–50 and Note 9 below). Ólafur Halldórsson suggests to me in private communication that a reading *Kári* is palaeographically improbable. And he prefers to read *Kati* (spelt 'katí') rather

*Var þar mikit hof ok eignat Þór*). Gunnarr is able to conceal his origins. The boy is called Rauðr after the colour of the red tunic he was wearing when found. When his adopter dies childless, Rauðr is his heir and maintains his cult of Thor. He puts such a spell on his image of the god that it is able to converse with him and walk with him around the island. Rǫgnvaldr's wife, Sigríðr, leaves her husband, seeks out Óláfr Tryggvason (in England in *RRÓT*, in Garðaríki in *RR557*) and is baptised. She tells Óláfr of the events which have passed and begs him to convert Rǫgnvaldr and Rauðr when he returns to Norway. She dies abroad in great sanctity.

[Cf. *RRÓT*, 325/12–327/4; *RR557*, 99/22–100/12] After Óláfr has returned to Norway, he seeks out Rǫgnvaldr at Ærvík and preaches the faith to him. Rǫgnvaldr, however, refuses to be baptised, implying that events have befallen him which he cannot confess to. Óláfr makes him his prisoner.

[Cf. *RRÓT*, 328/9–332/17;[3] *RR557*, 100/12–101/35] Óláfr makes for the island where Rauðr lives (now referred to as Rauðsey).[4] Rauðr urges his image of Thor to put up a resistance by producing a head

---

than *Káti*. He thinks that the name *Kati* in our text might have arisen as some sort of misunderstanding of the word *kati*, 'small ship, boat', perhaps used in some manuscript of the vessel in which Gunnarr arrived at the island where the man to whom the name is applied is said to have lived. We note also that *kate* in Norwegian dialect can mean 'small boy' (see Aasen, 1918, s.v.; *ÍO*, 450). *Kári* is, of course, a relatively common name in Old Norse (see Lind, 1905–1915, s.v., and Lind, 1931, s.v.). *Káti* is much rarer (see Lind, 1905–1915, s.v., and Lind, 1931, s.v.); it also appears as a byname (see Lind, 1920–21, s.v.).

[3] AM 62, fol. and Gl. kgl. sml. 1005, fol. (Flateyjarbók) have chapter headings referring to the content of *RR* at a point corresponding to *ÓT*, I, 328/1, that is, before this third passage from *RR* really begins (see textual variants to 328/1 in *ÓT*, I; *Fms*, I, 302/5; *Flat*, I, 296/1; *Flat²*, I, 327/31).

[4] It is doubtless pointless to attempt to identify Rauðsey in *RR* with any known place. And I have yet to discover any real place-name along the Norwegian coast (e.g. a *\*Raudsøya* or *\*Rødsøya*) which might reflect an Old Norse *Rauðs-ey* (i.e. genitive of a personal name *Rauðr* compounded with *ey*, 'island'; cf. Lind, 1905–1915, and Lind, 1931, s.v. *Rauðr*). On the other hand, *Raudøya/Rødøya* is the name given to a large number of islands off the Norwegian coast (cf. *NS*, 263) referring either to the redness of their rock or their vegetation (e.g. red heather) and it is not impossible that some such name was at the back of the author's mind here. In locating the scene of heathen

wind against Óláfr's ship. This proves to be of no avail in the long run and Óláfr eventually gets to the island. He then preaches Christianity to Rauðr and his people at length (*RRÓT*, 329/13–330/19), stressing amongst other things the impotence of heathen images. In response to this, Rauðr arranges a tug-of-war contest between the king and Thor over a fire to establish who is most powerful. This ends with the king pulling Thor into the fire and the idol being burnt to ashes. Despite this, Rauðr still refuses to be baptised although all the other people of

---

practice on an island off northern Norway (*ey ein norðr fyrir Hálogalandi*, *RRÓT*, 322/12), the author is probably following the literary conventions of the 'conversion-*þættir*' (on these cf. (D) below, p. 33); another such 'conversion-*þáttr*', *Vǫlsa þáttr*, is staged on a headland (*andnes*) in northern Norway, and this is a place where King Óláfr Haraldsson discovers a pagan cult and subsequently converts those practising it. Northern Norway was, of course, a place conventionally associated with the practice of magic and witchcraft. And in 'Rauðs þáttr ins ramma', which has close affinities with *RR*, Rauðr lives on the island (or islands) Goðey (or Goðeyjar) in the fjord Sálpti in Hálogaland and this/these can be identified modern Godøya in Saltfjorden (cf. Appendix, p. 161 below). Offshore islands, then, like remote headlands and forests, were thought of in literary tradition as places where heathendom persisted longest (cf. *Flat*$^2$, II, 441, 446); and such ideas doubtless to some extent reflect reality. And there is, in all probability, a basis in reality for the idea in *RR* that the cult of Thor was practised on islands. A number of theophoric place-names in mainland Scandinavia are of the type Old Norse *Þórs-ey*, Swedish *Tor(s)-ö* (cf. *NG*, 412, 438–439; *NK*, XXVI, 33, 54; *AR*, II, 117, 119; Munch, 1922, 230, 238; cf. also *VH*, 108, for such names in Ireland and for an island in the Seine). It is very possible that Thor was worshipped on at least some of these islands. And it is also possible that Thor was worshipped on an island or islands in the vicinity the Dnieper Rapids (cf. p. 73 below) and also on the island mentioned by Saxo (350; cf. Note 7 below) which must have lain off the Swedish coast. It may also be noted here in the context of the general discussion of this study that islands seem to have been favoured places for meteorological magic, wind-raising and the like. On the island mentioned by Saxo just referred to, attempts were made to produce thunder by the use of large Thor's hammers (cf. Note 12 in Chapter 3). In Scotland the most likely place to find wind-sellers was on the islands, the Hebrides, Orkney and Shetland (Cameron, 1903, 301). Lyall Watson (1984, 118) writes: 'The island of Sena off ancient Gaul was said to have a priestess . . . who could produce winds to order', but gives no references. And the Greek Aeolus, fabled as warden of the winds as well as inventor of the sail, lived on the Aeolian Islands (Isole Eolie) and kept the winds imprisoned in a cave there.

the island submit. Óláfr takes Rauðr prisoner and now has both him and Rǫgnvaldr in his custody.

[Cf. *RRÓT*, 349/13–351/7; *RR557*, 101/35–102/32] In a final episode, Óláfr brings Rǫgnvaldr and Rauðr together. He tells them that he knows from Sigríðr of the circumstances of Þórólfr's death and offers Rǫgnvaldr a pardon if he will accept the Christian faith. Rǫgnvaldr confesses his misdeed. Both he and Rauðr are baptised and discover their relationship to one another. They then return to their respective estates.

**(D) Sources, analogues and parallels**

*RR* may reasonably be placed amongst what have been called the 'conversion-*þættir*' (see e.g. Strömbäck, 1940, 15; Harris, 1980, 162–167; *DMA*, XII, 2). Without attempting any detailed definition of *þættir* of this type, we may broadly describe their theme as the conversion of the central character or characters to Christianity, usually under the influence of one of the two 'missionary' kings of Norway, Óláfr Tryggvason or Óláfr Haraldsson. Details of heathen practice prior to conversion are sometimes given and then often rather scornfully or satirically. The majority of such *þættir* are found embedded in the longer sagas of the two kings and are preserved not least in Flateyjarbók. As representative examples of the type, we may mention *Sveins þáttr ok Finns* (*ÓT*, II, 102–114), *Tóka þáttr* (*Flat*, II, 135–138) and *Vǫlsa þáttr* (*Flat*, II, 331–336). A number of such tales are alluded to in Ljungberg's work of 1938 (particularly on pp. 98–158) although they are there regarded more from the point of view of historical reality than as literary phenomena.

In a contribution published in *Folklore forum* (1980), Joseph Harris approached *RR* from the point of view of its parallels in the corpus of international folktale. Harris notes, for example, the motifs of 'Exposure in a boat' and 'Foundling hero' with reference to Gunnarr/Rauðr and his treatment by Rǫgnvaldr. He draws particular attention to Celtic material, not least in connection with the story of Rǫgnvaldr's burning of Þórólfr. In the story of Gunnarr/Rauðr being set afloat in a small boat, we may have a reminiscence of the story of Moses's treatment by his mother after his birth (Exodus 2: 3; cf. p. 164 below). Ólafur Halldórsson (personal communication) draws attention to the story of Hamlet as something of a parallel to Rǫgnvaldr's dealings with his father's killer. And for Gunnarr being named Rauðr from the colour of the tunic he wore when found, Ólafur notes the story in *Jómsvíkinga saga* where the foundling son of Arnfinnr is called *Knútr* by his childless foster-father Gormr *fyrir þá sök er fingurgull . . . hafði knýtt verið í enni sveininum þá er hann fannst* (*Jómsvíkinga saga*, 1969, 61–63).

Of particular significance as an analogue to *RR* is the story of Rauðr inn rammi in chs 78–80 of *Óláfs saga Tryggvasonar* in Snorri Sturluson's *Heimskringla* (*Hkr*, I, 324–328). Further information about 'Rauðs þáttr ins ramma' is given in the Appendix (pp.161–164 below). In both *RR* and 'Rauðs þáttr ins ramma', we find a heathen called Rauðr who lives on an island (or islands) off Hálogaland. The two Rauðrs seem to have, either directly or indirectly, some control over the wind and try to use this to prevent Óláfr Tryggvason reaching their islands. Even so, Óláfr Tryggvason gets to the island in each story and attempts to convert Rauðr there to Christianity (although with rather different results in the two stories). There is clearly some connection between *RR* and the story told in *Heimskringla*. It should also be noted that earlier in his *Óláfs saga Tryggvasonar* Snorri mentions: (a) 'Rǫgnvaldr ór Ærvík af Staði' as one of the followers of Sveinn Hákonarson at the Battle of Hjǫrungavágr (ch. 40; *Hkr*, I, 279); (b) Þórólfr skjálgr, son of Ǫgmundr, son of Hǫrða-Kári and father of Erlingr of Sóli (ch. 54; *Hkr*, I, 304). He makes, however, no connection between Rǫgnvaldr and Þórólfr and Rauðr. Precisely what relationship exists between *RR* and *Hkr* (and *ÓTOdd*, to which Snorri is probably indebted to a certain extent for his 'Rauðs þáttr ins ramma'; cf. pp. 163–164 below) is uncertain. Finnur Jónsson (1920–24, III, 85) described *RR* as 'en udvidelse af en ældre kort beretning om Rauðr på Hálogaland, der findes hos Snorre'. If I understand Finnur correctly here, he certainly appears to imply that *RR* borrowed from Snorri's *Óláfs saga Tryggvasonar* in *Heimskringla*, although, if so, this view seems to be a little inconsistent with his suggestion expressed elsewhere (Finnur Jónsson, 1930a, 123) that *RR* was the work of Gunnlaugr Leifsson who died in 1218 or 1219 (cf. below). Dag Strömbäck (1940, 15–16) had a different opinion. He thought that Snorri built up his 'Rauðs þáttr ins ramma' in *Hkr* on the similar tales in *ÓTOdd* but that he also knew *RR*, from which he borrowed at the least the name Rauðr. Strömbäck may well be right in this, although if he is, one might perhaps have expected to find more of the events or characters of *RR* mentioned in *Hkr*. As far as can be seen, then, the issue of whether *RR* borrowed from *Hkr* or *Hkr* borrowed from *RR* is a problematic one which must be left open. The possibility that *Hkr* represents a source for *RR* cannot be excluded. And the author of *RR* may, of course, also have known *ÓTOdd* (although again the converse is also a possibility).

### (E) Date of *RR*; authorship

The oldest extant text of *RR* (i.e. in the main part of AM 61, fol.) probably dates from the period 1350–1375. We have here, then, the most reliable *terminus ante quem* for the writing of *RR*. But there are reasons for thinking that *RR* was probably written well before 1375. Since the interpolated version of *RR* must have been in the archetype of *ÓT*, the date of the compilation of *ÓT* would also constitute a sound *terminus ante quem* for the writing of *RR*. In his article of 1990 (47–55), Ólafur Halldórsson sees no reason for rejecting the attribution, based on a notice in Bergsbók (cf. *ÓT*, I, 1, variants), of *ÓT* to Bergr Sokkason, abbot of the monastery of Munkaþverá in northern Iceland during the second quarter of the fourteenth century. Ólafur's conclusion on this point seems acceptable and, if correct, implies that *RR* must have been written quite some time before the death of Bergr. And we last hear of Bergr in 1345. We may therefore date *RR* to before about 1330. As noted, it is not possible to say whether *RR* influenced Snorri's *Heimskringla* (written about 1230) or *Heimskringla* influenced *RR* and thus to establish respectively a *terminus ante quem* or a *terminus post quem* related to the date of *Hkr* (although again, further investigations may help to do so).

The possibility that *RR* originated from the lost saga of Óláfr Tryggvason written in Latin by Gunnlaugr Leifsson has been somewhat debated (cf. Finnur Jónsson, 1930a, 123; Bjarni Aðalbjarnarson, 1937, 117 and references; Strömbäck, 1940, 16; Ólafur Halldórsson, 1990). If Gunnlaugr did write *RR*, then it must of course be dated to before his death, i.e. to before 1219 at the latest; indeed, various critics think Gunnlaugr's saga was written before about 1200 (cf. *Hkr*, I, xiv; Whaley, 1991, 68). But the arguments on this matter (which cannot be rehearsed fully here) appear to be rather tenuous. There seems little or nothing to suggest that *RR* was originally written in Latin and subsequently translated into Icelandic (cf. Ólafur Halldórsson, 1990, 53). Further, as is noted in the Appendix (p. 164 below), the story of Rauðr inn rammi may well have had a place in Gunnlaugr's lost saga and provided a source for 'Rauðs þáttr ins ramma' in Snorri's *Heimskringla*; if it did, then it is perhaps rather unlikely that it also contained the story of Rauðr, son of Rǫgnvaldr, which has so many elements in common with it (although it is, of course, not impossible; *ÓT* has both tales). All in all, then, there appears to be no particularly strong evidence for us to ascribe *RR* to Gunnlaugr Leifsson.

Our conclusions here must be that in the present state of research the writing of *RR* can, unfortunately, not be dated to within narrower limits than to between about 1180 (when, as far as is known, works of its type began to be written in Iceland) and about 1330 (i.e. before the compilation of *ÓT*). Nor, unfortunately, is it possible to point to any known person as author.

The above gives some account of *Rǫgnvalds þáttr ok Rauðs*. Attention may now be focused on the passage in it which has special interest in the present context. This is the account of Óláfr Tryggvason making for the island where Rauðr lives and Rauðr urging Thor to hinder this by producing a head wind against the king's ship(s). The texts of both versions at the relevant place may be quoted.

(1) *RR557* (100/12–24 (= AM 557, 4to, f. 37r, lines 24–37); angle brackets inserted by R.P. to indicate corrupt text):

> Sidan fer hann [i.e. Óláfr Tryggvason] nordr fírir land ok ætladí til Ravds eyiar. ok þann myrgín er konungr ætladí at kuolldi i eyna. þa fer Ravdr til hófs síns ok ueittí Þór honum eíngí anndsvavr eptir þvi sem hann var vanurr þetta þóttí honum vnndarlígt ok leítadi a marga uega orda uid hann ok spurdí hvat til bar. Þór kvat þat eigi vm sakleysí ok kvat ser þraungt míók i þeirra manna til kvǫmv er þa var þanngat a leid er var Olafr konungr. ‹Ravdr kvat þat ecki mundu tiða. eigi lítíd. færr i mót honum skeggbrǫdda þína ok gaunngum ut i mótí þeim.› hann kvat þat ecki mundu tiða ok forv þó vt. bles Þór i kampana i motí þeim ok kom konungi i anndvidrí ok hellt hann aptr ok fór svǫ nauckurvm sinnvm. enn konungr eggiadízt a at meír at kǫma þvi fram er hann uílldí ok uard hann rikarí i sínum kraptí enn sía fianndí er i moti stod.

(2) *RRÓT* (328/9–329/5 (= AM 61, fol., f. 34ra, lines 22–37; see Figure 2), here in normalised form with one minor emendation unnoted; localisation of two words by page/line reference to *RRÓT* is given in square brackets):

An episode in Rǫgnvalds þáttr        37

En er konungr kom norðr fyrir Naumudal, þá ætlaði hann út í Rauðseyjar. Þann morgin gekk Rauðr til hofs síns sem hann var vanr. Þórr var þá heldr hryggiligr ok veitti Rauð engi andsvǫr, þó at hann leitaði orða við hann. Rauð þótti þat mjǫk undarligt ok leitaði marga vega at fá mál af honum ok
5 spurði, hví þat sætti. Þórr svarar um síðir ok þó heldr mœðiliga, sagði þetta eigi fyrir sakleysi,—'því at mér er,' segir hann, 'mjǫk þrǫngt í kvámu þeira manna er hingat ætla til eyjarinnar ok mjǫk er mér óþokkat til þeira.' Rauðr spurði, hverir þeir menn væri. Þórr sagði, at þar var Óláfr konungr Tryggvason ok lið hans. Rauðr mælti: 'Þeyt þú í mót þeim skeggrǫdd
10 [328/19] þína, ok stǫndum í mót þeim knáliga.' Þórr kvað þat mundu fyrir

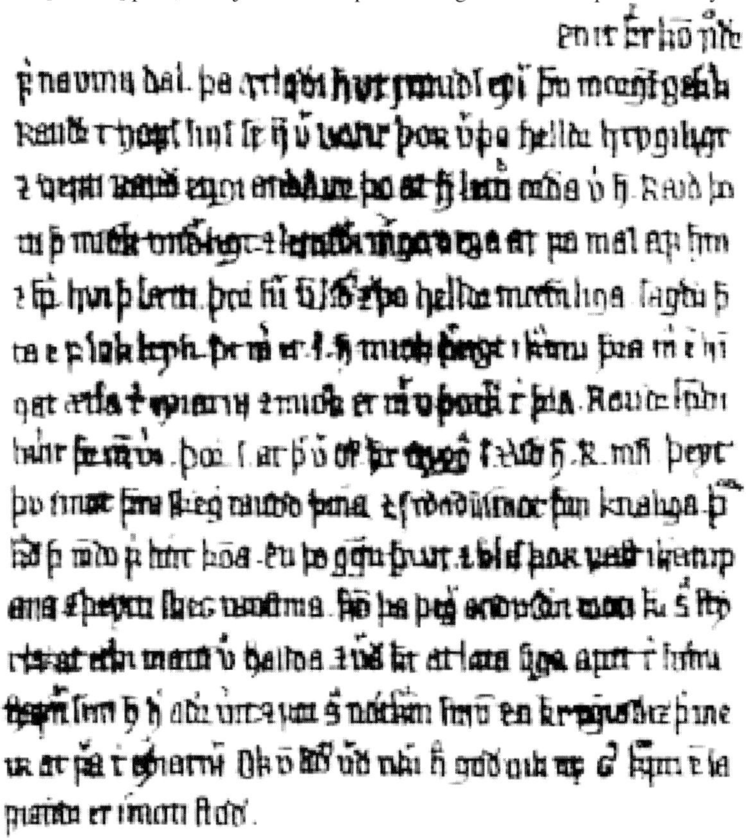

Figure 2: AM 61, fol., f. 34ra, lines 22–37. Thor blows into his beard to raise a wind against Óláfr Tryggvason. (Photo: Det arnamagnæanske Institut, Copenhagen.)

lítit koma. En þó gengu þeir út ok blés Þórr fast í kampana ok þeytti skeggraustina [328/21]. Kom þá þegar andviðri móti konungi svá sterkt, at ekki mátti við halda ok varð konungr at láta síga aptr til sǫmu hafnar sem hann hafði áðr verit, ok fór svá nǫkkurum sinnum. En konungr
15 eggjaðisk því meirr at fara til eyjarinnar ok um síðir varð ríkari hans góðvili með Guðs krapti en sá fjandi er í móti stóð.

(Some textual variants: Line 1 *út í*] *til* Bergsbók, Húsafellsbók, AM 325 IX 1 b, 4to, Flateyjarbók; *í* AM 62 fol. (There is no suggestion elsewhere in the narrative that Rauðr is chief man of a group of islands, nor is the plural form *Rauðseyjar* found elsewhere in *RR*. The reading *til* is therefore more acceptable and is also found in *RR557*. It is adopted for the purposes of the translation given below.) Line 9 *skeggrǫdd*] *skeggraust* AM 325 IX 1 b, 4to; *skeggbrodda* Flateyjarbók).

Some criticism and interpretation of the two texts is appropriate here.

Although, as suggested above, *RR557* may be the more original of the two redactions by virtue of its independence, I have also suggested (a) that it may represent a shortened version of the original; and (b) that the scribe of AM 557 4to was rather careless. At all events, as far as the passage under scrutiny is concerned, I regard the text of *RR557* as less original (and less interesting) than that of *RRÓT*. In particular, the words enclosed in angle brackets may, as suggested, be regarded as corrupt. Attempts could be made to emend them (or at least explain how the corruption arose) but these would be speculative and probably irrelevant to the present argument.

We turn to the question of which of the three words *skeggbroddar*, *skeggrǫdd*, *skeggraust* to accept. As will be seen from the above:

(a) at *RRÓT*, 328/19, AM 61, fol., Bergsbók, Húsafellsbók and AM 62, fol. all agree on having the reading *skeggrǫdd*. AM 325 IX 1 b, 4to has *skeggraust*. Flateyjarbók has *skeggbrodda* (which, as will be seen, is also the reading of *RR557*).

(b) at *RRÓT*, 328/21, all extant manuscripts of *RRÓT* have *skeggraustina*. There is no parallel passage in *RR557*. *Skeggrǫdd* and *skeggraust* would be translated 'voice of one's beard' (cf., for example, Sephton, 1895, 207); *skeggbroddar* (nominative plural), 'bristles of one's beard' (cf. C–V, 542), or simply 'beard'.

Here four points may be made:

(1) While, as shown below, the word *skeggbroddar* appears elsewhere in Icelandic (and moreover in the expression *at þeyta skeggbrodda(na)*), the words *skeggrǫdd* and *skeggraust* are *hapax legomena* found only

in this passage. As *hapax legomena* they are to be regarded as *lectiones difficiliores* and deserve respect as such. (It is, of course, a rule of thumb of textual criticism to prefer a *lectio difficilior* to a *lectio facilior*.)

(2) Given the fact that (as has and will be shown) a word *skeggbroddar* (plural; singular: *skeggbroddr*) did exist, it is not difficult to see how a reading *skeggrǫdd*(-) might be corrupted to *skeggbrodd*(-) in textual transmission.

(3) That a word *skeggrǫdd* did, however, also exist is suggested by the appearance of what seems to be more or less a synonym, *skeggraust*, which, as noted, is found not only in all manuscripts of *RRÓT* at 328/21, but also as a variant to *skeggrǫdd* at 328/19 in AM 325 IX 1 b, 4to.

(4) While the reading *skeggbrodda* in one manuscript of *RRÓT* (namely Flateyjarbók) is also found at the corresponding place in *RR557*, the distribution of the different readings in the various manuscripts is difficult to explain if we assume that it was the reading *skeggbrodda* which was in the original text of *RR* or, at any rate, in the original text of *RRÓT*. If, at a point corresponding to *RRÓT*, 328/19, the original of *RRÓT*, like Flateyjarbók, had the reading *skeggbrodda*, then it is a little odd that AM 62, fol., the manuscript of *RRÓT* closest to Flateyjarbók, does not also have that reading but has *skeggrǫdd*.

In view of these four considerations, I am a little unwilling to jettison, as C–V suggests we might, the readings *skeggrǫdd* and *skeggraust* (cf. C–V, 542, which has: 'the skeggröddina and skeggraustina . . . is prob. only a false reading for skeggbroddana'). I think *skeggrǫdd* and *skeggraust* could well have been found in the original version of the *þáttr*. It is true that, as will be noted below, the expression *at þeyta skeggbrodda(na)* is found elsewhere in Icelandic. But an expression *at þeyta rǫdd* is also found (in *Thómas saga erkibyskups*; see below) and C–V (s.v. *þeyta*), perhaps rather inconsistently, seems quite prepared to regard this as a parallel to *at þeyta skeggrǫdd* in our passage. In fact, then, for the purposes of what follows, I think it reasonable to place the three readings *skeggbrodda*, *skeggrǫdd* and *skeggraust* on equal footing and to recognise them as they appear in the main texts of the two redactions of *RR*. And whichever of these three readings we accept probably makes no very great difference to the broader point being made in the present study.

Attention may be given to the vocabulary of the passage from *RR* in question under three headings as follows:

(α) First, we may consider the expression *blés í kampana* found in both texts. In his Latin translation of the passage, Sveinbjörn Egilsson (1828–1829, I, 325) translated the words *blés Þórr fast í kampana* in *RRÓT* as 'Thor buccas fortiter inflaret,' suggesting that what the god was doing was puffing out his cheeks. This interpretation should not be entirely dismissed; it could well be right. But somewhat against it speaks the consideration that the adverb *fast* in *RRÓT* does not perhaps seem particularly apposite to the action of puffing out one's cheeks. On the whole, one should probably prefer the interpretation suggested by other translators of the passage (who are probably in the majority); Rafn (1826–1827, I, 273) has 'Thor blæste stærkt i Skægget' and Sephton (1895, 207) 'Thor blew a hard blast into his beard.' Cf. Schomerus (1936, 92), who paraphrases: 'Thor . . . bläst gewaltig auf seinem Bart.' Harris (1980, 186) paraphrases: 'Thor puffed hard into his moustaches.' In this connection, it should be noted that the word *kampr* can certainly be used of facial hair both above and below the mouth. We may compare this passage from *Qrvar-Odds saga* (1888, 134): *Qgmundr . . . skattgildi alla konunga í Austrvegi á þann máta, at þeir skyldu allir senda honum á tólf mánuðum hverjum kampinn ǿfra ok neðra af sjálfum sér*. Here in *RR*, *kampar* would seem to refer to the hair below Thor's mouth, (and) his beard. Thor cannot, of course, be blowing straight ahead. And we need hardly entertain the idea that he is blowing upwards into his moustache; that would hardly be consistent with the following *ok þeytti skeggraustina*. And the plural form *kampar* can certainly be used of hair which, while it may be rooted above the mouth, ends below it (cf. ch. 244 of Snorri Sturluson's *Óláfs saga helga* in *Hkr* (II, 404), which refers to Bishop Grímkell's treatment of Óláfr helgi's dead body: *Síðan tók byskup sǫx ok skar af hári konungsins ok svá at taka af kǫmpunum. Hann hafði haft langa kampa, svá sem þá var mǫnnum títt.*). While, then, Sveinbjörn Egilsson's translation can by no means be entirely dismissed, what Thor seems to be represented as doing here is blowing down into his beard.

(β) Second, attention may be given to the verb *þeyta* which, as has been seen, appears on two occasions in the passage in *RRÓT*, at 328/18 and 328/21, but not at all in the passage in *RR557*. In both cases in *RRÓT* it has an object in the accusative. In the present context, it is probably best translated 'to make something sound (loud)', 'to sound something (loud)'. (The sense Fritzner (III, 1017) gives for it is 'bringe til at lyde'; and C–V (735) has 'to make sound'.) What must be noted here is that instances of this verb cited in the dictionaries (e.g. C–V and Fritzner) and in the unpublished collections of the Ordbog over det norrøne prosasprog show that where this verb appears elsewhere in Old Norse in this sense, it is used in the vast majority of cases of the blowing or sounding of a wind-instrument (e.g. *horn*, *lúðr* or *pípa*). Two examples of its use in this sense are: *Þeyta nú hvárirtveggju lúðra sína ok herhorn svá at bylr í ǫllum fjǫllum, þeim er í nánd eru* (*Alexanders saga*, 1925, 36), and *Hlaupa þeir þá á hendr þeim með þeyttum lúðrum ok háreysti miklu* (*Byskupa sǫgur*, 1938–1978, 393). It is true that in *Karlamagnus saga ok kappa hans* (1860, 181) the verb *þeyta* is used with *heróp* as an object (*þeyta kristnir menn hvellt heróp*; although even here the use of wind-instruments may be thought of as involved). But even in a case where the object of *þeyta* is *rǫdd* (which is therefore of particular interest in the present context), the comparison is made between this object of the verb and a wind-instrument: *Kalla þú með staðfesti, þeyt rödd þína sem móthorn, segjandi fólkinu glæpi sína* (*Thómas saga erkibyskups*, 1875–1883, I, 424, translating a letter from Pope Alexander III to King Henry II of England: *Clama, ne cesses, quasi tuba exalta vocem tuam, et annuntia populo meo scelera eorum* (*PL*, CC, 486; cf. Isaiah 58: 1)). It is not surprising, then, that in the glossary to *Thómas saga erkibyskups*, 1875–1883 (II, 564), *þeyta* is glossed 'to blow (a wind instrument)'.[5] It should also be remembered that the weak verb *þeyta* is a causative of the strong verb *þjóta* (cf. *ÍO*, 1177), and two points may be made in this connection. First, the verb *þjóta* can also have the sense 'blow (a wind instrument)'. This admittedly rare meaning is found, however, on at least two occasions in Old Norse: in verse 18 of *Hamðismál*, *áðr halr hugfullr / í horn um þaut* (*Edda*, 271), and in a verse ascribed to Máni skald in *Sverris saga*, 1920, 91, *sás þýtr í trumbu* (cf. *LP*, s.v. *þjóta*). (The ancient connection between the verbs *þjóta* and *þeyta* on the one hand and wind-instruments on the other is suggested, *inter alia*, by Gothic *puthaurn*, 'trumpet' (verb *puthaurnjan*, 'to trumpet').) Second,

---

[5] As the following quotation from *Norðanfari* (10th February, 1870, 12) shows, one could, in modern Icelandic at any rate, sound one's nose (*að þeyta nefið*) and produce a trumpet-like sound: *Saura-Mangi . . . hafði nef svo hvast og hart sem moldvörpueyra, og er hann þeytti nefið, hvein það svo hátt, sem þá er margir herlúðrar gjalla í einu.*

and perhaps more interestingly, *þjóta* (as well as being used of thunder) is used, sometimes more or less proverbially, of the wind (see e.g. *Grágás*, 1992, 457–458; cf. *LP* and Fritzner, s.v.). And a *nomen agentis*, *þjótr*, is found with the sense 'wind' (cf. *LP*, s.v.) The verb *þeyta* could, therefore, have had a sense 'to make, produce a sound similar to that of the wind'.

(γ) As suggested above, the two words *skeggrǫdd* and *skeggraust* are to be regarded as more or less synonymous (cf. *NO*, 375, which gives a translation 'røyst, stemme som høyrest gjennom skjegget' for both words). The noun *rǫdd* can be used of the noise made by a wind-instrument (such as a *móthorn*; see Fritzner, II, 739, for examples). It is perfectly possible that *raust* could have been used in the same sense although no examples have been found.

From the preceding discussion, it appears that Thor is being asked to blow down into his beard, to 'play' it as one might play some sort of wind-instrument. He complies and in so doing he presumably produces some sort of noise, that of his *skeggbroddar* or *skeggrǫdd* or *skeggraust*. This sound may, quite plausibly, be thought of as resembling the noise of the wind. But whatever noise he is thought of as making, what he does do is produce a head wind which impedes the progress of Óláfr Tryggvason's ships. The words *at þeyta skeggbrodda* may, then, be translated 'to sound one's beard' and *at þeyta skeggrǫdd/skeggraust* 'to sound the voice of one's beard'.[6]

On the basis of the preceding considerations, I translate *RRÓT*, 328/9–329/5, as cited above, as follows:

> And when the king [Óláfr Tryggvason] got north of Naumudalr, he determined to go out to Rauðsey. That morning, Rauðr went to his temple (*hof*) as was his habit. Thor was rather downcast and gave Rauðr no reply even though he addressed him. This seemed very strange to Rauðr and he tried in many ways to get Thor to talk and to find out what the matter was. Eventually Thor answered, albeit in very weary tones, that he had good reason for his mood,—'for,' he said, 'I am put in a very difficult predica-

---

[6] We may here note the Norwegian expression *å blåse i barten(e)*, 'to be angry, gruff', literally 'to blow into one's moustache'. The word *bart* comes from German and in the modern language normally means moustache. Cf. *Nynorskordboka*, 1986, 43: '*bart*... (ty.) skjegg på overleppa; ofte i fl pga dei to delane: *ha b-ar og hakeskjegg / blåse i b-en*, vere sint, brysk'. Whether this expression has any connection with the Old Norse one under discussion is difficult to say.

ment by the intended visit to our island of those men for whom I have the greatest loathing'. Rauðr asked who those men might be. Thor said it was King Óláfr Tryggvason and his force. Rauðr said: 'Sound (*Peyt þú*) the voice of your beard (*skeggrǫdd/skeggraust þína*; or, if we accept Flateyjarbók's *skeggbrodda þína* (also found in *RR557*) 'sound (the bristles of) your beard') against them and let us resist them doughtily.' Thor said that that would be of little use. Even so, they went outside and Thor blew hard down into his whiskers (*blés Þórr fast í kampana*; or, less probably, 'puffed out his cheeks') and sounded the voice of his beard (*þeytti skeggraustina*). Straightaway there arose a head wind against the king so strong that it could not be withstood and he had to retire to the same harbour as he had set out from. This happened several times and the more it happened, the more the king felt spurred on to get to the island. And eventually, through the power of God, the king's good intentions prevailed over the devil who was offering him resistance.

We have, then, in the passage from *RR* just discussed, the notion that by blowing into his beard (i.e. *at þeyta skeggrǫdd/skeggraust/skeggbrodda*) the god Thor was able to produce a wind. These questions now arise. Is this idea just the isolated invention of the author of *RR*? Or was it more widely current and then perhaps as an established belief of Norse heathendom? This issue has been given detailed attention and the conclusion reached that it is the second of these two alternatives that must obtain. In the following, evidence is produced in support of this conclusion under three headings (A), (B) and (C), as follows:

(A)

First we may briefly consider, mainly on a comparative basis and item by item, the various objects and actions involved in the process by which Thor is represented as producing the wind against Óláfr Tryggvason. This will sometimes be done within the context of comparisons with ideas from outside Iceland (or at least from outside *RR*) as to how wind might be produced by powerful or supernatural figures (and the like) or by magical methods. It must be noted that the investigation on this matter makes no claim to be exhaustive; that would, of course, have involved wide-ranging work in the mythologies, folklores and literatures of many nations. What is offered here are a few random parallels based, to no small extent, on Lyall Watson's somewhat popular book of 1984 and the works cited by Watson (which include those of James Frazer). This, in turn, will be done under six headings as follows:

(1) As has been noted above (p. 40), an interpretation of the words *blés Þórr fast í kampana* as 'Thor buccas fortiter inflaret' should not be entirely dismissed and would suggest that in blowing into his beard (cf. (2) below), Thor puffed out his cheeks. At all events, the wind or winds have, of course, been represented pictorially since the Middle Ages as bodiless heads blowing with puffed-out cheeks (cf. Watson, 1984, 254; the vignettes in OM, 20, 26, 28, 32). Note also the personified south-west wind of *Konungs skuggsjá* (1920, 91) who *bælger hvapta*. In Shakespeare's *King Lear* (Act III, Scene ii), we find: 'Blow, winds, and crack your cheeks! rage! blow!' We may note also verse 33 of *Ýmisríma* by Eiríkur Hallsson (1614–1698) (see *Stakar rímur*, 1960, 59):

> Því sagt var mér um Hræsvelgs ham,
> hvoftana kunni þeyta,
> Neptunum þann gusta gram
> get eg að láti heita.

(2) The idea of the wind as an emission from the mouth (or other orifice, for example, nostrils) of some being, often powerful, supernatural or divine, must be very common (cf. Watson, 1984, 327–329). Pictures of blowing faces (for instance at the corners of old maps) have been mentioned in (1). In the section on the winds in the thirteenth-century Norwegian *Konungs skuggsjá* ([1955], 69–73), winds from the eight points of the compass are quite elaborately personified and produce their blasts by blowing, puffing and sighing; such verbs as *blása, gusta* and *andvarpa* are used. For example, the north wind *setur á höfuð sér ískaldan hjálm yfir jökluðu skeggi, blæss stríðlega að haglsfullum skýfjöllum*. And the north-east wind *situr reiðulega með snjódrifnu skeggi og gustar kaldlega vindþrotnum nösum, eitlar augum undir hrímfrosnum brúnum, snerkir kinn undir kaldskýjuðu enni, hvetur hvofta með ískaldri tungu, blæs af þjósti með smuglegu rennidrifi*. In 'Rauðs þáttr ins ramma' (cf. Appendix, pp. 161–164 below), it seems to be implicit that Rauðr's fortune in having a following wind is to some extent a result of his ability to blow through his mouth. Frazer (1911, I, 322) refers to Hagen (1899, 269) and writes: 'The natives of the island of Bibili, off German New Guinea, are reputed to make wind by blowing with their mouths. In stormy weather the Bogadjim people say, "The Bibili folk are at it again, blowing away".' In *The*

*Independent* (newspaper) of 8th April, 1989, Bridge writes this of a windy vexation for sunbathers at a holiday resort on the south coast of Crete: 'There was something faintly absurd in the sight of rows of naked bodies wincing in unison as they were lashed by salvo after salvo of sand and stones on the beach at Damnoni. "Gaddafi is blowing," say the Cretans of the wind that sweeps north across the Mediterranean from Libya. If that was the colonel blowing, I would hate to catch him in a rage.'

(3) Three of the eight winds of *Konungs skuggsjá* (cf. above) appear to have beards. The Boreas of Greek mythology was often represented with a beard. And the beard was, of course, part of the traditional iconography of Thor as well as being a symbol of his power (cf. *NK*, XXVI, 22). Grimm (1875, I, 147) suggests that it had meteorological assocations in, for example, Frisian folklore. And one might well imagine that when, as in the first stanza of *Þrymskviða* (*Edda*, 111), Thor got into a rage and shook his beard (*scegg nam at hrista*), this was thought of as having meteorological consequences. Cf. Gjærder, 1964, 102; Ellis Davidson, 1964, ch. 3.

(4) As noted above, the verb *þeyta* is used particularly of the blowing of wind-instruments. In the passage under consideration Thor appears to 'play' his beard like a wind-instrument. The idea of the wind as a figure playing a wind-instrument or the sound of the wind as the noise produced by such an instrument is quite an understandable one (cf. Watson, 1984, 242, 245, 254). Boreas, the north wind, was represented as an old man with grey locks blowing a conch-shell trumpet. In Shakespeare's *Henry IV, part 1* (Act V, Scene i), the scene is set with these words:

> The southern wind
> Doth play the trumpet to his purposes,
> And by his hollow whistling in the leaves
> Foretells a tempest and a blustering day.

And for examples of the noise of the wind as that of supernatural or unearthly musical instruments (e.g. pipes or trumpets), see *HWDA*, IX, col. 655, and references.

(5) In what precedes, it has been noted that mimetic magic is often invoked to produce a wind, e.g. by 'whistling for the wind' (cf. p. 11 above); it has also been noted that a verb which could be used more or

less proverbially in Old Norse for the blowing of the wind was the strong verb *þjóta* 'to emit a whistling sound' (so C–V); thirdly, it has been suggested that the causative form of *þjóta* (strong verb; < *\*þeutan*) is *þeyta* (weak verb; < *\*þautian*), the verb we are, of course, treating in the present context. There might well, then, be some idea of sympathetic magic here: by causing his beard (*skeggbroddar*) or the voice of his beard (*skeggrǫdd, skeggraust*) 'to sound' (*þeyta*) (or perhaps 'to vibrate'), Thor could well have been encouraging the wind to blow.[7] And here the following points may be worth making: First, that a bull-roarer might sometimes be referred to in Icelandic by the

---

[7] For some sort of parallel to the mimetic weather-magic connected with Thor suggested here (although to induce thunder rather than wind), we note the following passage in Saxo (350) about a raid in the 1120s by the Danish prince Magnus (Nielsen) apparently off the east coast of Sweden: *Magnus inter cetera trophæorum suorum insignia inusitati ponderis malleos, quos Ioviales vocabant, apud insularum quandam prisca virorum religione cultos, in patriam deportandos curavit. Cupiens enim antiquitas tonitruorum causas usitata rerum similitudine comprehendere, malleos, quibus cæli fragores cieri credebat, ingenti ære complexa fuerat, aptissime tantæ sonoritatis vim rerum fabrilium specie imitandam existimans. Magnus vero, Christianæ disciplinæ studio paganam perosus, et fanum cultu et Iovem insignibus spoliare sanctitatis loco habuit. Et adhuc quidem eum Sueones perinde ac cælestium spoliarum raptorem sacrilegum autumant.* (I am grateful to Robert Ireland for clarifying certain points in the following translation of this passage, any flaws in which are, however, my responsibility.) 'Magnus took care to have sent home, amongst other remarkable trophies, certain hammers of unusual weight, which they call 'Thor's hammers' (*mallei Ioviales*) and which were held sacred by the old religion of men on a certain island. For the ancients, seeking to explain the causes of thunder in terms of a resemblance to familiar objects, had hammers sheathed in heavy bronze; with these, they believed that the crashings of the heavens might be brought about, and considered that such powerful sounds might be most aptly imitated by the analogous din of the smith's workshop. But Magnus, in his love for Christian teaching and his antipathy towards paganism, considered it an act of piety to deprive the temple of its holiness and Thor (*Iupiter*) of his emblems. And indeed even to this day the Swedes count him guilty of sacrilege as if he were a robber of spoils from heaven.' Ellis Davidson (1965, 3) suggests that, when the model goat-drawn Thor's chariot in the temple in Trøndelag (cf. p. 97 below) described in *ÓT* (I, 378–386) was pulled along on its wheels, the intention was to imitate the noise of thunder. This, as far as I can see, is reading rather more into the text than is warranted, but the idea is interesting. Certainly thunder was interpreted as the noise made by Thor's vehicle; cf. *NK*, XXVI, 124; *MRN*, 99.

word *þeytispjald* (or *-speldi*). Second, that bull-roarers appear to have been known in Scandinavia since the Stone Age (cf. Helgi Guðmundsson, 1979, and references). Third, that as observed above (p. 11), bull-roarers were often used elsewhere in the world in an attempt to influence wind and weather by sympathetic magic. For example, Frazer (1911, I, 324) writes: 'In some islands of Torres Straits the wizard made wind by whirling a bull-roarer; the booming sound of the instrument probably seemed to him like the roar or the whistling of the wind.' It seems quite possible, then, that bull-roarers might have been used in Scandinavia to induce winds and then perhaps referred to in Old Norse by a word containing the element *þeyti-*.[8]

(6) The passage under discussion seems to suggest that the wind might be equated with the voice of Thor (cf. the elements *-rǫdd*, *-raust*). The idea of the (noise of the) wind as the voice of some supernatural being is doubtless to be found in mythologies and folklores elsewhere in the world. (It is, of course, closely related to the idea of the wind as the blowing (etc.) of some supernatural being; cf. (2) above.) Certainly Watson (1984, 261) argues this to be the case, although some of the references he gives are rather unconvincing on closer examination. One of them, however, may be noted here, that to Howitt's articles of 1884. As just noted, the bull-roarer (which might have been referred to as *þeytispjald* in Icelandic) can be used in meteorological magic, especially in wind-magic, and not least by the aboriginal peoples of Australia. It is therefore of interest that the Australian tribe(s) referred to by Howitt made frequent use of the bull-roarer (known as the *mŭdji*) and believed it originally to have been created by Daramulun who seems to have been a sky-god and in control of thunder (cf. Howitt, 1884a, 192–193). And Howitt (1884b, 446) writes of the *mŭdji* that 'the noise made by it is the voice of *Daramūlŭn*, calling together the initiated, and, moreover, it also represents the muttering of thunder, which is said to be his voice "calling to the rain to fall and make the grass grow up green"'.

---

[8] Gomme (1894–1898, II, 291; cf. I, 51) records the bull-roarer in Scotland in the nineteenth century where it was used under the name 'Thun'er spell' in a children's game and as an instrument of meteorological magic to protect oneself against 'the thun'er bolt' during thunder-storms (cf. Spence, 1947, 84–85). Cf. H395. (It should be remembered that 'like repels like', as well as like producing like; cf. H423; pp. 57–58 below.)

(B)

A second, perhaps rather more compelling body of evidence in this context comes from a somewhat unexpected source, namely from later Icelandic folk-tradition as reflected in post-medieval Icelandic poetry and other writings. Following up a reference from Sigfús Blöndal's Icelandic-Danish dictionary (1920–1924, 968, s.v. *þeyta*), we find that Matthías Jochumsson (1835–1920), in his poem *Þórs-mál*, has this verse (Matthías Jochumsson, 1902–1906, III, 202, verse 4):

> Lítið lograstir
> leiftra við himin;
> Þór er að þeyta
> þrúðga skeggbrodda,
> hljóðar húmstormur,
> hræðist kyn þjóða.

Matthías's *Þórs-mál* is based on Longfellow's *The Challenge of Thor* (in his *Tales of a Wayside Inn*), which, however, has no exact equivalent to the verse just cited. Cf. Longfellow, 1904, 364–365; verse 4 reads:

> The light thou beholdest
> Stream through the heavens,
> In flashes of crimson,
> Is but my red beard
> Blown by the night-wind,
> Affrighting the nations!

Now one might at first sight surmise that Matthías picked up the phrase *að þeyta skeggbrodda* solely from one of the nineteenth-century printed editions of *RR* which existed in his time (e.g. from *Flat* (I, 296), where *skeggbrodda* appears in the main text; or even from the edition of *Óláfs saga Tryggvasonar in mesta* in volumes I–III of *Fms*, where, on p. 303 of vol. I, Flateyjarbók's (*skegg*)*brodda* is given as a variant to *skeggravdd*). But such a proposition is in itself far from probable. And from a consultation of the collections of the Orðabók Háskólans in Reykjavík, we can safely infer that the expression *að þeyta skeggbrodda* was more widely used than in the instances so far cited. It is used of supernatural beings capable of producing winds, perhaps mainly of Kári.[9] The parallel material found (and there is probably more) may be itemised as follows:

(1) In *Höddu-ríma* by Eggert Ólafsson (1726–1768), it is said of

---

[9] The reference to Kári in three of the instances cited from modern Icelandic here is noteworthy. Kári appears in Old Icelandic sources (see *ÍF*, XXXIV, 3;

Kári that he *óðum blès í skegg-broddana* (see *Kvæði Eggerts Ólafs-sonar*, 1832, 202); we are told that 'þessi ríma var gjörð í góðum byr, á ferð frá Kaupmannahöfn til Vestmannaeya, árið 1750'.

(2) Þorlákur Þórarinsson (1780, 287) in a section headed 'Skegglof' has these words (unnormalised): *Skegg=Broddaña þeyter.* (Þorlákur lived 1711–1773. The first edition of *Nokkur ljóðmæli* of 1775 does not appear to have contained the relevant section and phrase.)

(3) In a poem headed 'Ljóðabréf Björns Stephensens á Esjubergi til Magnúsar bróður síns, síðar konferenzráðs, ort nálægt 1800' (Björn Stephensen, 1914), we find these two lines: *Brodda þeyta kári kann, / köldum fleytir anda.* The substitution of *brodda* for *skeggbrodda* suggests that the expression *að þeyta skeggbrodda* was well known. Björn Stephensen lived from 1769 to 1835.

(4) An Icelandic translation of Hans Christian Andersen's *Paradisets Have* published in *Iðunn*, 1887, has this: *jeg* [i.e. Norðri, the north wind] *þeytti skeggbroddana, lagði fram drekum mínum, hinum fjallháu jökum, og ljet þá merja sundur bátana* (Andersen, 1887, 50). (The Danish here has: 'jeg blæste op, lod mine Sejlere, de klippehøje Isfjelde, klemme Baadene inde'; cf. *H. C. Andersens Eventyr og Historier*, I, 1905, 174.) Cf. the reference to the bearded north wind in *Konungs skuggsjá* cited on p. 44 above.

---

*SnE* 1998, 183; *Flat*[2], I, 22 (where it is said that *hann réð fyrir vindum*) and 241). Although we are told so little about him, he appears to represent the wind or control it (cf. *AR*, I, 250; *KL*, s.v. *Vær og vind; Ægir*). Now in Dalin's Swedish dictionary of 1850–1853 (I, 802) we find this entry: 'KAJSA. *Blås, Kajsa!* uttryck, vanligt på sjön, då man önskar frisk vind i seglen, och upp-kommet af *Blås, Kåre!* hvilket sednare ord man af okunnighet förvexlat med *Kari. Kare* (deraf vårt *Kåre*) betyder i fornspråket: vind.' It is true that the name *Kajsa* in the expression *Blås Kajsa!* does not appear to go back to *Kåre*; as noted (p. 12 above), Norlén (1972) has shown that *Kajsa* must, in fact, be derived from the name of St Katherine of Alexandria (Swedish: *Katarina av Alexandria*; cf. *KL*, VIII, cols 335–343). Even so, one tentatively wonders if some such expression as *Blås, Kåre!* addressed to some *male* figure repre-senting the wind might not have existed in Swedish in post-Reformation times (cf. the statement in Dalin's dictionary and the unpublished source from Bohuslän cited by Norlén, 1972, 73). Certainly in Swedish in recent times *kåre* is used of a breeze suitable for sailing. And in view of the references to Kári in these Icelandic sources, Norlén's statement (74) that 'han omnämnes inte heller under någon annan tidsepok i folktraditionen efter uppträdandet i den forn-nordiska mytologien' may need some reconsideration. Cf. also Note 2 above.

(5) Perhaps the latest analogue is found in the works of Theodóra Thoroddsen (1863–1954); in her *Bjarni í Skemmunni*, there is a reference to *vindstrokurnar, sem hann gamli Bárður Snæfellsás sendir okkur úr skeggbroddunum* (see Thoroddsen, 1960, 156).

Finally, in adducing modern analogues to the phrase *at þeyta skeggbrodda*, and while we have that personification of the wind, Kári, in mind, we may also note a modern parallel to the phrase *at blása í kampana* (*RRÓT*, I, 328, lines 20–21). In a ditty for children in Páll J. Árdal's *Ljóðmæli og leikrit* (1951, 92–93), we find this verse: *Kári blæs í kampana, / klórar nöglum frerann, / skefur ofan skaflana, / skuggalegur er hann*. Páll Árdal lived 1857–1930. (We may also note that in the instance from Eggert Ólafsson's *Höddu-ríma* cited above under (1), the verb of the expression *at blása í kampana* appears.)

(C)

From (A) and (B) it is already clear that the notion that a wind could be produced by a supernatural figure (such as Thor) blowing into his beard was not peculiar to the author of *RR*. It was obviously more widespread. And there is no reason for supposing that we have other than a genuine folk-belief here, which was current at least as early as the time of the writing of *RR*. What we may consider here in (C), however, is to what extent we may have a genuine *heathen* belief. And here attention may be drawn to two factors of possible relevance, as follows:

In ch. 3 of Tacitus's *Germania* (1961, 34), we find the well-known reference to the mysterious *barditus* of the Germani (which is clearly some sort of battle-cry):

> Fuisse apud eos et Herculem memorant, primumque omnium virorum fortium ituri in proelia canunt. sunt illis haec quoque carmina, quorum relatu, quem barditum vocant, accendunt animos futuraeque pugnae fortunam ipso cantu augurantur; terrent enim trepidantve, prout sonuit acies, nec tam voces illae quam virtutis concentus videntur. affectatur praecipue asperitas soni et fractum murmur, obiectis ad os scutis, quo plenior et gravior vox repercussu intumescat.

Of this passage, the following translation is offered, based heavily on those in Tacitus, 1961 (35; Önnerfors) and Tacitus, 1970 (103; Mattingly/Handford):

> It is said that Hercules has also visited them [i.e. the Germani] and they sing of him as the foremost of all heroes when they are about to engage in

battle. They also have those songs which they chant to kindle their courage. These songs they call *barditus* and, from the sound of such songs, they forecast the outcome of an imminent battle. For they are either able to terrify their foe or they themselves become frightened according to the character of the noise their company makes; and they regard it not merely as so many individual voices chanting at the same time but rather as a choral unison expressing their valour. They seek especially to attain a harsh and intermittant roar by holding their shields in front of their mouths so that, by this, the sound of their voices resounds and grows to a full and deep crescendo by the reverberation.

In his commentary to the *Germania*, Müllenhoff (1900, 136) hazarded an explanation of the word *barditus* relating it to the Germanic word for 'beard' (cf. Old High German *bart*, Old English *beard*, Old Icelandic *barð*); Hercules would be an *interpretatio Romana* for Thor (or an earlier counterpart of corresponding name). Müllenhoff continued his argument:

> *barditus* wäre demnach 'die bartrede' und zwar des Hercules, des donnergottes, den die Germanen *ituri in proelia canunt.* altn. wird *skeggrǫdd* 'bartruf' vom unwetter gebraucht, das Þórr gegen die feinde sendet . . . *barditus* bedeutet also ein donnerähnliches getöse, ein getöse in dem die stimme des gottes nachgeahmt wird. je nach dem ausfall erfuhren die krieger, ob der gott, den sie eben angerufen, ihnen beistehn wolle und gegenwärtig sei . . . für mehr als einen versuch, den dunklen ausdruck aufzuhellen, möchte ich aber diese erklärung nicht ausgeben.

I cannot here enter into a full discussion of Müllenhoff's suggestion. Suffice it to say that neither it nor, it should be noted, any other explanation of the word *barditus* has found general acceptance (cf. *RGA*[2], s.v. *Barditus* and references). But it is perhaps not to be entirely dismissed; Harris (1980, 186–187), for example, thinks it has 'great merit'. The point to be made here then is that if Müllenhoff's conjecture is by any chance correct, then it would, of course, suggest that the idea of Thor raising a wind by blowing into his beard may have had very ancient origins and then, of course, heathen ones.

The second point of relevance here is this: It has been noted above (p. 33) that in the so-called conversion-*þættir*, details of heathen practice are often given and this sometimes in a rather satirical or scornful manner. Now it can be shown that in certain cases the information in question represents genuine reminiscences of pagan customs, beliefs and superstitions. Two clear-cut examples may be given (cf. Harris, 1980, 187): In *Ǫgmundar þáttr dytts* (see *ÍF*, IX, 99–115), which certainly comes close to being a conversion-*þáttr*, there is some account of the cult of Frey and the way an effigy of the god was carried in a chariot around the provinces of Sweden. By comparison with various independent sources (and not least with ch. 40 of Tacitus's *Germania*, 1961, 88–91), the information given can be shown to contain authentic traces of worship of the god (cf. *MRN*, 165–175). Again, in the bizarre but colourful *Vǫlsa þáttr* preserved in Flateyjarbók (cf. p. 33 above), there can be little doubt that we have memories of phallus-cult in heathen Scandinavia (cf. *KL*, s.v. *Falloskult*; *MRN*, 256–258). So, as Harris (1980, 187) suggests, there is no reason why the story in *RR* of Thor producing a wind by blowing into his beard should not be a genuine pagan survival.

CHAPTER THREE
# THREE BEARD-CLUTCHING FIGURES

THE ARGUMENTS of the previous chapter have suggested that, in the Old Norse world, Thor was thought capable of producing a wind by blowing into his beard. Now in *RR*, Rauðr is able to persuade his image of Thor to raise a *head wind* against Óláfr Tryggvason and his ships by blowing into his beard; what one might wonder is, whether it was also believed possible for Thor (or images of him) to raise a *favourable wind* (and then for sailing) by this same procedure. In the light of the discussion so far, the proposition seems far from improbable and we shall return to it shortly. Before doing this, however, we may broaden the discussion, and digress somewhat, in order to take account of various more general factors. This will be done under five headings as follows:

(1) *The existence of amulets*. Amulets seem to have existed during at least the last three millennia, more or less everywhere throughout the world, including Norse Scandinavia. The following brief notes give examples mainly from outside Scandinavia, some typical, some random, some of relevance in the present context. They are based to no small extent on the article 'Charms and amulets' in volume III of James Hastings's *Encyclopædia of religion and ethics* (1910, 392–472; abbreviated H) (cf. also *HWDA*, s.v. *Amulett, Talisman*; Grieg, 1954; *KL*, s.v. *Amulettar*; *RGA*$^2$, s.v. *Amulett*; Meaney, 1981).

Through the agency of amulets, superstitious man believes himself able to influence the world around him by magical means. Amulets may be prophylactic, they may be productive, or they may be malevolent (cf. H416–421; p. 10 above). They may bring 'luck' in general. They have, however, many specific purposes (cf. H393): for example, they may afford protection against disease, falls, the pangs of childbirth, the evil eye, shipwreck or drowning (cf. H400 and p. 8 above), death in battle, lightning (cf. Note 8 in Chapter 2). Or they may give success in journeys and seafaring, in trade (cf. H466), in hunting and fishing (including, for example, seal-hunting and whaling), in love, even in winning lawsuits and gaining access to potentates (cf. H413) or becoming invisible (H439). They may allow one to control the actions of the tide (H450; *Nihongi*, 1956, I, 103; cf. pp. 3–4 above). And amulets (and the like) were often used in the regulation of meteorological conditions, rain, sunshine, hailstorms and not least, as indicated above (pp. 10–12), the wind (cf. H419, H466 and *passim*).

The material of amulets might be almost anything, animal, vegetable or mineral. Metals were especially valued, partly because of the relative difficulty in obtaining them, partly because of the aura of mystery surrounding the smith's craft (H395); amongst metals, bronze was particularly favoured (see e.g. H410, H412, H413, H437, H441, H464; Meaney, 1981, 190 and *passim*). But amber was another material often used (cf. e.g. H413, H422; *KL*, s.v. *Rav*; Meaney, 1981, 67–71; *VH*, 278). An amulet might, then, take the form of a simple natural object, for example, a stone, (part of a) plant or the claw of an animal. Or it might be some rarer natural object, for example, a double walnut or a nodule of coal. But amulets might, of course, also be man-made (and manufactured objects, elaborately wrought, sometimes in ritual circumstances, might be thought of as more efficacious; cf. H397). For example, a coin or medallion (e.g. bearing the image of St Christopher) or bracteate might be an amulet. Prehistoric stone implements were often used as amulets (H395; cf. *KL*, s.v. *Torvigg*) as were strings, threads and knots (cf., for example, H444, H463; cf. pp. 11–12 above). And they very often took the form of representations of parts of the body, such as eyes (particularly to counter the effect of the evil eye; cf. H398 and *passim*), legs (Andrews, 1994, 71–72; *VH*, 278), phalluses; or of animals (e.g. scarabs, snakes, whales), ships or weapons. Many amulets would be associated with religion; they might be miniature images of gods (e.g. Buddhas (cf. H468); cf. H410 (Assyrian), H437 (Greek), H450 (Japanese) and Andrews, 1994, 14–35 (Egyptian)), or symbols or attributes of gods (cf. H413, H456). The Christian cross often served, of course, as an amulet (H426–427). Amulets could carry inscriptions (often magical or religious; cf. H397–398), for example, the name of a deity (e.g. the Tetragrammaton) or an invocation of a deity (cf. the runic amulet from Ribe with its inscription mentioning Odin, and the amulet, also runic, from Södra Kvinneby, Öland, with its invocation of Thor). And various magical words, signs or symbols might also appear on amulets (e.g. the swastika; cf. H445; *DR*, cols 774–777, 1005–1008).

Amulets were positioned in various places and attached to various objects (cf. H393), for example, at thresholds and doorways, under pillows, on household furniture (H393), on ships (cf., for example, H402, H445, H450), in places where livestock was kept or crops grown, at boundaries (cf. H447 and Strömbäck, 1970, 159–162), places of burial and cross-roads. But they were most frequently attached to the human body; hence, of course, the fact that they were small and portable (cf., for example, H438). They were very often hung around the neck (see, for example, H399, H437, 446), often inside the shirt (H453), carried in pouches at the belt or hung from the belt (see, for example, *HWDA*, I, col. 381; H406), sewn into the clothes, carried around the arm. Amulets might also be attached to domestic animals or livestock.

The active use of amulets for magical purposes was frequently accompanied by oral incantations, the rehearsal of spells, etc. (see H *passim*).

(2) *Miniaturisation*. As just suggested, amulets were, in general, small and portable. For this reason, and as noted, they frequently took the form of miniaturisations of larger objects, and not least of miniature effigies of gods, of symbols of gods or of other supernatural objects. As far as medieval Scandinavia is concerned, there is ample evidence for such miniaturised objects in both the archaeological material and the literary sources (cf. Arrhenius, 1961; Fuglesang, 1989; *VABC*, 173). Actual miniatures of spears, swords, axes and scythes have been found and also of chairs. These are probably to be regarded as amulets, some probably symbols of gods (e.g spears as symbolic of Odin).[1] And

---

[1] About a dozen Viking-Age amulets representing miniature chairs (sometimes in the form of so-called 'log-chairs') are known from Sweden and Denmark (cf. Fuglesang, 1989, 16). They seem to have been found particularly in women's graves (cf. Arrhenius, 1961, 150: 'miniatyrstolarna äro hittills endast påträffade i kvinnogravar'). According to Anne-Sofie Gräslund (*VH*, 190), 'de kubbstolsformiga hängena kan eventuellt sättas i samband med asagudarna—stolen skulle symbolisera guden på sin tron; såväl Oden som Tor har föreslagits'. Certainly a connection is made between these objects and *Odin* in both Arrhenius (1961, 157) and Drescher and Hauck (1982, 289). But I wonder if a connection with *Thor* is not more appropriate. Some reasons might be: (a) It is clear that Thor was conventionally represented as *sitting*, either on a throne (as in Adam of Bremen's account of the temple in Uppsala) or in his chariot; cf. also Ljungberg, 1947, 218. (b) At least two of the chairs of this type mentioned by Drescher and Hauck (1982, 255, 267–270) have

numerous miniature Thor's hammers have been found in places throughout the Norse world (cf. *KL*, s.v. *Torshamrar*). The well-known figurine found at Rällinge, Södermanland (SHM 14232) is between 6 and 7 cm. high and is generally thought to be a miniature representation of the god Frey. The silver effigy of Frey in *Vatnsdæla saga* was also so small that it could be kept in a pouch (see *ÍF*, VIII, 29). Snorri (*SnE*, 124) says that, if Thor so wished, his hammer could be so small that he could keep it inside his shirt (cf. *ÓTOdd*, 174; H453). And as noted (p. 17 above), the ship Skíðblaðnir not only always had a following wind, but it (or its sail?) could be folded up like a cloth and also carried in a pouch (*SnE*, 123).

(3) *Belief in the efficacy of amulets*. Various ideas, relating to both magic and religion, lie behind the belief in the efficacy of amulets in fulfilling their purposes (cf. (1) above). Belief in a supernatural potency, often referred to (if only for convenience) by the Melanesian word *mana*, is a feature of many primitive peoples. Whatever its source was conceived of as being, *mana* was a magical force which might be possessed in varying degrees of strength by a person or god or animal or object. Certainly amulets were thought of as having *mana* which gave them their efficacy. An object acquired this special efficacy and thus became an amulet in various ways (cf. H392–398). A stone, for example, may simply have attracted attention because of its special shape or some other feature which distinguished it from others (e.g. that it was naturally perforated); or an object might be regarded as having *mana* because of its rare material or elaborate manufacture; or simply because it had been kept and carried for a long time, perhaps (as amulets often were) handed down from person to person or from

---

been found in close proximity to miniature Thor's hammers (cf. Skovmand, 1942, 54–58; Ekelund, 1956, 152–153). (c) In ch. 23 of *Fóstbrœðra saga* (*ÍF*, VI, 243–245) a large chair is mentioned; on it an image of Thor is carved and it is owned by a woman (cf. Arrhenius's remark quoted above). It is placed *á stufugólfi miðju* (cf. Adam of Bremen's *in medio triclinio* of Thor's throne; cf. also Ljungberg, 1947, 128); when the fugitive Þormóðr Kolbrúnarskáld sits in it he becomes invisible to his pursuers (cf. the *empty* chair of the miniatures). Cf. H439, with its mention of Greek charms thought to confer the gift 'of becoming invisible or indiscoverable (the wish of runaway-slaves)'. (d) In anticipation of the conclusions of this chapter, we note that LI, which we identify as an image of Thor, sits on a log-chair. Cf. Trotzig, 1983, 365–366, and pp. 63 and 103–104 below.

generation to generation as an heirloom (H465; cf. *ÍF*, VIII, 26–27); or because it had come from a distant or special place (e.g a shrine or other religious centre; cf. H446). But there would also have been more specific and often more formal ways by which it was thought possible to endow an object with *mana* (or similar divine power). For example, it might be, as suggested, manufactured under ritual circumstances. Spells or incantations might be recited over it. Or it might be marked with special symbols or words. Cf. (4) below and Note 3.

According to H395, 'the Nicobarese set up images of ships to attract traders when their coco-nuts are ready for sale, and images of crocodiles to prevent crocodiles from attacking them while bathing'. Two common ideas, however vaguely conceived, lie behind such methods (cf., for example, Frazer, 1963, 14). First, there is the idea that 'like produces like', that the imitation of a phenomenon in some way will have the effect of producing that phenomenon. As noted (p. 11 above), by whistling and thus making a noise resembling the noise of the wind, one might give rise to a favourable wind. A seal-hunter might use a stone whose shape reminds him of a seal as an amulet to attract seals and therefore give him success (H395). Images of legs were meant to replace a lost limb or bestow power of movement on an existing one. Eyes were 'drawn on ships and boats as a sort of mimetic charm to enable them to see their way at night and avoid shoals and rocks' (H445). And by acting upon an object's symbolic representation, it was believed that one might act upon that object itself (cf. Falk, 1927, 35: 'En gjenstands mana gikk også over i dens dobbeltgjenger, den billedlige fremstilling av den. Fölgen herav var at man ved å besverge billedet kunde påvirke dets original'). Thus, of course, by sticking needles into the waxen image of a person it was thought to be possible to bring sickness on that person (cf. H423). And the intention of a number of Stone-Age petroglyphs in Scandinavia which show animals such as deer and elk heading towards precipices and lakes was to encourage the animals themselves to do likewise and thus make themselves easy prey. But second, perhaps paradoxically, the idea existed that 'like repels like' (cf. again H423). As noted, the Nicobarese seek to repel crocodiles by setting up images of them. The best scarecrows were, in fact, figures of crows. Flies might be kept away by setting up images of flies. And a particularly common application of the idea of like repelling like is in amulets against the evil eye: these often took the form of representations of the human face with eyes, often particularly large or piercing, intended to counter or divert the evil glance (cf. p. 54 above).

(4) *Old Norse terminology*: at magna, blótskapr, *etc*. As noted on p. 31 above in the summary of *RR*, when his adopter dies childless, Gunnarr/Rauðr maintains his cult of Thor and puts such a spell on the image of the god that it appears to be able to converse with him and walk around the island. The words used are (*RRÓT*, 320/12–15): *Ok er svá sagt, at hann magnaði með miklum blótskap líkneski Þórs þar í hofinu, at fjándinn mælti við hann ór skurðgoðinu ok hrærði þat svá at þat sýndisk ganga úti með honum um dǫgum ok leiddi Rauðr Þór optliga með sér um eyna*. In this context we must, of course, be on the lookout for both Christian tendentiousness and literary borrowing.[2] But even so, it is reasonable to say that both the verb *at magna* and the noun *blótskapr*, or at least the noun *blót*, belong essentially to heathen rather than Christian terminology. Now Hjalmar Falk (1927, 34–35) has given attention to the word *magna*. His arguments suggest that the Old Norse word for *mana* is *megin*, '(supernatural) power, strength'. According to him, 'gjennem trylleformler og blot (besprengning med blod) kunde en gjenstand bli ladet med mana eller bli et kraftcentrum. Det tekniske uttrykk herfor er *magna*.' In this way, ordinary stones (for example) could be endowed with apotropaic powers as amulets (cf. *Grágás*, 1992, 19: *Menn skulu eigi fara með steina eða magna þá til þess að binda á menn eða fénað*). But an object which had been *magnat* might have more active powers. For example, Falk (1927, 34) refers to the tree-stump (*rótartré*) in *Grettis saga* (*ÍF*, VII, 249–251)

---

[2] It should be stressed here that the following passages from the works cited in this context show verbal likenesses to the passage in question from *RR* which could well suggest verbal borrowing between the texts. *Ǫgmundar þáttr dytts* (*ÍF*, IX, 112): *Þar váru blót stór í þann tíma, ok hafði Freyr þar verit mest blótaðr lengi, ok svá var mjǫk magnat líkneski Freys, at fjándinn mælti við menn ór skurðgoðinu*. *Þorleifs þáttr jarlsskálds*, ch. 7 (*ÍF*, IX, 225–226): *lét hann* [i.e. Hákon jarl] *drepa einn mann ok taka ór hjartat ok láta í þenna trémann* [i.e. an image he has had made out of a piece of drift-timber; cf. the passage from ch. 79 of *Grettis saga* quoted in Note 3 below], *færðu síðan í fǫt ok gáfu nafn ok kǫlluðu Þorgarð ok mǫgnuðu hann með svá miklum fjandans krapti, at hann gekk ok mælti við menn*. *Ynglinga saga*, ch. 13 (*ÍF*, XXVI, 13): *Óðinn tók hǫfuðit* [i.e. Mímir's head] *ok smurði urtum þeim, er eigi mátti fúna, ok kvað þar yfir galdra ok magnaði svá, at þat mælti við hann ok sagði honum marga leynda hluti*.

which was *magnat* by an old woman and which assumes very active powers, including the ability to move, defying wind and weather, and eventually to play an important part in Grettir's downfall.³ Here we note that Thor's *megin* is not infrequently referred to: he has his *ásmegin*, 'divine strength', and his *megingjarðar*, 'belt of strength'. He is, we may assume, also *almáttugr* (*inn almáttki áss*) and *máttr* is a concept closely related to *megin* (cf. the expression *máttr ok megin*; *MRN*, 86, 263–268). Thor also has a son called *Magni*. On *magna*, see also *AR*, I, 275–279 and references. And, as has been seen, Rauðr is said to employ *blótskapr* to put a spell on his image of Thor. The word *blót* and related words, although of uncertain etymology, were, of course, very much part of the terminology of Norse heathendom and Old Norse magic (cf. p. 19 above; *KL*, s.v. *Blot*). As is remarked in *VAch* (401): 'The noun *blót* meant the act of worship or sacrifice, and was later used of any object or practice designed to give someone supernatural power—a clay image of a human being used in witchcraft, for example, could be called *blót*' (see C–V, s.v. *blót*, for injunctions in the Norwegian laws against ownership of such objects; also Grieg, 1954, 169–170). In, for instance, *Vǫlsa þáttr* (*Flat*, II, 331–336), the related word *blæti* is used of the fetish Vǫlsi.⁴ Cf. further *AR*, I, 414–415 and references.

---

³ *ÍF*, VII, 249–250 (ch. 79): *Þá beiddi kerling, at henni skyldi aka til sjávar . . . Þar lá fyrir henni rótartré svá mikit sem axlbyrðr. Hon leit á tréit ok bað þá snúa fyrir sér; þat var sem sviðit ok gniðat ǫðrum megin. Hon lét telgja á lítinn flatveg, þar gniðat var; síðan tók hon kníf sinn ok reist rúnar á rótinni ok rauð í blóði sínu ok kvað yfir galdra. Hon gekk ǫfug andsælis um tréit ok hafði þar yfir mǫrg rǫmm ummæli. Eptir þat lætr hon hrinda trénu á sjá ok mælti svá fyrir, at þat skyldi reka út til Drangeyjar, ok verði Gretti allt mein at . . . Vindr var útan eptir firði, ok hóf rót kerlingar í móti veðri, ok þótti fara eigi vánu seinna.* (On p. 256, the tree-stump is referred to as having been *magnat*.) We note certain verbal likenesses here to the account of Þórólfr Mostrarskegg's high-seat pillars (cf. pp. 24–25 above; *ÍF*, VII, 250, note 1). But *Grettis saga* may well give some idea of the realities of the way in which an object was *magnaðr* according to heathen practice. And we may more generally compare the log of *Grettis saga* with high-seat pillars. Cf. Note 2 above.

⁴ Another word, also used of Vǫlsi and also discussed by Falk, is the adjective *aukinn*. In this connection we note *RR557*, 98/26–28 (corresponding to *RRÓT*, 320/12–15): *En Rauðr . . . lét eigi hofit niðr falla heldr lét hann auka orði, sem áðr hafði verit, ok svá gat hann magnat Þór, at hann leiddi hann eptir sér um eyna.*

(5) *'Living images'*. From *Grágás* we understand that one might put spells on (*magna*) stones, in *Grettis saga* the old woman puts a similar spell on a piece of wood. But it was also thought possible to animate images of men and of gods. The Thor of *RR* was an image (*líkneski*) of the god which Rauðr brought to life by such means and over which he had no small measure of control. Thus the very vigorous and full-sized image (*líkneski*) of another god, Frey, which Gunnarr helmingr encountered and eventually overcame in Sweden, was animated by magic (*magnat*; cf. *ÍF*, IX, 112). In *Þorleifs þáttr jarlsskálds*, the pagan Hákon jarl has a human heart placed in a wooden image, the image is charmed (the verb is *at magna*) and sent to Iceland where it kills Þorleifr at the Alþingi (*ÍF*, IX, 225–227). (Here one is reminded of the *sendingar* of later Icelandic folklore.) In ch. 4 of *Ynglinga saga* (*ÍF*, XXVI, 12–13), Odin takes Mímir's decapitated head and uses charms (*magnaði*) so that it speaks to him and tells him secrets. And the miniaturised image (*hlutr*) of Frey in the first chapters of *Vatnsdœla saga* (although the word *magnaðr* is not used of it) is 'living' enough to make its own way from Norway to Iceland and, once there, to move around to find an auspicious place for its owner to settle (*ÍF*, VIII, 26–42; cf. *ÍF*, I, 217–219). (In this, it somewhat resembles Þórólfr Mostrarskegg's high-seat pillars; cf. pp. 24–25 above.) In the examples just cited, we are, of course, very much in the realm of fantasy. We must again be on the watch for literary motif. And we must beware of Christian tendentiousness; Christian writers would, of course, have been only too ready to represent the heathen gods as graven images brought to life by pagan sorcery. But the basic ideas underlying these stories are ones which were also held in reality; it was doubtless believed that images could, at least to some extent, 'come to life'. After all, even in the twentieth century, numerous 'weeping Madonnas' have been reported. And as recently as 1995, images of the elephant-headed Hindu god Ganesha, an insatiable glutton (and, incidentally, often invoked at the beginning of journeys), were believed to have started drinking milk in many places round the world (cf., for example, Brown, 1995).

Finally in the present context, and as a sixth factor, the following may be recalled:

(6) *Certain conclusions arrived at in Chapter 1*: That the practice of wind-magic, which included the use of, *inter alia*, wind-amulets (cf. (1) above), existed in medieval Scandinavia (as well as in various other

societies); that the need for a favourable wind for sailing was as great as in other societies and possibly much greater than in many or most of them; and that Thor was thought of as a god who had control of the wind.

We now return to the idea put forward in Chapter 2, that it was believed that Thor was capable of raising a fair wind by blowing into his beard. On the basis of the various factors just mentioned, it would now not be unreasonable to hypothesise as follows: *that there existed in Norse Scandinavia images of Thor blowing into his beard which were believed to help their manipulators produce favourable winds; that these images were not 'full-size' but represented the god in miniaturised form; such images would, then, have served as wind-amulets; as amulets, they may have been thought to have some special supernatural power; and this special power may, to some extent, have been thought to have been conferred on them by magical means* (blótskapr). It is true that in making these suggestions at this point and in view of what follows, I might be regarded as guilty of special pleading. Nevertheless, on the basis of the evidence adduced so far, they do not *a priori* seem at all improbable. I shall in what follows consider these suggestions in the light of three archaeological finds belonging to the Viking Age. Before doing this, however, I briefly return to the story of Hallfreðr vandræðaskáld's conversion mentioned on pp. 13–14 above.

In ch. 5 of *Hallfreðar saga* (*ÍF*, VIII, 151–152) we find Hallfreðr amongst a ship's company at Agðanes sacrificing to the heathen gods for a fair wind to escape from Óláfr Tryggvason's newly-converted Norway. No wind comes, and they are forced to sail into Þrándheimr, where Hallfreðr is baptised, perhaps somewhat reluctantly, at the instance of the king and with the king himself standing sponsor. The poet then stays with Óláfr, although not in altogether happy circumstances; Óláfr takes exception to the heathen content of some of his poetry. Also Hallfreðr quarrels with two of the king's courtiers, Óttarr and his brother Kálfr. He kills Óttarr, is condemned to death, and, although this sentence is subsequently commuted, relations remain strained. Then we find the following episode in ch. 6 of the saga (*ÍF*, VIII, 162–163; from the Möðruvallabók text with readings in square brackets from the version of the saga in *Óláfs saga Tryggvasonar in mesta*; cf. *ÓT*, I, 394–395; *Hallfr*, 55–56; Perkins, 1999, 186–187):

> Eitt sinn var þat, at konungr spurði hvar Hallfreðr væri. Kálfr segir: 'Hann mun enn hafa vanða sinn, at blóta á laun, ok hefir hann líkneski Þórs í pungi sínum af tǫnn gǫrt, ok ertu of mjǫk dulinn at honum, herra, ok fær hann eigi sannreyndan.' Konungr bað Hallfreð þangat kalla ok svara fyrir sik. Hallfreðr kemr þar. Konungr mælti: 'Ertu sannr at því, er þér er kennt, at þú [hafir líkneski Þórs í pungi þínum ok] blótir?' 'Eigi er þat satt, herra,' segir Hallfreðr; 'skal nú rannsaka pung minn; hefi ek hér ekki undanbragð mátt hafa, þó at ek vilda.' Nú fannsk engi sá hlutr í hans valdi, er til þess væri [líkligr, sem Kálfr hafði sagt á hann].

Later in the same chapter, Hallfreðr gets his revenge for the slander by blinding Kálfr in one eye.

Now it would doubtless be reading too much into the text of *Hallfreðar saga* to suppose that its author intended a connection between (on the one hand) any part Hallfreðr may have had in the sacrifices at Agðanes to the heathen gods, including Thor, for a fair wind and (on the other) the image of Thor which Kálfr so slanderously asserted he had in his possession and continued to worship after his conversion. This is not, of course, to deny that in terms of the narrative of the saga, Hallfreðr must have had some record of active pagan practice before his baptism to make Kálfr's calumny in any way plausible. And the episode in ch. 6 of *Hallfreðar saga* is, in itself, far from unrealistic. Doubtless the newly baptised often did waver and revert to their former pagan belief. Sometimes they (or those still unbaptised) may have carried idols of gods or their emblems surreptitiously (cf., for example, Meaney, 1981, 159). And there would, of course, also have been false accusations of recidivism. (One may recall here the story of the seventeenth-century Guðríður Símonardóttir, 'Tyrkja-Gudda', wrongfully rumoured to have worshipped an idol in Iceland after her years of captivity in Muslim Barbary.) Certainly, as suggested, there is good evidence that amulets and small images of divine figures were carried in purses or pouches.[5] But what is of greatest interest in the present context is the fact that a small figure of a man

---

[5] Amulets, figurines of gods, etc., seem, in the Old Norse world as elsewhere (cf. p. 56 above), to have been kept in pouches. As noted, Ingimundr appears to have kept his figurine of Frey in a pouch. Salin (1913, 408) argues that wear on RI may indicate that it was also kept in some sort of pouch. And other archaeological finds suggest that Thor's hammers and other amulets were kept in pouches; cf. Ström, 1984, 136 (Birka); *KL*, XVIII, col. 504 (Kaupang); Grieg, 1954, 188.

made of walrus-ivory (i.e. in Old Icelandic *af tǫnn gǫrt*) has indeed been discovered and that this has been interpreted by at least one scholar as an image of the god Thor. We now turn to it.

The object in question (abbreviated LI) was found in 1936 during the digging of foundations not far from the cathedral in Lund (see Figures 3 and 4; cf. *VArt*, 24–25 (to which the following description is partly indebted) and *VH*, 387). This small figurine of a man is made of walrus-ivory. He sits with his arms resting on his knees and holding his long beard with both hands. The eyes are large and round and the mouth and nose clearly represented. Apart from parallel lines on the top of the head which may indicate a skull-cap (but which may also indicate short hair), there is no sign of clothing. The figure is seated on a so-called 'log-chair' (Swedish: *kubbstol*; cf. *KL*, s.v. *Kubbestol*). Down the back of this there is a line of three rings-and-dots above a circle of five more; and there is a single ring-and-dot on the back of each of the figure's shoulders. The object is some 4.7 cm. high. LI is dated by Graham-Campbell (*VArt*, 24–25) to the 'Late Viking Period' (i.e. second half of the tenth century to the beginning of the twelfth century). It is now in Kulturen in Lund (KM 38.252).

In an article published in 1963, Ivar Lindquist appears to offer three reasons for a possible recognition of LI as an image of Thor:

(1) The figure of LI is seated on a chair. This, Lindquist suggests, is a characteristic feature of the representation of Thor and he compares Adam of Bremen's account (470) of the heathen temple at Uppsala which has Thor seated on a *solium*. Lindquist also compares the chair described in ch. 23 of *Fóstbrœðra saga* (*ÍF*, VI, 245–247; cf. Note 1 above) which has an image of Thor carved on it and which (he suggests) may, like the chair of LI, be a log-chair. Certainly Lindquist is on firm ground in his arguments here and we shall return to this feature of the representation of Thor below (pp. 103–104).

(2) Lindquist compares the eyes of LI with those of what he regards, with some justification, as a 'porträtt' of Thor on the runic rock at Norra Åby, Södermanland (Sö 86), and which he describes as 'hieratiskt arkaiskt cirkelrunda'.[6] Certainly large (or piercing or staring) eyes can be said to be of central importance in the iconography of Thor. This is a

---

[6] The location of the runic rock in question is sometimes given as 'Södra Åby' or simply as 'Åby'. In using 'Norra Åby', I follow the official notice at the site in 2001.

Figure 3: Walrus-ivory figure from Lund, Sweden (= LI; KM 38.252; height: 4.7 cm.). (By permission of Kulturen, Lund.)

# Three beard-clutching figures

Figure 4: Walrus-ivory figure from Lund, Sweden (= LI; KM 38.252; reverse). (By permission of Kulturen, Lund.)

point made on various occasions in Ljungberg's discussion of the matter ('Tor i bildframställningen', Ljungberg, 1947, 91–156) and again one which, together with the face on Sö 86, will also be treated in greater detail below (see pp. 101–102 and 123 below). We can, however, say here that Lindquist's view on this point again appears justified.

(3) Lindquist's remaining argument relates to the ring-and-dot pattern on the reverse of LI and is more controversial. It perhaps only succeeds in a slightly varied interpretation proposed by Gjærder (1964, 97–99). Lindquist saw the upper five rings-and-dots in their T-formation as the head and shaft of a hammer and, like others, the lower five as forming a larger ring. He presents a photograph of the reverse side of LI with white lines drawn in to make his point (his 'bild 5'). The hammer Lindquist quite confidently identified with Thor's hammer Mjǫllnir, the larger ring much more tentatively and less justifiably with Baldr's ring Draupnir. Gjærder developed this idea with the suggestion that the larger ring was rather the chain or cord to which amulets of the Thor's hammer-type were often attached or the loop like that from which the Thor's hammer on the rune-stone at Stenkvista, Södermanland (Sö 111), is suspended (Figure 21). Certainly the lines drawn in by Lindquist are suggestive of a Thor's hammer and of a ring; for purposes of comparison on this point, I juxtapose a picture of the Thor's hammer from Läby, Uppland (SHM 131), and Lindquist's 'bild 5' as my Figure 5. And just as the image of Thor with his hammer is carved on the back of the chair in ch. 23 of *Fóstbrœðra saga*, so Lindquist's and Gjærder's Thor's hammer is (partly) on the back of the chair in which the figure of LI is sitting. Lindquist's original suggestion on this point receives, then, some measure of acceptance from Gjærder and, for example, from H. R. Ellis Davidson (1967, 134). Other scholars appear more sceptical (see, for instance, *VArt*, 24–25; *VH*, 387).[7] And a perhaps more acceptable interpretation of the larger ring on the back of LI will be suggested on p. 76 below).

---

[7] What appear to be representations of the Thunder God's hammer, found in Kent and taken to be Anglo-Saxon, are now in National Museums and Galleries on Merseyside (Liverpool Museum). At least one of these is on a ring and has a series of small circles on its head and shaft in the form of a T with three circles for the head (see Ellis Davidson, 1965, 10 and plate I; Meaney, 1981, 149–150). For stylised signs of Thor's hammer in the form of a T in Danish runic inscriptions, see *DR*, cols 1007–1008. Meaney (1981, 147) refers to T-shaped bones used as amulets in modern times to bring general good

# Three beard-clutching figures

Figure 5. Left: Reverse of walrus-ivory figure from Lund (KM 38.252) with white lines drawn in by Lindquist. (Reproduced from Lindquist, 1963, 77, by permission of Kulturen, Lund.) Right: Thor's hammer from Läby, Uppland, Sweden (SHM 131). (Reproduced from Stephens, 1878, 41.)

Now any one of these three arguments suggested by Lindquist is probably, by itself, not strong enough to be decisive (although LI's large eyes are relatively indicative in the context). Taken together, however, they must be regarded as much weightier and make it reasonably probable that LI was intended to be a representation of Thor. And we may note certain minor factors of relevance: Graham-Campbell (*VArt*, 24) rightly describes LI's nose as 'fully modelled' and a prominent nose may well have been part of the accepted iconography of Thor (cf. p. 102 below). Thor was, of course, traditionally bearded (cf. p. 103 below) and so is LI. Finally, of course, Lindquist

---

luck and also to save fishermen from drowning; according to her, some have seen a connection between these and Thor's hammers. The silver Thor's hammer from Rømersdal, Bornholm (DNM 597; cf. *VH*, 276) is also attached to a ring and also has small circles on its head and shaft although not in a **T**-formation. Cf. also *KL*, I, fig. 16. On the back of a bronze statuette from Køng, Fyn, there are the remains of a runic inscription (cf. Moltke, 1976, 77–78, 101–102); one wonders if the intention here was to identify the object as some deity or to endow it with some special power.

is able to refer to the passage in ch. 6 of *Hallfreðar saga* for a parallel example of a miniature image of Thor made from the same material as LI.[8] A rival theory that LI is a playing-piece fails to explain various idiosyncratic details of the object under discussion.

The second item of interest is a small amber figure discovered during World War II while land was being ploughed on Feddet, the tongue of land on the eastern side of Præstø Fjord (Roholte parish) in southern Sjælland (see Figure 6; abbreviated FI; cf. Gjærder, 1964, 99–100; *OA*, 186–187, 203; *VH*, 202–203, 247). This has been in National-museet in Copenhagen since 1944 (DNM C24292). FI is about 4.6 cm. high, with a round head, a large ear (on its right-hand side) and a large place for an ear (on its left-hand side), oval eyes with wrinkles (it seems) at the corners, a broad, rather clumsy nose and a rectangular hole representing an open mouth. The man appears to be bald but has a long cylindrical beard which he clasps with both hands in much the same way as the Lund figure clasps his beard. FI was made terminating at the hips and according to Gjærder 'has never been longer'. Roesdahl (*OA*, 203) dates FI to the tenth or eleventh century. There are certain factors which suggest that this object may indeed be intended to portray Thor. There is, of course, the general likeness to the Lund figure which for stronger reasons can be taken as representing Thor. The two objects were found relatively close to each other, Feddet being less than 100 km. from Lund. Gjærder (1964, 100) certainly suggests that FI could have been an amulet. He notes that 'the back part of the head shows two bore-holes which may have served as a fastening for a chain or cord round the neck' (cf. *VH*, 247). (Threading holes are, of course, a feature of amulets; cf., for example, Andrews, 1994, 8.) And in *KL* (XIII, s.v. *Rav*) Birgitte Kjær also suggests we have an amulet here and, by implication, compares the Rällinge image (RI) and the

---

[8] We note that it is at Niðaróss/Trondheim that Hallfreðr is accused by Kálfr of possessing an image of Thor made of walrus-ivory. Trondheim seems to have been something of a centre for work and trade in walrus-ivory in the medieval period; cf. *VH*, 202–205, 390–391. The greatest supply of this material would, of course, have come from northern Norway. And one wonders if LI itself may not have been carved in Norway and then perhaps precisely in Trøndelag. For example, Claes Wahlöö (*VH*, 390) remarks that while there are a few signs that walrus-ivory was worked in Lund, a fragmentary walrus-ivory gaming-piece found there is more likely to have come from a Norwegian workshop. Cf. Perkins, 1999, 193 and note 2.

Figure 6: Amber figure from Feddet, Roholte parish, Sjælland, Denmark (= FI; DNM C24292; height: 4.6 cm.). (By permission of Nationalmuseet, Copenhagen.) See also cover illustration.

Eyrarland image (EI), which have been taken to be respectively Frey and Thor (and both of which will be dealt with later in this study). (It should, however, be noted that both Gjærder and Kjær also suggest that FI might have been a playing-piece.) Certainly miniature Thor's hammers, if not miniature Thors, made of amber have been found elsewhere, for example at Lindholm Høje (Ramskou, 1956, 180); at Paviken (Lundström, 1981, 67, 95, although this is possibly an axe); at Wolin (*VH*, 296); and at Birka (Ström, 1984, 136; probably kept in a pouch like Kálfr's invented *líkneski Þórs*; cf. Note 5 above). And amber was a favoured material for amulets (cf. p. 54 above). Its electrical properties might perhaps have been regarded as particularly appropriate to the god of thunder and lightning. But perhaps the feature of the object from Feddet which is of most interest in this context is the physique of the man it portrays. The impression of Thor one reasonably gains from the literary sources is that he is the strong man of the gods, a muscle man, a tough guy, something of a bruiser. And FI seems to represent such a figure: the amber figure has a bull-neck, rugged nose, a none too elegant ear, ample biceps and a bald head. It seems to portray not only the sort of person one might expect to see engaged in all-in wrestling in present-day Britain but also Thor as we might reasonably imagine him. It is true that Gjærder refers to the 'primitive shape' of the figure, perhaps suggesting technical incompetence. But I am more inclined to think that the creator of the figure consciously intended it to represent a man endowed with a robust physique and considerable strength and then quite possibly the god we are discussing. As Roesdahl rightly says (*OA*, 186), the figure radiates power, and this is precisely what one might expect of an image of Thor. There are, then, various factors to suggest that the figure is indeed meant to be a likeness of Thor (cf. Magnusson, 1976, 68). And there is nothing, as far as I know, which speaks against the proposition. The suggestion that the object was primarily intended as a playing-piece (also put forward in *OA* and *VH*) again fails to explain its idiosyncratic features and not least the two bore-holes at the back of the neck.

We turn thirdly to an object found at Chernigov in northern Ukraine (on the River Desna, about 130 km. north-north-east of Kiev) (Figure 7; for further illustrations, see Rybakov, 1949, 45; Pushkina, 1984, 87; *VH*, 308). Chernigov (Ukrainian: Chernihiv) was one of the chief cities of medieval Russia, probably second in importance only to Kiev. And

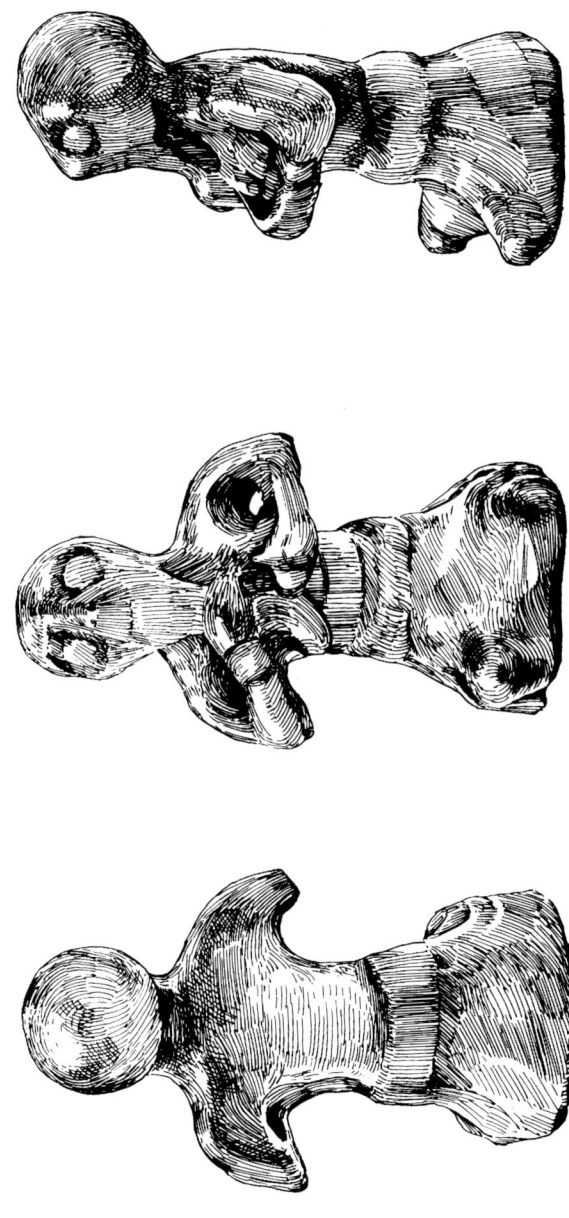

Figure 7: Bronze figure from Chernaia Mogila, Chernigov, Ukraine (= CI; GIM 76990/1539/77; height: 4.6 cm.). (By kind permission of the artist, Elena Kruchina.)

it was here, in the 1870s, that D. Samokvasov excavated one of the most important burial mounds of pagan Russia, the Chernaia Mogila ('Black Grave'; cf. Arbman, 1955, 90–94 and references). Alongside other finds, often somewhat more impressive, a small bronze statuette was discovered, heavily oxidised. This, Samokvasov (1908, 199) suggested, was an idol, possibly a Buddha. It was not, however, until the 1980s that satisfactory conservation work was carried out on the object at the Gosudarstvennyi Istorichii Muzei ('State Historical Museum') in Moscow, where it has the number 76990/1539/77 (abbreviated CI). The work (reported by Pushkina, 1984) revealed the image of a seated man, round-headed and bearded. His hands are raised to his chest and with his right hand he holds his beard, close to the mouth. His left hand also appears to touch (the end of) his beard but also seems to have held an object which has not been preserved. On his right wrist there is a bracelet. His mouth is represented by a small slit and the eyes are round and particularly large. According to Pushkina, the man is dressed in a caftan. Around his waist a broad belt is clearly discernible, the ends of which hang down to the right and left. The object is about 4.6 cm. high and now weighs slightly over 39 gm. In *VH* (308) CI is dated to the tenth century.

In her article, Pushkina finds two main reasons for making a positive identification of this figurine as Thor. First, she notes its beard. Thor's beard was, as has already been suggested above (p. 67), one of the god's main attributes. Second, Pushkina rightly draws attention to the broad belt which is such a relatively conspicuous feature of the figure. This she reasonably interprets as Thor's *megingjarðar*, specifically said by Snorri (*SnE*, 29) to be one of the god's special possessions and alluded to in skaldic poetry, including the *Þórsdrápa* ascribed to Eilífr Goðrúnarson (see Ljungberg, 1947, 218). And there are other factors of relevance: Pushkina herself notes the 'round, somewhat staring eyes' ('круглые, слегка выпащенные глаза') of the figure, which are also very large. As has been suggested in the discussion of the Lund figure above (cf. also pp. 101–102 below), large, 'cirkelrunda' (to borrow Lindquist's epithet), staring eyes are features of representations of Thor, a point stressed, as noted, by Ljungberg (1947, 125–126) in his study of the iconography of Thor (cf. again *MRN*, 83). Lastly it will be observed that CI has a particularly large and prominent nose and this, again as noted, may well have been part of the traditional iconography of Thor (cf. pp. 67 above and 102 below).

As we see, then, Pushkina interprets the statuette from Chernigov within a Scandinavian context, as an image of the god Thor. And there is no reason why she should not do so. She feels herself able to argue that there is nothing similar to it amongst Russian antiquities of the relevant period, nor elsewhere in Europe apart from Scandinavia. Now this, of course, is scarcely the place to discuss Scandinavian elements in the cultural and ethnic composition of tenth-century Kievan Russia or, more specifically, amongst the finds in the Chernaia Mogila. But a few points may be made in connection with the cult of the Norse gods in Russia, particularly that of Thor. What could well be a bronze image of Odin has been found at Staraia Ladoga (*VH*, 150, 298; cf. *VH*, 276 and Note 10 in Chapter 4 below). Thor's hammer rings have been found, for example, at Gorodishche, at Gnëzdovo and, particularly relevant in the present context, at Shestovitsa, a site on the Desna less than 15 km. downstream from Chernigov (see Novikova, 1992). Various of the personal names of men from Kiev, Chernigov and other places which appear in the Russo-Byzantine treaty preserved in *The Russian primary chronicle* for the year 945 contain the element *Þór-* (*RPC*, 73; Thomsen, 1877, 134, 140; cf. *MRN*, 86, on the name-element *Þór-* amongst settlers of Iceland and its evidence for Thor worship).Thor appears to have been venerated in Kievan Russia also under the Slavonic name *Perun*. For example, we are told in *The Russian primary chronicle* of the oaths the Rus swore by Perun and at least one of these can be shown to be typically Scandinavian in form and suggests belief in Thor (*RPC*, 74, 77; cf. *MRN*, 96 and references). Under various entries for the tenth century, *The Russian primary chronicle* tells us of idols of Perun erected in Kiev (*RPC*, 77, 93, 116–117). Constantine Porphyrogenitus (*DAI*, I, 60–61) describes the rites performed by Rus merchants on the so-called Island of St Gregory (Khortitsa) in the River Dnieper, and Mansikka (1922, 323–324) suggests that these represent a Scandinavian Thor-cult. It should not, then, unduly surprise us to find an image of the Norse god Thor in a grave-mound in Chernigov.

We now move to the main conclusion of this chapter. In what precedes, attention has been drawn to three small figures, two of them from Scandinavia (Lund, Skåne; Feddet, Sjælland), the third from Ukraine (Chernaia Mogila, Chernigov). These figures have been interpreted by certain scholars (albeit with varying degrees of conviction and authority) as images of the Norse god Thor. Arguments that the figure from Sjælland portrays Thor are perhaps weakest, those for the figure from Chernigov possibly the strongest. But the combined evidence that all three objects represent the god is stronger than the sum of that for the individual items. And, of course, a single explanation for all three objects is desirable. I can only conclude, then, that LI (KM 38.252), FI (DNM C24292) and CI (GIM 76990/1539/77) were all intended to represent the Norse god Thor (or possibly, in the case of CI, of Thor under the name *Perun*). And with that said, we turn straightaway to the one very obvious feature which all three figures have in common but which has not yet been discussed: all three of them are holding their beards. To my knowledge no real attempt has been made to explain this feature, either by those who interpret the individual figures as representations of Thor (e.g. Lindquist, Pushkina) or by those who, like Roesdahl (*OA*, 186) and Wahlöö (*VH*, 387), see two of them as playing-pieces (rather than images of Thor). What, one might ask, is Thor doing with his beard? My answer to this question, doubtless now already implicitly apparent from what precedes, may now be stated explicitly. It seems to me that what the three Thors are represented as doing is what the same god is said to have done in the passage from *Rǫgnvalds þáttr ok Rauðs* discussed in Chapter 2: each appears to be blowing into his beard (*at blása í kampana*), each 'sounding the voice of his beard' (*at þeyta skeggrǫddina*, etc.). Obviously it was not easy to represent a small figure as performing this act in terms of the plastic arts. And the creators of the figures had recourse, to some extent, to stylisation. What was important was to portray the god holding his beard with at least one hand and to ensure that the mouth was in some way indicated. And at least the carver of FI has achieved what I take to be his aim with admirable success: the amber figure has his mouth well open, and is clearly intended to be either blowing or shouting or a combination of both. He holds his beard very much as one might a wind-instrument and the cylindrical form of the beard is also suggestive. And we may now further move on to an interpretation of the three figures in terms of the hypothesis ventured on p. 61 above. In the three figures, LI, FI, and CI, we have, I would argue, examples of the type of wind-amulet envisaged there: all three, as just concluded, represent the god, in 'miniaturised' form, blowing into his beard. They were used, I would suggest, by Norse sailors as wind-amulets, in the hope of obtaining that particularly desirable benefit, a favourable wind for themselves (or perhaps an unfavourable wind for their competitors or adversaries). They are all portable objects which could easily be carried in pouches, or, in the case of FI, hung around the neck. And they and their possible use may be considered a little further, and perhaps in more speculative terms. When used aboard ship, it seems possible that they would have been given the appropriate orientation and maybe held behind the sail; we hear of such orientation elsewhere in connection with wind-magic (cf., for instance, p. 11 above); and we have, in the sources, a case where an effigy of Thor is mentioned aboard a ship (although then rather as a figure-head; cf. *ÓTOdd*, 220–222; *AS*, 41). The use of the objects in the way envisaged was quite possibly accompanied by the recitation of an oral spell or formula or even a prayer or hymn. We recall in this connection Þórhallr veiðimaðr's *skáldskapr* in ch. 8 of *Eiríks saga rauða* (cf. pp. 25–26 above), although this was probably improvised poetry; and Máni skáld's prayer for a wind in *Sverris saga* (cf. p. 15 above). The latter may represent a Christian substitute for something heathen; and we note its request for a wind from a stated direction. Perhaps a wind of a particular strength was also requested.[9] With regard to the materials of the three objects, we note that amulets were typically made of bronze (so CI) or amber (so FI; cf. p. 54 above). Amber may also, as noted, conceivably have had some significance in connection with the god of thunder and lightning (cf. p. 70 above). And the comparative rarity and cost of walrus-ivory might well have made it an appropriate material for amulets (cf. LI). Lastly we return to the belt around the waist of CI interpreted as Thor's girdle of strength

---

[9] In connection with the idea that it was thought possible to get a wind of a desired direction and strength by manipulation of an image of the god Thor, compare Watson, 1984, 303–304: 'In ancient Chinese lore, the god of the wind is Feng Po ['the Earl of Wind'], an old man with a white beard and a blue cap. He holds a yellow sack . . . and points its mouth in any direction he pleases. And in Japan he becomes Fu Jin, also dressed in blue, who carries a large bag from which he pours the wind in any required strength, according to how wide he opens the neck.' Cf. *New Larousse encyclopedia of mythology*, 1968, 384. As noted, it was also thought possible to regulate the strength of a wind by the use of 'wind-knots' (cf. p. 11 above).

(*megingjarðar*). It was clearly important (as suggested above, pp. 58–59) for an amulet to be endowed with a certain magical potency (for which the Old Norse term was probably either *máttr* or *megin*). One wonders if, then, by giving an image of Thor (the father, we remember, of Magni) its *megingjarðar*, one was in effect increasing its potency as an amulet. After all, if the god himself could increase his divine strength (*ásmegin*) twofold by assuming his *megingjarðar* (*SnE*, 29), any image of him may have been thought to have increased potency (to be *magnat*) by bearing a representation of that same attribute. And in this connection we may also return to LI. Just as CI, as an image of Thor, might have been thought of as having special efficacy by virtue of carrying a representation of the god's *megingjarðar*, so LI, also as a Thor, might have been thought of as endowed with special potency by virtue of (the symbol of) the god's hammer incised on its reverse side. And here a further possibility presents itself. As also discussed above (p. 66), while the upper five rings-and-dots on the reverse side of LI (cf. Figure 4) have been fairly confidently seen as representing a Thor's hammer by both Lindquist and Gjærder, the two scholars found it more difficult to explain the larger circle formed by the lower five rings-and-dots; as noted, Lindquist guessed at Odin's ring Draupnir, while Gjærder suggested the ring from which a Thor's hammer might have been suspended. On the other hand, it seems not at all impossible, in view of the evidence of CI, that it was rather intended to represent the god's *megingjarðar*, albeit in stylised form. If this were so, LI would then have carried (symbols of) two of Thor's attributes as mentioned by Snorri (*SnE*, 29) and would, as a result, doubtless have been thought of as possessing much enhanced potency.

It would greatly support the conclusions put forward in the previous paragraph as to the nature and function of the three objects under discussion if examples of images of gods used as wind-amulets (and then not necessarily in early Scandinavia) could be pointed to as parallels. And in this context one item of interest has come to light from Lithuania.[10] This might, if we were to accept *HWDA*'s definitions (I, col. 375), by virtue of being comparatively large, perhaps be regarded

---

[10] I would conjecture that another type of Norse wind-amulet might well have been a representation either of the ship Skíðblaðnir itself or of its sail. As noted, Skíðblaðnir always had a following wind, but it could be folded up like a cloth and kept in a pouch (cf. p. 17 above).

more as a 'talisman' than an 'amulet' (if indeed either term is applicable).[11] The object in question was noticed and described by the sevententh-century cleric Matthäus Praetorius who himself was born in Memel (now Klaipėda) very close to the place where he observed it. Praetorius lived from some time in the 1630s until 1707. His *magnum opus*, referred to as *Deliciae Prussicae* (or *Preußische Schaubühne*) was finally completed in 1703 but has unfortunately never been published in its entirety. The manuscript (designated R165) is now housed in Vilniaus Universiteto Mokslo Muziejus in Vilnius. In this work, Praetorius covers many aspects of Prussian folklore, superstition and religion and not least discusses the pagan Prussian gods. Excerpts from *Deliciae Prussicae* are published in Pierson, 1871, and, as far as they concern the pagan gods, in Mannhardt, 1936. Now in referring to the god of merchants, Perdoytus, Praetorius writes this (quoted, with minor adjustments, from Mannhardt, 1936, 542; cf. Pierson, 1871, 27–28):

> Indem ich dieses [i.e. presumably, Perdoytus] gedenke, fällt mir ein, was ich einsmahls bey einem Fischer in dem Dorf Karkel [modern Karklė, just north of Klaipėda] gesehen. Derselbe hatte anstatt der Fahnen aufm Mast seines Boots eine Statuam beym Ruder aufgerichtet. Er hatte nemblich von Borken gemacht ein Bild eines Menschen, dass am Kopff zweene Gesichter, eins fornen, eins hinten waren; an beyden aber war das Maul aufgesperret. An den Schultern waren ziemblich grosse Flügel, dabeneben er seine Hände ausgestrecket, die rechte aufwärts, die linke erdwärts. In dieser seiner linken Hand hält er einen Fisch, in der rechten ein Fässchen; auf dem Kopfe war ein Hahn gemacht. Das Bild nennete er Wejopattis, gleichsam nach der deutschen Sprache Herr des Windes. Ich mutmasse, dass vordem die alten Preussen dem Perdoytus eine solche Statuam mögen gesetzet haben. Weil aber der Handel und Wandel zur See vermittelst der Winde in esse kompt, hat dieser Fischer denselben Wejopatis einen Herrn des Windes genannt, vielleicht weil den alten Preussen als seinen Vorfahren verboten worden die andern bekandte Götter zu nennen.

---

[11] In *HWDA* (I, col. 375), we read: 'Vom Talisman . . . unterscheidet sich das A[mulett] höchstens dadurch, daß das Wort Talisman gelegentlich auch auf größere Gegenstände wie Bildsäulen angewandt wird.' I have not seen this distinction made elsewhere, nor with reference to the English words *amulet* and *talisman*. Indeed entirely different possible definitions of the two English words are suggested in H393. But generally the notion of objects such as high-seat pillars (*ǫndvegissúlur*) or statues of gods simply as large amulets is perhaps not an uninteresting one in the present context (cf. the remarks on miniaturisation on pp. 55–56 above).

> Denselben Fischer, der diesen Herrn des Windes auf seinem Boote führet, hielte der weiland Pfarrer daselbst N. Isingius vor einen recht alten Preussischen Heyden und den er nicht vermögen köndte, dass er zur Kirche oder zum Tische des Herrn ginge. Wenn dieser Fischer den Wejopatis ansahe, hub er seine beiden Hände auf, insonderheit wenn es ungestümes Wetter war. Denselben soll er auch Wejpons, auch öfter Wejdiews, Windgott, genennet haben. Sonsten wurde der Kerl damalen vor den reichsten Fischer gehalten und schrieb man den Reichtum seiner Hexerei zu, dass er wüste den Wind zu besprechen und die Fische in sein Garn zu locken, wiewol er auch eine ziemliche und des Orts ungewöhnliche Kupezyste, i.e. Kaufmannschaft, triebe. Was aber bey dieser Statua vor Aberglauben mögen geschehen seyn habe ich nicht von selbigem oder sonsten erfahren können.

This passage is preceded in the manuscript by a pen-and-ink drawing of the the object in question which we may assume is the work of Praetorius himself and which is here reproduced as Figure 8.

In the fisherman mentioned by Praetorius, we seem, then, to have a figure similar to the Oddr Ófeigsson of *Bandamanna saga* (cf. pp. 5–8) in this respect: both were men whose success in fishing and trade were to some extent related to their luck with the wind. We also note that the Prussian is still worshipping his heathen Vėjopatis in Christian times (and indeed in general the heathen Baltic religion was relatively persistent after the official introduction of Christianity). And here, in the object described by Praetorius, we would seem to have something similar to what I have suggested LI, FI and CI are. Usener (1900, 329, footnote 4), doubtless correctly, visualises the image of Vėjopatis as placed at the helm of the boat. The wind would, of course, have been thought of as blown through the two mouths of the god, one wind a *ventus secundus*, the other a *ventus adversus*. The Lithuanian object differed from the three Scandinavian items in various ways; as suggested, it seems to have been larger. It had two faces; there is no mention of any beard. But essentially it had the same purpose as I posit LI, FI and CI would have served, to raise a favourable wind for its owner. It may be regarded as something of a parallel to the three objects in the function that I believe they served.

In this context other considerations are relevant. The place where Praetorius saw Vėjopatis, on the coast of what is now Lithuania, lies in an area which, in the Viking Age, had, of course, particularly close connections with Scandinavia. Modern Karklė lay in the old Kurland (cf. *KL*, s.v. *Kurer*) which had, at least for certain periods during the

Viking Age, been under Scandinavian suzerainty. It also lies between what had been the Scandinavian colonies at Wiskiauten (just north of modern Kaliningrad) and Grobiņa (Grobin; now in Latvia). This second place had special significance as a Scandinavian trading centre in the early Viking Age, with contacts both with Gotland and central Sweden.

Figure 8: Vėjopatis. Pen-and-ink drawing from a manuscript of Matthäus Praetorius's *Deliciae Prussicae* (R165 in Vilniaus Universiteto Mokslo Muziejus, Vilnius).

And further up the Latvian coast lies the harbour at Ventspils which would have had the same connections with Scandinavia (and may have been known by some such Norse name as *Vindøy*, which, in turn, may be interpreted as 'platsen där man . . . får god segelvind'; cf. Jansson, 1987, 53–56; Modéer, 1932, 142). To the west from Kurland lay a sea-route across the southern Baltic to, for example, Sjælland where the amber FI was discovered; to the east, well-frequented river-routes led initially along the Daugava/Dvina and Nemunas/Neman, and on to Kiev and to Chernigov, where CI was found (cf., for example, maps in *RPC*, x, and Nerman, 1942, 111). Doubtless pagan Vikings practised their religion in the area; for example, an iron hammer of remarkable size reported by Aeneas Sylvius (238) in Lithuania has been interpreted as a Thor's hammer (cf. Note 7 in Chapter 2); and miniature amber axes, probably indicative of Nordic heathendom, have been found in Latvia, for example, in one of the Viking graves at Grobiņa (see *KL*, XIII, col. 683; Nerman, 1942, 55–56; cf. Jensen, 1991, 51). And heathen Scandinavia was close at hand. Just across the Baltic, for example, in Öland, the theophoric place-name *Torslunda* is suggestive of the worship of Thor, quite possibly at a largish cult-centre;[12] an unusually large number of miniature Thor's hammers has been found on Öland (*VArt*, 156; cf. the Bredsätra-pendant (SHM 101) mentioned on p. 119 below); and an amulet discovered at Södra Kvinneby on Öland mentions Thor by name as well as his hammer and may well have belonged to a fisherman, conceivably one seeking favourable weather conditions from the god (see Nilsson, 1976, especially 241–242; cf. Trotzig, 1995, 37). And the few harbours along the island's long east coast would doubtless have received at least occasional visitors from Kurland (cf. Jansson and Lundberg, 1987, 168; the name of one of them, *Kårehamn*, may even reflect this fact; cf. Hallberg, 1985, 116). There would, then, have been ample scope for cultural and religious contacts and influences between Balts and Scandinavians and not least,

---

[12] It is certainly tempting to think of Torslunda, more or less at the centre of Öland, as the place where Saxo's men of the old religion, using Thor's hammers, performed their meteorological magic and to identify his 'certain island' as Öland (cf. Note 7 in Chapter 2). On the other hand, when Saxo intends to refer to Öland, he seems to do so by name (cf. Saxo, 605, s.v. *Ølandia*). At all events, the island mentioned by Saxo in this context probably lay not too far from Öland.

of course, amongst sailors, fishermen and merchants, who travel more than others. And there is possibly even a further, more ancient affinity. *WM* (431 and 447) invites us to compare Vėjopatis with the Old Lithuanian thunder-god Perkūnas; in turn, on p. 434, the same work, in connection with Perkūnas, draws attention not only to the Slavonic deity Perun, but also to the Germanic Thor. Here we touch on the question of the extent to which an equation is to be made between Perkūnas, Perun and Thor. Some scholars have seen a linguistic connection between the names of the Old Lithuanian *Perkūnas*, the Old Russian *Perun* and the Norse deities *Fjǫrgynn* and *Fjǫrgyn*, this last said to be the mother of Thor (*Edda*, 13, 87; cf. *ÍO*, 183). This is not a matter that can be discussed in detail in the present context; the reader is referred to *MRN*, 94–98, for some survey of the arguments (cf. also, for example, Lorenz, 1984, 178; *RGA*$^2$, s.v. *Fjǫrgyn, Fjǫrgynn*). But in presenting Praetorius's Vėjopatis as a *parallel* to the three objects which it is suggested are all wind-charms and representations of Thor (i.e. LI, FI, CI), we must note that the deity venerated by the Lithuanian fisherman may also conceivably have some other, more intimate connection with the Scandinavian god which goes further back in time.[13]

---

[13] The cock on Vėjopatis's head is of interest and probably something more than just an indicator of the direction of the wind. Meyer (1891, 110–111) finds a connection between the cock and meteorological superstition in Germanic tradition; and Mansikka (1922, 323–324) suggests that the cult of Thor may have involved the sacrifice of cocks. But sacrifice of the cock probably existed amongst other peoples, for example, the pagan Balts and Slavs (see e.g. Mannhardt, 1936, 644, s.v. *Opfer. Hahn*, and references; cf. *DAI*, II, 55). One wonders if, in Vėjopatis's two faces, there may not be some solution to the problem of the three- and four-headed 'gods' (on which cf. *OA*, 110–111) found in the Baltic area, for example in Bornholm, or the four-headed Svantovit (Suantovitus) mentioned by Saxo (465–473). Svantovit's image was housed in a temple on an island, Arkona, on the northern tip of the island of Rügen, probably a suitable place for attempts at wind-raising (cf. Note 4 in Chapter 2); miniatures representing Svantovit have been found along the southern shore of the Baltic, at Wolin and Riga (cf. *VABC*, 13, 261–262).

CHAPTER FOUR

## THE EYRARLAND IMAGE

> Ekki... er... enn fenginn fullur skilningur á Eyrarlandslíkneskinu.
> LISE G. BERTELSEN
>
> Eiendommelige og overmåte sjeldne ting må ha sin selvstendige mening.
> HAAKON SHETELIG
>
> The measure of a theory is what it explains.
> CAROL J. CLOVER

THE EYRARLAND IMAGE (EI) in Þjóðminjasafn Íslands (National Museum of Iceland; inv. no. 10880) will be known to most students of Viking and Old Norse-Icelandic studies, to most Icelanders and to many of the tourists who find their way to Iceland and its national museum during the summer months. Pictures of it are readily available. To give some random examples: in Turville-Petre's *Myth and religion of the North* (*MRN*, illustration 15); in definitely larger-than-life size in Bertil Almgren's *The Viking* (1966, 144); in the handbook *Iceland 1986* (1987, picture 16); and in the form of postcards issued by the Þjóðminjasafn. In the summer of 1994, for example, passengers on Icelandair planes were able to buy a gold-plated reproduction of EI (see *Saga boutique*, 1994, 15) and less sophisticated replicas are often to be found in souvenir shops in Reykjavík. Also in 1994 Mjólkursamsalan í Reykjavík featured EI (with, of course, an illustration) in a series on Icelandic antiquities on some of their one-litre milk-cartons.

EI was discovered in Eyjafjörður in northern Iceland, while digging for other purposes was in progress, at some time in the years 1815–1817. According to Matthías Þórðarson (1930), it was found 'rjett hjá bænum á Eyrarlandi', on which statement Kristján Eldjárn (KE1983, 64) writes: 'Ekki getur talist fullvíst hvort átt er við Eyrarland rétt fyrir innan Akureyri eða Eyrarland í Öngulsstaðahreppi.' The first farm called Eyrarland referred to by Kristján (and often called Stóra-Eyrarland) lay within the limits of the present town of Akureyri on the *western* side of the inner end of Eyjafjörður; its land abutted on that of the farm Naust to its south (see *HTB*, II, 110; Jón Hjaltason, 1990,

The Eyrarland image 83

30–31). The other Eyrarland (known also as Litla-Eyrarland) lies on the *eastern* side of the valley at the end of the fjord (cf. *HTB*, II, 126). Kristján's doubts on this matter were not shared by Kålund (*HTB*, II, 110, note 1). Kålund firmly connects EI with the first of the two places. It is true that he was writing some sixty years after the object was found. But he was probably informed in what he says and, in the absence of any evidence to the contrary, one must accept his statement as correct (cf. Kålund, 1882, 76).[1]

Wherever EI was found, it seems to have been acquired by Jóhann Gottlieb Gudmann, a prominent merchant in Akureyri at the time, who, apparently through the mediation of Finnur Magnússon, presented it to Det Kongelige Museum for nordiske Oldsager (so officially designated from 1819) in Copenhagen and here it was lodged by late 1817. We have two early descriptions of EI. The following is from Thorlacius and Thomsen (1820, 363–364):

> Fra islandsk Kiøbmand J. Gudmand indsendt i Nov. 1817 og foræret: ... En liden Idol af Metal, funden 1817 i Jorden paa Island, $2^1/_2$ Tom. høj, siddende paa en Stol med en Hue paa Hovedet, med Knebelsbarter, holdende med begge Hænderne et korsformet Instrument, maaskee Thors Hammer. Paa Ryggen Spor til Forgyldning, temmelig raat Arbeide.

As Kristján Eldjárn (KE1981, 75; KE1983, 65) points out, this last remark about the quality of the workmanship is scarcely justified. The second early account of the object is from *Collegial-Tidende* of 10th February, 1821 (p. 98):

> Aar 1817 skjænkede Kiøbmanb [sic] Gudmand fra Island igjennem Professor Magnussen et paa denne Øe fundet lidet Metal-Idol, som engang har været forgyldt. Det har en Slags Hammer i Haanden, en Pileus paa Hovedet, og er maaskee Guden Thor.

From these two sources, it is clear that at least some people in Copenhagen at the time believed that the object was once at least partly gilded.

---

[1] Kålund collected much of the material for *HTB* during travels in Iceland in the years 1872–1874 (cf. the introductory statement to the first volume of his work). He presumably visited Akureyri in these years. At that time Friðrik Carl Magnús Gudmann (1821–1879), son of Jóhann Gottlieb Gudmann (died 1858) (cf. the following), was still alive. But there were doubtless many other channels through which he could have received correct information on the point in question. Stóra-Eyrarland appears to have been the property of Stefán Þórarinsson amtmaður between 1796 and 1823. Cf. Jón Hjaltason, 1990, 30–31, 46, 72, 149 and *passim*; Klemens Jónsson, 1958, 79.

We may note the first published picture of EI. The object was not only mentioned in the two Danish periodicals just cited, but also in the Swedish *Iduna*, the organ of Götiska Förbundet in the first quarter of the nineteenth century. In a contribution from 1820 (full title in Bibliography), J. G. Liljegren gives some account of the various antiquities and manuscripts housed in the libraries and museums of Copenhagen at the time. Among these (pp. 145–146), the Eyrarland image is given passing attention, described as a 'metallbild, som man anser wara Thors', and illustrated as 'Tab. 2, Fig. 3'. The illustrations in question (reproduced as Figure 9 below) are actual size, and give views from front and rear. In the view of Kristján Eldjárn, this is 'fairly true to nature' and 'sýnir líkanið að mestu leyti eins og það er' (KE1981, 76; KE1983, 65).[2]

Figure 9: The oldest pictures of the Eyrarland image (= EI; from Liljegren 1820 (*Iduna*)).

[2] In the same article in *Iduna* (8, 1820, 145–146), Liljegren writes: 'Åstundas afgjutning af sjelfwa bilden, må ansökning derom göras hos Commissionen [i.e. Commissionen for Oldsagers Opbewaring].' Here we seem to have an offer of a museum replica from as early as the first quarter of the nineteenth century.

The Eyrarland image remained in the museum (renamed 'Nationalmuseet' in 1892) in Copenhagen until 1930 (where, according to Bertelsen, 1994, 59, it had the museum number 'NM LXV'). In 1930 it was moved to Þjóðminjasafn Íslands together with various other items discovered in Iceland (cf. Matthías Þórðarson, 1930).

A short description of the Eyrarland image follows (cf. Frontispiece and Figures 9–11). This, it should be noted, is as much or more based on previous descriptions as on original observations. It owes much, for example, to the descriptions by Kristján Eldjárn (in *KH*, 362–363; KE1981; KE1983) and James Graham-Campbell (*VArt*, 25). It has also benefited from information kindly provided by Þór Magnússon in correspondence and in conversation. It will be somewhat complemented by information presented in the subsequent discussion of the individual features of EI.

The Eyrarland image is of cast bronze, produced by the method referred to as 'the lost-wax process' (French: *cire perdue*). It is 6.7 cm. high and a fully three-dimensional figure of a man sitting upright on an armless chair with a low, tripartite back. Apart from a hat or cap or helmet of conical shape, the man is naked and unshod and his bare toes are a prominent feature of the object. Ears, eyes and nose are boldly represented. The man has a large moustache which develops into two parts on each cheek; the upper parts reach outwards over the cheek and upwards towards the outer corners of the eyes where they end in curled terminals. The lower parts are thick and somewhat drooping. The mouth appears to be open. The chin carries a heavy beard extending downwards and 'the man apparently splits his beard in two and grips the halves with his clenched fists' (KE1981, 74). Below his fists the beard develops, perhaps rather unexpectedly, into a cross-like object with rounded ends; the transverse arms of this object rest firmly on the man's knees, the vertical part extends down between them. The whole object has a remarkable symmetry and, as Kristján Eldjárn suggests, bears witness to considerable technical competence. Kristján also writes that 'in spite of its smallness the image, as a sculpture, is endowed with a quality of greatness and might with success be considerably enlarged' (KE1981, 75). In *KH* (383), EI's weight is given as 114.914 gm. Þór Magnússon points out, however, that a small hole has been bored in the bottom of the image, presumably for sampling purposes and while it was still in Copenhagen. It would, therefore, probably have originally been very slightly heavier than it is now.

86 Thor the wind-raiser

Figure 10: Bronze figure from Eyrarland, Eyjafjarðarsýsla, Iceland (= EI; Þjms 10880; height: 6.7 cm.), side view. (Photo: Gísli Gestsson; by permission of Þjóðminjasafn Íslands, Reykjavík.)

# The Eyrarland image

Figure 11: Bronze figure from Eyrarland, Eyjafjarðarsýsla, Iceland (= EI; Þjms 10880; height: 6.7 cm.), front view. (Photo: Gísli Gestsson; by permission of Þjóðminjasafn Islands, Reykjavík.)

An attempt at dating EI on art-historical grounds has been made by two scholars with reference to the shape of the man's moustaches/ beard. Shetelig (1937, 215) dated it to about the year 1000. Kristján Eldjárn, on the other hand (KE1983, 70), put it somewhat later and thought it was 'frá 11. öld og geti vel verið frá miðbiki þeirrar aldar'. Kristján's arguments will be referred to again below. Suffice it to say here that Kristján himself put them forward very tentatively. Graham-Campbell (*VArt*, 25) dates the object to his 'Late Viking Period' which runs from the second half of the tenth century to the beginning of the twelfth, and a broader dating of this kind is probably safest.

We shall return to the question of EI's provenance (i.e. place of manufacture) below (pp. 139–144).

In what immediately precedes, EI has been described and some views as to its age have been noted. These fundamental questions now present themselves: What is the Eyrarland image? What did its creator intend it to be? For what purpose was it originally manufactured? Various suggestions (referred to now, largely for want of any better term, as 'Theories') have been made or may be made on this issue. These may be first set out in list form as follows.

EI might have been intended to be:

1. A statuette of the god Thor (Þórr). (This is a theory held by a number of scholars ever since the object was found in the early nineteenth century; cf. pp. 83–84 above).
2. A statuette of the god Frey (Freyr).
3. A playing-piece (used, for example, in the board game *hneftafl*).
4. A child's toy.
5. A weight.
6. A statuette of a musician playing an instrument which has a close affinity to a double flute.
7. None of the things mentioned under Theories 1–6, but something else.
8. A combination of two or more of the things mentioned under Theories 1–7 (though some combinations, e.g. of Theories 1 and 2, are not really possible).
9. Finally, a view on EI expressed by Bertelsen in 1994 should be noted. This is that while it is virtually impossible to say what EI is, the object resting on the knees of the figure is in all probability a Christian cross.

Some assessment will now be offered of these different Theories. This is done in varying degrees of depth and also partly on the basis of a process of elimination. No consideration will be given to anything which might fall under Theory 7.[3] And only one or two of the permutations presented by Theory 8 will be considered (cf. Note 4 and pp. 137–139 below). At all times in the following discussion, one should bear in mind Carol Clover's remark (albeit made in an entirely different context), cited as one of the mottoes to this chapter, that 'the measure of a theory is what it explains' (Clover, 1986, 37).

## Theory 5

We may begin with Theory 5. Kristján Eldjárn suggested that EI might conceivably be a weight (see *KH*, 383; KE1981, 81–82; KE1983, 71–72). This he did largely, it seems, on the basis of the passage in *Jómsvíkinga saga* where Hákon jarl gives Einarr Helgason a pair of scales which can be used for divinatory purposes and the weights of which appear to have anthropomorphic form (cf., for example, *Jómsvíkinga saga*, 1969, 179; *Flat*, I, 188–189). But the scales in question would seem to belong rather more to the world of fiction than reality. It is true that weights could take the form of animals, particularly horses (e.g. the so-called 'Håkon den femtes messinghester'); or, as suggested by an apparently unique example from Denmark, of knights on horses; cf. *NK*, XXX, 165–167. But if EI really was a weight in anthropomorphic form, one would expect to find other examples and no such have been found. One would also have to attempt to answer the question of what unit of weight (or proportion or multiple of what unit of weight), the Eyrarland image of about 115 gm. was intended to represent. Kristján Eldjárn himself appears to prefer another explanation of EI's function to this one (cf. discussion of Theory 3 below).[4]

---

[3] No detailed attention is given to Kålund's suggestion (cf. Note 6 below) that EI is 'en middelalderlig kunstgenstand' if this refers to anything other than a playing-piece (cf. the discussion of Theory 3 below). I would dismiss it as too vague to be of much value.

[4] In the version of *Jómsvíkinga saga* translated into Latin by Arngrímur Jónsson (ed. Jakob Benediktsson in *BA*, IX), the weights in question seem to appear in the form of the Norse gods (*BA*, IX, 133). One might therefore entertain the idea that EI was meant to serve two purposes, as a weight and as the image of a god (cf. Theory 8). And it is true that weights in the form of

## Theory 4

It might be argued that the Eyrarland image is a toy of some sort. (On toys in general in medieval Scandinavia, cf. *KL*, s.v. *Leketøy* and references.) But EI represents a rather static object (i.e. a seated man), unlike, say, the toy horses or toy boats which are archaeologically attested. It was also probably rather expensive to produce. It seems, then, unlikely that EI was specifically manufactured to serve as a child's plaything.[5]

## Theory 3

The suggestion that EI is a playing-piece (Theory 3) was made at least as early as the 1880s.[6] And because it has been argued relatively recently and in some detail by Kristján Eldjárn (d. 1982), it will be given, in the form it takes in Kristján's contributions, careful critical examination in the present context. Kristján first published his views on this matter in an article (= KE1981) in the memorial volume for Gabriel Turville-Petre, *Speculum norroenum*, which appeared in 1981; and an Icelandic version of this article, with some revisions and alterations (= KE1983), appeared in *Árbók Hins íslenzka fornleifafélags 1982*. Kristján's views may be summarised as follows (with particular reference to KE1981).

After introductory remarks, Kristján offers a useful description of EI (cf. above). He then cites the two early descriptions of EI, from Thorlacius and Thomsen (1820) and *Collegial-Tidende* (1821), and reproduces the picture of EI from Liljegren's article in *Iduna* (1820). He observes that the most widely held interpretation of EI, that it represents the god Thor, probably stems from Thorlacius or Thomsen

---

horses were sometimes employed as amulets or at least for magical purposes in Norway of more recent times (cf. Grieg, 1954, 207, note 76). But Arngrímur's text is of doubtful authenticity here (cf. *BA*, XII, 137–138). And the same difficulties apply here as apply to the assumption that EI was simply a weight (i.e. Theory 5).

[5] A toy horse of brass or bronze is, for example, mentioned in ch. 12 of *Víga-Glúms saga* as having existed in Eyjafjörður. But this at any rate might have been originally manufactured as a weight. Cf. *ÍF*, IX, 40–41 and note 5.

[6] In *HTB*, II, 110, note 1, where Kålund writes of EI that while it was originally seen as 'et Torsbillede', it was regarded at the time he was writing as 'en middelalderlig kunstgenstand (skakbrik?)'.

or Finnur Magnússon (or two or all of them) and must rest on the interpretation of the object held by EI as Thor's hammer (cf. Thorlacius and Thomsen, 1820: 'maaskee Thors Hammer'). But, Kristján argues, the object held by EI only bears 'a very faint resemblance' to a Thor's hammer and the only item known to him which has a certain likeness to it is the silver pendant found at Foss in Hrunamannahreppur, Iceland (Þjms 6077; Figure 12 below; cf. *VArt*, 156, 307; *VH*, 314).[7] The Foss pendant itself, Kristján argues, is, however, very unlike a Thor's hammer and is more likely to be a Christian cross; it cannot, therefore, be used as evidence in the present context.

Kristján next attempts to date EI the basis of art-historical criteria. After an interesting comparison of EI's moustache with the leaf-decoration of other objects (a walking stick from Lund, KM 59.126:795, see *VH*, 232; the weather-vane from Källunge, Gotland, now in Gotlands Fornsal), he is inclined to conclude that 'the Eyrarland image is solidly anchored among the monuments of the fully developed Ringerike style' and should therefore be dated in the first half of the eleventh century and perhaps near the middle of it. But Kristján also admits the uncertain nature of this dating. He notes that the leaf-decoration he has drawn attention to is 'also found among the Mammen style monuments', and reasons that 'since the Mammen style and the Ringerike style merge and very likely overlap not a little in time, it would be hazardous to venture anything like a precise dating of the Eyrarland image on stylistic grounds' (p. 80). Even so, his general impression is that EI is eleventh-century work. Given this conclusion (Kristján argues), we must certainly have doubts about EI representing Thor since it unlikely that Icelanders were still manufacturing and worshipping

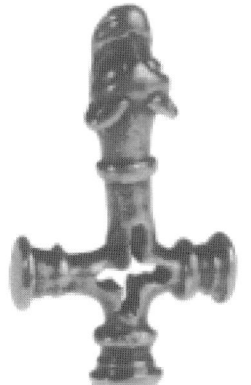

Figure 12: Silver pendant from Foss, Árnessýsla, Iceland (Þjms 6077). (Photo: Ívar Brynjólfsson; © National Museum of Iceland, Reykjavík.)

---

[7] For further pictures of the pendant from Foss, see KE1981, 78; KE1983, 67; *KH*, 326; *MRN*, illustration 16; Magnusson, 1976, 71; Page, 1990, 13. In Bæksted, 1986 (54), pictures of the pendant and EI are juxtaposed for purposes of comparison.

pagan idols half a century or so after Christianity had been officially adopted in Iceland. Nor does Kristján let the analogy of the ithyphallic bronze statuette from Rällinge in Sweden (SHM 14232; cf. p. 97 below and Note 9) affect his conclusion. Although this is normally thought to be a representation of the god Frey, and although it represents much the same artistic tradition as EI (and is therefore probably of much the same date), it should be remembered (Kristján stresses) that Sweden remained pagan long after Iceland had been converted.

So much for the first part of Kristján Eldjárn's arguments. He now goes on to the question of what the Eyrarland image is if it is not an image of Thor. He first considers the possibility that it is a weight (cf. above). He is not, as noted, inclined to favour this explanation, and turns to another. EI, he observes, finds a close parallel in the whalebone figure found in what seems to be a pagan grave at Baldursheimur, Mývatnssveit, Iceland (Þjms 6; cf. *VArt*, 25, 214). Both figures hold their arms in the same way, both grasp their split beards with clenched fists. Now Kristján finds reason for thinking that Þjms 6 was a *hnefi* in the board game *hneftafl*: it was found alongside twenty-four simple playing-pieces and a dice. Kristján stresses that he had accepted the identification of Þjms 6 as a *hnefi* in *KH* in 1956 and that he continues to hold to this view. He notes, however, that certain scholars, e.g. Shetelig (1937) rejected it. And if Þjms 6 is a *hnefi*, Kristján reasons, so too may EI be. It is true, Kristján concedes (KE1981, 84), that the objection might be made that EI 'is far too exquisite, too noble, to be simply a gaming-piece from a common *hneftafl*'. But he also points out that the time-span between EI and the Lewis chess-set with its elaborately carved pieces is not great; and he thinks there is something in the demeanour of the seated persons of the Lewis chess-set (cf. *VH*, 390–391), not least the kings, which is reminiscent of EI. Kristján concludes by stressing 'the weaknesses' of his argumentation, not least its failure to offer any explanation of the cruciform object resting on the knees of EI.

Some criticism of Kristján Eldjárn's arguments may be offered. First, some remarks on his dismissal of the proposition that EI is a representation of Thor.

(1) It is true that the interpretation of EI as Thor as initially put forward within five years of its discovery could well have rested *largely* on the interpretation of the object the man is holding as a hammer. But as the following investigation of Theory 1 will show, it certainly does

## The Eyrarland image

not do so entirely. And as has been seen from Chapter 3, it is probably possible to identify the figures from Lund (LI), Feddet (FI) and Chernigov (CI) with Thor on considerations quite separate from the possibility that the first-mentioned of the three (i.e. LI) has a ring-and-dot configuration on its reverse side which might be interpretable as a Thor's hammer. Further, as will also be shown in the following, it may, at any rate, very well be possible to interpret the object EI is holding as a Thor's hammer (cf. pp. 106–118 below).

(2) As Kristján appears to admit himself, his dating of the Eyrarland image on the basis of art-historical considerations is somewhat hazardous and, interesting though his observations on the shape of EI's moustache are, it would be misguided to draw close and firm conclusions from them. Shetelig's dating of EI to 'omkring år 1000' (1937, 15), also on the basis of the shape of the man's moustache, has been noted. And as will be suggested below (pp. 102–103), a moustache of the shape of (the upper part of) EI's moustache may, in fact, be a feature of the iconography of Thor (or of the Norse gods in general).

(3) Kristján appears to assume that the cult of Thor died out abruptly with the acceptance of Christianity at the Alþingi in 999/1000. But such an assumption is probably not entirely warranted. The cult of Thor appears to have been very well established in the Iceland of the tenth century. It is rather unlikely that it suddenly came to an end simply as the result of an act of the country's none-too-powerful assembly. The chief source for our knowledge of the conversion of Iceland, Ari Þorgilsson's *Íslendingabók*, itself hints that certain heathen practices lived on for at least some years after the conversion (*ÍF*, I, 17). And the studies of, for example, Hans Kuhn (1969–1978, II, 296–326, 378–386) have shown that forms of heathendom (and the practice of magic connected with it) lived on in Scandinavia (including Iceland) well after the Conversion. Some random indications of this survival may be noted from Iceland and mainland Scandinavia. In the first decades of the twelfth century, Bishop Jón Ǫgmundarson of Hólar found it necessary to rule against remnants of pagan practice and magic which were still alive in his diocese. (We may here recall the stubborn Lithuanian fisherman mentioned by Praetorius, still worshipping his Vėjopatis long after the introduction of Christianity, and regarded by a local priest as 'a real old Prussian heathen'; cf. p. 78 above.) As noted above (p. 22), Thor was still held responsible for the weather in Småland in the seventeenth century. In Iceland the so-called *Þórshamar*

was used as late as the nineteenth century as a charm to detect thieves (see *MRN*, 84 and references; cf. p. 110 below). Amulets known in Sweden as *torviggar* and closely associated with Thor were owned and prized in Scandinavia down to fairly recent times (cf. *KL*, s.v. *Torvigg*).

(4) Throughout his contributions (KE1981; KE1983) Kristján Eldjárn seems to assume that EI is of native Icelandic manufacture and so it may well be. But an object like EI was also easily portable and one wonders if, whatever its date of manufacture, it could not have been produced in a Scandinavian country other than Iceland and then perhaps one where the cult of Thor was still practised. The question of the provenance of EI will, as noted, be discussed below (pp. 139–144). But it may be noted here that it is far from improbable that EI was produced in Sweden. And as remarked above, Kristján himself notes (KE1981, 81) 'that the Swedes remained pagan long after the Icelanders had accepted Christianity'.

For the reasons just suggested, then, it is difficult to accept Kristján's objections to Theory 1. And it is unfortunate that his rejection of Theory 1 on less than justifiable grounds seems, as it were, to lead him to a far less acceptable proposition than Theory 1, namely, Theory 3, the supposition that EI is a playing-piece. It is, of course, reasonable that Kristján should draw attention to the whalebone image from Baldursheimur (abbreviated BI) in his discussion of the Eyrarland image. Obviously EI and BI have features in common which make a single interpretation of both of them an attractive idea. But I am not convinced that BI was primarily intended as a playing-piece. This is a matter I shall return to later in this chapter. And quite irrespective of what BI is, three reasons may be adduced for tending to dismiss the theory that the Eyrarland image is a playing-piece:

(A) The image is made of bronze, which is rather a heavy material; as noted, it weighs over 110 gm.; in medieval (as well as in modern) times, playing-pieces tended to be made of lighter materials than metals. Thus a playing-piece in medieval Scandinavia would typically have been made from wood or bone or horn or walrus-ivory (although sometimes they were made of glass, which is, it is true, probably a heavier material than those just mentioned, though not as heavy as bronze). It is also true that in *Schach* (103) we find pictured a chess-piece (a pawn, it seems) from Nuremberg in Germany (dated about

1570) which is made of bronze (and gilded bronze at that; cf. p. 83 above). But in addition to being well-shod, the man is fully and elaborately dressed (cf. (B) below). And he stands on a proportionally large, flat, circular base (cf. (C) below). Thus, while the piece has one feature in common with the EI, it differs from it in two other relevant respects.

(B) Kristján Eldjárn himself writes (KE1981, 83): 'The rules of the play [of *hneftafl*] are unknown now, but it is clear that some major role was played by a main piece, different from the others, bigger and more stately and in some way distinguished as an important person in the game.' Now it would be difficult to deny that the Eyrarland image has an impressive appearance. But if the artist who made it was really trying to produce some sort of equivalent to the kings of modern chess-sets or even of the Lewis chess-set, would he have left his figure more or less naked? And would he have left his 'stately' and 'important' figure (to use Kristján's own words) unshod, with his bare toes presenting themselves as what literally is the foremost feature of his creation? The notion is improbable. Gods might well be represented as naked (see below); the 'kings' of chess-sets (and the like) surely only rarely so. Kings, like emperors, with nothing on tend towards the ridiculous.

(C) But a third argument in this context perhaps weighs heaviest. Looking at Figure 10, for example, and comparing EI with what we otherwise know about playing-pieces, one gets a distinct impression that, relatively speaking, EI is not a particularly stable object. It is rather tall and its four-legged base seems rather small compared to its height. And with its large head, it would seem to have a relatively high centre of gravity. When one inspects (pictures of) individual playing-pieces (or sets of them) from both early and more recent times and from various places in Europe and Asia, one finds that in the vast majority of cases they have one thing in common: *playing-pieces nearly always have flat bases or are set on platforms or plinths*. As far as I have been able to discover, a playing-piece on four legs like the Eyrarland image would be a very rare exception to this general rule.[8]

---

[8] Grieg (1954, 184; cf. his figure 7) dismisses the proposition that an animal figure from Østre Alm in Hedmark is a playing-piece on the grounds that, with a height of 5.8 cm. (cf. EI's 6.7 cm.), it would have been 'for *høy* til å

Any one of the three considerations just presented (and particularly the third) weighs fairly heavily in this context. Taken together, they can be regarded as more or less decisive: they suggest that it is highly unlikely that EI was manufactured with the intention of its serving primarily as a playing-piece. And Theory 3 does nothing to explain the idiosyncratic features of EI. In view of these factors, then, we may confidently and permanently dismiss it.

## Theory 1

We now turn to Theory 1, which is that EI was intended to be an image of the god Thor. This theory was, as noted, suggested within a decade of EI's discovery in modern times, i.e. in 1820 by Thorlacius and Thomsen. And it has been accepted with varying degrees of certainty by a number of scholars, not least from about 1930 onwards. Grieg (1954, 181), for example, states it as a virtual fact (cf. p. 106 below). But it has not gone uncontested. For example, again as noted, Kålund says that while the object was originally taken to be an image of Thor, it was regarded at the time he was writing as 'en middelalderlig kunstgenstand', or perhaps a chess-piece (see Note 6 above). I am not able to offer here a full account of the changing views in the nineteenth and twentieth centuries as to how far EI is to be regarded as an image of Thor. It is perhaps interesting, however, that when George Stephens wrote his monograph of 1878 which was much concerned with the iconography of Thor (see below), he left EI entirely out of account, even though it is difficult to believe that he did not know of it and even though it would have greatly reinforced his arguments if regarded as an image of the god. And as recently as the 1980s, no less an authority than Kristján Eldjárn disputed that EI was intended to portray Thor. It

---

brukes sammen med de vanlige spillebrikker fra vikingetiden'. At a special exhibition, 'Board games of the world', held at the British Museum in London in 1990–1991, a large number of playing-pieces from different board games from many places around the world were on display. Apart from instances where unmanufactured objects were used (e.g. pebbles, shells, beans), the playing-pieces almost exclusively had flat bases (i.e. were not, like EI, on legs), although some had peg bases for insertion into holes on the board. While, it is true, there were a very few pieces made of metal (though these were rather small), the majority were made of lighter materials, bone, horn, ivory, wood (cf. (A) above).

cannot, therefore, be taken for granted that EI is a representation of Thor. The proposition needs renewed examination.

Such an examination follows. Its approach is this: Some thirteen features (or what will referred to for convenience as 'features') of EI which could have relevance to the issue of whether the object represents Thor or not will be isolated. These features will be discussed within the context of what we otherwise know about the iconography of Thor and the Norse gods, and about images of other gods and about amulets in general. Comparative evidence takes three main forms: (i) the evidence of the literary sources; (ii) that of pictures on rune-stones; (iii) that of other miniature representations of Norse gods or of objects connected with them (e.g. Thor's hammers). As far as (i) is concerned, there are the two well-known references to idols of Thor in the sagas of the two missionary kings of Norway, one said to have been at Mære (Mærin) in Trøndelag (*ÓTOdd*, 163–164; *Hkr*, I, 317–318; *ÓT*, I, 378–386; *Flat*, I, 319–322; *Flat²*, I, 353–357), the other at Hundorp (Hundþorp) in Gudbrandsdalen (*ÓHLeg*, 29–35; *Hkr*, II, 183–190; *ÓH*, 271–282; *Flat*, II, 188–192; *Flat²*, II, 279–284). Needless to say, these must be regarded with circumspection. The Eddic poems (more particularly *Þrymskviða*), Snorri's *Edda* and the *Íslendingasögur* also have evidence to offer in this context. And, amongst non-West-Norse sources, Adam of Bremen's account (470–472) of the heathen temple at Uppsala with its idol of Thor (amongst other gods) is of especial value. Of pictures on rune-stones, what appears to be a representation of the pagan gods at Ragnarǫk on the stone at Ledberg Church in Östergötland (Ög 181) is of special interest (Figures 13 and 14; cf. Moltke, 1976, 135, 199–200). And what is generally accepted to be the face of Thor on the rune-inscribed rock at Norra Åby in Södermanland (Sö 86) is of particular significance (cf. pp. 122–124 below). As far as items falling under (iii) are concerned, problems of identification inevitably arise. For purposes of the present discussion, however, the little ithyphallic bronze image from Rällinge in Södermanland (RI; Figure 15) is of great interest and will be regarded by me, as it is by many others, as a representation of the god Frey (so Salin, 1913; cf., however, pp. 134–135 below).[9]

---

[9] Pictures of RI are widely found elsewhere; cf. Grieg, 1954, 182; *KL*, I, fig. 17; Lindquist, 1963, 74; Gjærder, 1964, figure 1; *MRN*, illustration 13; Ellis Davidson, 1967, plate 59; Magnusson, 1976, 75; *VArt*, plate 513; KE1981, 82; KE1983, 71; Jansson and Lundberg, 1987, 282; Page, 1990, 29; *VH*, 147

Figure 13: Rune-stone at Ledberg church, Östergötland, Sweden (Ög 181), probably depicting the heathen gods at Ragnarǫk. (Photo: Bengt A. Lundberg; © Riksantikvarieämbetet.)

# The Eyrarland image

Figure 14: Reverse of rune-stone at Ledberg church, Östergötland, Sweden (Ög 181), probably depicting the heathen gods at Ragnarǫk. (Photo: Bengt A. Lundberg; © Riksantikvarieämbetet.)

Figure 15: Bronze image from Rällinge, Lunda parish, Södermanland, Sweden, probably a representation of Frey (= RI; SHM 14232; height: 6.9 cm.). (By permission of ATA, Stockholm; © Riksantikvarieämbetet.)

With rather less certainty, a small bronze figure from Lindby, Skåne (SHM 13701; Figure 16) will, for example, be identified as Odin.[10] Some further points should be made in this context: In drawing parallels with the comparative material in question, we must naturally be on our guard against the circular arguments which are sometimes difficult to avoid. We have also to note that various of the individual features in question are, naturally, more widespread than in representations of

---

(though in mirror image); Trotzig, 1995, 35 (with photograph of the back of the object). The most detailed discussion of RI is in Salin, 1913; cf. also *VArt*, 153; *VH*, 276.

[10] The reason for identifying SHM 13701 as Odin is the fact that the figure appears to have only one eye (cf., for example, Page, 1990, 8). Neil Price (private communication) kindly assures me that the same feature is present on a small bronze male head from Staraia Ladoga (cf. *VH*, 150, 298). It has been suggested that a one-eyed carved head in Hegge stave-church in Norway might also be intended as Odin (see Holtsmark, 1970, 129). Other pictures of SHM 13701 are found in Arne, 1909, 185; Magnusson, 1976, 59; *VArt*, 307 (cf. 154); Page, 1990, 8. The one in Trotzig, 1995, 36, is in mirror image.

# The Eyrarland image 101

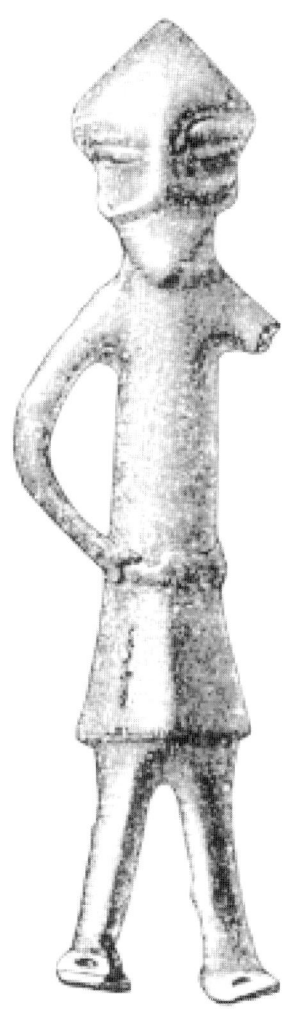

Figure 16: Bronze figure from Lindby, Skåne, Sweden, possibly representing Odin (SHM 13701; height: 6.9 cm.). (After Arne, 1909, 185.)

Thor or other Norse gods. Finally, it should be noted that in the following arguments relating to Theory 1 (as in the case of the other Theories), as little cognisance as possible will be taken of features of the three objects discussed in Chapter 3, i.e. the figures from Lund (LI), Feddet (FI) and Chernigov (CI). Nor will any comparisons be made with the whalebone figure found at Baldursheimur in northern Iceland (BI; Þjms 6). I shall, however, return to all four objects later in the discussion.

*Feature 1.* EI's head-gear is described by Kristján Eldjárn (KE1981, 74) as 'a cone-shaped cap or a hat', by Graham-Campbell (*VArt*, 25) as a 'conical helmet'. On the whole, Graham-Campbell's description seems the more acceptable. At all events, the likeness of EI's head-gear to that of RI has been noted by, for example, Ellis Davidson (1967, 134: 'the little man [i.e. EI] wears a conical hat, like the supposed image of Freyr'). And the head-gear of RI has been compared by Salin (who prefers to regard it as a helmet) to the helmets of the figures on the Ledberg stone (Salin, 1913, 406), interpreted by others, as noted, as Norse gods at Ragnarǫk. Further, the bronze figure from Lindby in Skåne, taken by some to represent Odin (Figure 16), also wears a 'conical helmet' (so *VArt*, 154).

*Feature 2.* The eyes of EI (and we must here, of course, beware of falling victim to mere impression) could reasonably be described as large and glaring (cf. Figure 11; Perkins, 1994, 656). There is satisfactory evidence in the literary sources that Thor was thought of as having glaring or piercing eyes. Thus the god's eyes are described as *ǫndótt*, 'fierce, frightening', in stanza 27 of *Þrymskviða* (*Edda*, 115) and perhaps elsewhere (see *LP*, s.v. *ǫndóttr*); and as *hvǫss* in *ÓHLeg* (33; cf. *Hkr*, II, 188; *ÓH*, 279; *Flat*, II, 191). In *SnE* (49), Þjálfi and Rǫskva's father is so terrified by what he sees of Thor's eyes (and that is not all of them), that *hugðisk hann falla mundu fyrir sjóninni einni samt*. Thor, then, excelled in glaring. We note also the 'cirkelrunda' eyes (so Lindquist, 1963, 76) of the face of Thor on the runic rock at Norra Åby which may be said to have a piercing effect. Cf. on the matter of Thor's eyes, Ljungberg, 1947, 125–130; *MRN*, 83; also Bjarni Guðnason, 1993, 99, note 5.

*Feature 3*. EI might be described as having a relatively large and prominent nose (cf. Figures 10–11). In his discussion of the iconography of Thor, Helge Ljungberg (1947, 125–126; cf. 145) finds evidence (which includes the testimony of Sö 86) that the god was represented as having a large or long nose.

*Feature 4*. Of the Eyrarland image, Kristján Eldjárn writes (KE1981, 74): 'He has a big moustache, which on each cheek develops into two leaves (or something which looks like leaves), the lower one rather thick and curving slightly downwards, the upper one reaching upwards, across the cheekbone and almost up to the corner of the eye, where it has a tightly curled terminal.' No exact parallel has been found to EI's rather impressive bipartite moustache in its entirety. But a slit on at least one side of the Rällinge image's moustache (on the left-hand side as seen from the front), suggests perhaps division into two parts (cf. Figure 15; *VArt*, 153). Moreover the upper part of EI's moustache certainly has parallels. Salin (1913, 406) refers to RI as having '"à la Kaiser Wilhelm" uppvridna mustascher'; like EI's moustache, that of RI is turned up and has curled ends. The four figures on the Ledberg rune-stone (Ög 181) taken as Norse gods also have moustaches not dissimilar from that of RI, and therefore not dissimilar from that of EI (cf. Salin, 1913, 406). Arne (1909, 185–186) notes the luxuriant upturned moustache on the bronze figure from Lindby (Skåne), and compares that of one of the figures on the Ledberg stone. And of particular interest here is the face of Thor on Sö 86 (Figure 20). This is also adorned with an upturned moustache not at all dissimilar from the upper part of EI's; this has a curled terminal, at least on the left-hand side of the face as seen from the front. The idol of the god Perun which Prince Vladimir is said to have set up in Kiev in about 980 (cf. p. 73 above), was, we are told, 'made of wood with a head of silver and a mustache of gold' (so *RPC*, 93; cf. Mansikka, 1922, 38).

*Feature 5.* Graham-Campbell (*VArt*, 25) refers to EI as a 'cast bronze figure . . . of a bearded man' and Kristján Eldjárn (KE1981, 74) says of it: 'the chin . . . seems to be profusely bearded'. Matthías Þórðarson (1930) notes EI's 'hökuskegg'. Various parallels are relevant. Salin (1913, 406) describes RI and at least one of the figures on the Ledberg stone as having the 'samma spetsiga hakskägg'. Stephens (1878, 33) refers to the 'peakt Beard' of Sö 86. The pointed beard of the figure from Lindby may be seen from Figure 16. But the evidence of the written texts is perhaps of greater interest. In ch. 21 of *Flóamanna saga* (*ÍF*, XIII, 278), when Thor appears to Þorgils in a dream to threaten him with a stormy passage to Greenland (cf. pp. 18–19 above), he is described as *mikill ok rauðskeggjaðr*. As noted (p. 26 above), Þórhallr veiðimaðr refers to Thor by the epithet *inn rauðskeggjaði* and this could well have had currency outside *Eiríks saga rauða*. And a passage in *ÓTOdd* (173–174; cf. *ÓT*, II, 136) suggests that Thor's beard itself may have been the object of special veneration; here the red-bearded Thor tells Óláfr Tryggvason how the people of the country, tyrannised by two giant women, *'tóku . . . þat til ráðs . . . at heita á þetta it rauða skegg til fulltings sér'* (so *KS*, I, 141). A beard, then, was one of Thor's more important attributes, invested, apparently, with special potency. Cf. Grimm, 1875, I, 147–148.

*Feature 6.* EI is, apart from his head-gear, naked. We may compare RI who, except for his helmet, is also naked (although here, if RI was meant to be the god Frey (cf. p. 127 below), he may have been represented in this way with the specific aim of displaying his erect penis). But generally gods are more likely to be naked than human beings. It has, for example, been noted above (p. 95) how unlikely kings (or 'kings' in board games) are to be portrayed without clothes. It is particularly the Greek and Roman gods we find presented to us unclothed in the statues and figurines of classical antiquity.

*Feature 7.* Kristján Eldjárn (KE1981, 74) describes EI as 'sitting upright on a four-legged chair with a three-peaked back but without arms'. Literary sources certainly seem to suggest that Thor was conventionally represented as sitting, either on some sort of seat or throne, sometimes in a boat (cf. U 1161), but perhaps more often on the seat of a carriage (*kerra*; *vagn*; *reið*), thought, presumably, to be goat-drawn (cf., for example, Ljungberg, 1947, 214–215, 218; *MRN*, 80–81). Ch. 4 of *Eyrbyggja saga* (*ÍF*, IV, 7) refers to *stallrinn, þar er Þórr hafði á setit* in Þórólfr Mostrarskegg's *hof* in Norway. Adam of Bremen (470) says that in the temple at Uppsala *Thor in medio solium habeat triclinio*. In Flateyjarbók (*Flat²*, I, 354) we find this description of the idol of Thor in the temple at Mærin: *Þórr sat í miðju . . . Sá var umbúnaðr Þórs, at hann sat í kerru. Hon var mjök glæsileg, fyrir henni váru beittir tréhafrar tveir, harðla vel görvir. Á hvelum lék hvárttveggja, kerran ok hafrarnir* (cf. *ÓTOdd*, 163; *Hkr*, I, 317; *ÓT*, I, 378). One of the mythological tags of Kormákr Ǫgmundarson's *Sigurðardrápa* is *sitr Þórr í reiðu* (*Skj*, A, I, 79; B, I, 69). In ch. 88 of *Brennu-Njáls saga* (*ÍF*, XII, 214), it is said of Víga-Hrappr, entering a temple, that *sér hann kerru Þórs ok tekr af honum . . . hring*; this implies an idol of Thor sitting in a carriage. And equally, when it is said of Thor in stanza 26 of *Vǫluspá* (*Edda*, 6) that *hann sialdan sitr, er hann slíct um fregn*, this perhaps implies that he was normally thought of as sitting.

The object on which EI is sitting could be taken as any sort of seat. But one wonders if it might not be especially intended to represent the seat of a ceremonial carriage in which an idol was placed and either kept in a cult-building or driven around a given area (in much the same way as an idol of Nerthus/Frey seems to have been; cf. *MRN*, 165–175). In a way, EI's chair is not too dissimilar from the loose seat (without arms) belonging to one of the Dejbjerg wagons from near Ringkøbing in Denmark (DNM C4738; cf. *RGA²*, s.v. *Dejbjerg* and references; Drescher and Hauck, 1982, 275–276 and fig. 25). The three peaks of the low back of EI's seat are to some extent reminiscent of the pillars on the seat of the Dejbjerg wagon.[11] On EI's chair, see, however, further pp. 146–149 below).

*Feature 8*. EI is made of bronze. Both RI and the figure from Lindby, thought to be respectively the gods Frey and Odin, are also made of

---

[11] Whatever the significance of the three prongs which form the back of EI's chair (cf. Figure 9), they (and particularly the middle one) released the object's creator from the need to represent the less attractive (or at any rate the iconographically less significant) parts of the man's body. They would also have protected the man's rear parts from assaults from behind, sexual or otherwise. A *gananda rassaklof* (cf. *ÍF*, VI, 242) was something scarcely to be revealed, cf. Meulengracht Sørensen, 1983, 71–73 and *passim*; *Bjarnar saga Hítdœlakappa*, ch. 17 (*ÍF*, III, 154–155). And Thor had to be no less careful than others in such matters.

bronze. Bronze images of non-Scandinavian deities (or the like) have been found in Scandinavia (Sweden): the Buddha from Helgö (SHM 25514:2200) and a statuette of Venus from Ösby, Öland (SHM 775; cf. Janson and Lundberg, 1987, 168). Bronze statuettes of the classical gods are, of course, widely known throughout Europe. Miniature Thor's hammers made of bronze have been found in e.g. Birka and Hedeby (cf. *KL*, XVIII, col. 504 and references); and apparently larger ones are reported by Saxo (cf. Note 7 in Chapter 2). Bronze was generally a favoured material for amulets and was thought to have prophylactic powers (cf. p. 54 above).[12]

*Feature 9*. This is a very minor point. As noted above (p. 83), the first modern descriptions of EI suggest that the object may originally have been gilded. While we might have considerable reservations on this point—there is little or no sign of gilding on the object now—, we should perhaps not entirely dismiss the possibility. And in this context, we may note that the images of Thor at Mærin and Hundþorp (see p. 97 above) are said to be adorned with precious metals. Of the former, Snorri (*Hkr*, I, 317) writes that he was *búinn með gulli ok silfri* (cf. *ÓT*, I, 378; *Flat*, I, 320); and it is said of the latter that *eigi skortir hann gull á sér né silfr* and that he was *allt gulli glæst ok silfri* (*ÓHLeg*, 32, 33; cf. *Hkr*, II, 187, 188; *ÓH*, 277, 279; *Flat*, II, 190, 191). It is true that in these two accounts we probably have more literary motif than reflection of reality (or at least considerable exaggeration); cf. *AR*, I, 386. Even so, it is not entirely impossible that idols of Norse gods (and not least Thor) were adorned with precious metals in some way or other (cf. also the idol of Perun mentioned in *RPC* (see pp. 102–103 above), which had 'a head of silver and a mustache of gold'). Certainly statues and statuettes of the gods of classical antiquity (often made of bronze) were frequently gilded. At all events, a miniature image of a god

---

[12] As noted (p. 85 above), EI seems to have been produced by the lost-wax process. This was probably relatively expensive and such objects could not be mass-produced. In considering whether or not EI was an amulet representing the god Thor, it is perhaps worth noting Carol Andrews's statement (1994, 104–105) with respect to ancient Egypt: 'The lost wax method was the most popular for metal amulets made during the last millennium BC, especially those in the shape of deities or sacred animals.' Perhaps such amulets produced by this method, however expensive, were particularly favoured in other civilisations. On the use of wax for implements of magic (though usually with malevolent intent), cf. H422–423.

is more likely to have been gilded than, for example, a weight (cf. Theory 5), a toy (cf. Theory 4) or a playing-piece (cf. Theory 3; note, however, pp. 94–95 above). And miniature Thor's hammers could be gilded (see for example Lundström, 1981, 67, 63; cf. Note 12 above).

*Feature 10.* The most important attribute of Thor was his hammer. There is more than ample evidence for this and only a few examples need be given. Dala-Guðbrandr says of his image of Thor that it has a large hammer in its hand ('*ok hefir hann mikinn hamar í hendi*', *ÓHLeg*, 32; cf. *Hkr*, II, 187; *ÓH*, 277; *Flat*, II, 190). In ch. 23 of *Fóstbrœðra saga* (*ÍF*, VI, 247), two people see a chair on which the image of Thor is carved: *þau sá Þór með hamri sínum skorinn á stólsbrúðunum*; the use of the reflexive possessive pronoun here is indicative and implies that Thor was frequently represented with a hammer (cf. here also *NK*, XXVI, 125 and references for the expression *Tor med tungum hamre* in mainland Scandinavian folk-tradition). In the pictorial representation of the story of Thor's fishing for the Miðgarðsormr on the rune-stone at Altuna, Uppland (U 1161), the god proclaims his identity by holding a Thor's hammer of a type known from elsewhere in Uppland (cf. the Thor's hammer from Läby (SHM 131; see Figure 5 above)). Olav Bø (*KL*, I, col. 287) can reasonably state: 'Sermerkt for Torsbileta var hamaren.'

We turn to EI. The object held by the man of EI has already been described. If this object held by this man could unequivocally be identified as a hammer, then this, of course, would be a very powerful argument in support of the proposition that the image itself was intended to represent Thor. But it is precisely this identification which has been called into question. It is true some scholars have had no difficulty in making it. Thus Sigurd Grieg (1954, 181) writes this alongside a picture of EI:

> Et slikt lite Torsbilde som Hallfred ble beskyldt for å ha, men altså ikke eide, er faktisk bevart [and here Grieg is thinking of EI and not LI; cf. pp. 61–68 above]. Det er av bronse, fremkommet på Island, og var opprinnelig i Nationalmuseet i København og er nå i Nationalmuseet i Reykjavik. Som vi ser er guden gjengitt i sittende stilling—han holder hammeren i hendene i omvendt stilling, skaftet er todelt og det går over i skjegget.

But quite a different view is expressed by Kristján Eldjárn (KE1981, 77–78) in his rejection of the proposition that the pendant from Foss is a Thor's hammer and can be compared with the object held by EI (cf. p. 91 above). This may be quoted in full:

Let us first look at the strange object (if an object it is) which has been taken for Thór's hammer and on which the identification of the Eyrarland image as Thór rests. All over the Scandinavian area small hammer-like objects, which certainly were carried on a string round the neck, have been found in great quantities. They are made of iron or silver, most of them very simple, but some quite elaborate, even with fine filigree work. These objects are, very reasonably, thought to be amulets in the shape of Thór's hammer. But the object on the Eyrarland image bears only a very faint resemblance to these amulets. The only object known to me, which has a certain likeness to it, is a silver cross, found at Foss in Hrunamanna-hreppur in south-western Iceland (Icel. Nat. Mus. No. [= Þjms] 6077), with a fine animal's head and a loop on the longer vertical arm, while the other three have discoid terminals [see Figure 12 and Note 7 on p. 91 above]. This quite unique object must certainly be looked upon as an amulet, but to explain it as Thór's hammer, as has been attempted many times, seems to be rather far-fetched, since it is in many ways very different from the well-known Thór's hammers. The object is decidedly cruciform, and the best explanation seems to be that it simply is the Christian symbol, intended to be worn round the neck, in the same way as the real Thór's hammers, true enough. Therefore it is by no means tenable to try to use the Foss silver object for identifying the mysterious unique object on the Eyrarland image as Thór's hammer and through it the image itself as the god Thór.

From these two statements, those of Grieg and Kristján Eldjárn, it is clear that there is an issue here to be addressed.

Now the reasons for the unwillingness of some scholars to make the identification of the object held by EI with Thor's hammer (which would be of such importance in this context) are probably the following four:

($\alpha$) the fact that the object in question has a double shaft; one would expect a single one.

($\beta$) the fact that the faces of the head of the hammer are rounded; one might expect them rather to be square.

($\gamma$) the fact that the vertical part of the hammer that goes down between the man's knees exists at all.

($\delta$) the fact that the object seems to be connected to the man's beard.

We shall return to these four objections below. Before doing this, however, three points ((A) – (C)) may be made which are relevant in the present context:

(A) However the object held by EI is to be interpreted, most people (including Kristján Eldjárn himself) would probably agree that it is, in fact, a combination of at least two objects, the man's beard and some other thing or things. This is, of course, certainly true of those who regard the lower part of the object as Thor's hammer. Thus, as noted, Grieg (1954, 181) clearly regards it partly as a hammer, the shaft of which 'går over i skjegget'. And Gjærder (1964, 101) writes of the beard that it is 'shaped like a cross, and one may without doubt interpret it as the hammer of Thor'. But here account must also be taken of another possibility or other possibilities. Halldór Laxness (1974, 38) describes EI (which he rather inaccurately refers to as 'íslenska myndin úr Eyrardal') as a representation 'af karli með mjög svo stílfærðar hreðjar áfastar karlmenskutákni sínu, skegginu'. And Margaret Clunies Ross (1994) makes a slightly different suggestion but one along the same lines. She thinks that Thor's hammer was not infrequently regarded as a phallic symbol. And she argues (62, note 17) that if EI 'really represents a bearded and seated Þórr with his hammer, the hammer clearly doubles as a phallus'. Clunies Ross could well be right in her suggestion. It is entirely possible that the object resting on EI's knees is intended to represent not only Thor's hammer but also his genitalia (i.e. two testicles either side of a member). (Indeed, I have myself developed the idea elsewhere and with reference to stanzas 30–31 of the poem *Þrymskviða*; cf. Perkins, 1994.) If we take cognisance of all suggestions on this count, it is not impossible that we must interpret the object held by EI as a combination of three things, not only the man's beard and his hammer, but also his genitalia. And such a combination of symbols need not surprise us unduly. The combination of symbolic emblems by, for example, superimposing one over the other is not an uncommon phenomenon in medieval art (cf., for example, Reuterswärd, 1982, 95). And with particular reference to EI, Gjærder (1964, 102), who fully appreciates the importance of Thor's beard (as well as his hammer) as one of the god's attributes, writes: 'Now, looking at the bronze cast again, we have reason to believe that the queer beard exemplifies a phenomenon which often occurs in medieval and in popular art, namely the combining of two signs or symbols in order to obtain a stronger magical effect or a heavier weight of thought.'

(B) A factor which may not have been given sufficient attention in the present context is *stylisation*. This needs special emphasis. The symbol of Thor's hammer would have been extremely common throughout pagan Scandinavia. Historically it probably had its origins

# The Eyrarland image

far back in time. It would have been found in numerous contexts and forms, for instance, as the sort of elaborate object represented by the well-known miniature silver hammer from Skåne (SHM 9822:810; Figure 24 below; cf. *VH*, 190, 276); or as a simple graffito, scratched on a coin or a loom-weight (cf. *KL*, s.v. *Graffiter*; *VH*, 315). Now the more common and familiar a symbol or symbolic object is, the more likely it is to be stylised; one notes how many different forms the symbol of the cross can take and how different many of these are from the reality of the object on which a man might be crucified. And portrayal of Thor's hammer was certainly subject to stylisation. Thus Skjølsvold (1951, 45) can write: 'Det forholdsvis store material av Torshammere som foreligger i Danmark og Sverige, viser at disse varierer sterkt i detaljene. Best går dette fram av de mange eksemplarer som er funnet i Birka, hvor nesten ingen av formene er helt like. Det samme er tilfelle med de forskjellige fremstillinger av lappenes "Tor", Horagalles, hvis hammertegn har de forskjelligste former. Alt tyder på at utformingen av disse hammertegnene ikke har vært særlig bundet av detaljer, som alltid når det gjelder symboler. Vi kjenner jo til fra vår egen tid hvorledes symboler kan forringes eller forenkles ved gjentagelser, dog uten å tape sin effekt.' And in connection with this last remark, it should be noted that a symbol can be *altered* and *elaborated* by the process of stylisation as well as *simplified*. (For remarks relevant to the stylisation of Thor's hammers, cf. also, for instance, Skovmand, 1942, 57, 63–65; *DR*, 1942, cols 1007–1008.) The evidence we have, then, certainly suggests that Thor's hammers could be given a variety of stylised forms by artists and artisans to suit their own artistic and technical purposes. Some exemplification may be given. The runemaster of the Swedish rune-stone Vg 113 (near Grästorp, Västergötland; see Figure 19) gave his hammer an abnormally long shaft to allow it to act as (part of) a frame for two long lines of runes. (He may also have given it an asymmetrical head because of a crack in the stone.) Quite the reverse situation is represented by many of the Thor's hammers intended as pendants. For example, the silver Thor's hammer from the Eketorp hoard in Närke (now in Örebro Läns Museum as ÖLM 22.461; see Figure 17; cf. Ekelund, 1956, 153, 169) has a shaft of proportionately minimal length and of triangular shape while the faces of the head are somewhat pointed and rounded.The Thor's hammers on the rune-stones from Norra Åby (Sö 86) and Stenkvista

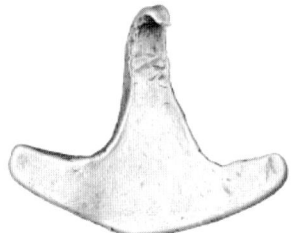

Figure 17: Silver Thor's hammer (pendant) from Eketorp, Närke, Sweden (ÖLM 22.461). (By permission of Örebro Läns Museum.)

church (Sö 111) in Södermanland (see Figures 20 and 21) have shafts, the ends of which are wider than the faces of the heads. (It is true that both stones are probably the work of one and the same rune-master.) Finally, attention may perhaps again be drawn to the Icelandic *galdrastafur* known as *Þórshamar* and used as a charm to detect thieves (Figure 18; see Jón Árnason, 1862–1864, I, 446 and cf. pp. 93–94 above). This swastika-like symbol has, of course, really very little resemblance to a hammer (or indeed to two hammers). For precisely what reasons it has been given this name is far from clear to me. But that it has surely bears witness to thought-processes in which ideas of stylisation played a considerable part.[13]

(C) It will be seen from the above that Kristján Eldjárn rejects the comparative evidence of the Foss pendant on the grounds that it is more likely to be a Christian cross than a Thor's hammer. If the Foss pendant is indeed a Christ's cross, he is of course right in so doing. This, however, is an issue which must be left aside at present (though we should perhaps not entirely dismiss the possibility that the Foss pendant is a Thor's hammer). What should be noted is that there is a set of objects which can be more or less definitely identified as Thor's hammers and which bear no small resemblance to the object held by the Eyrarland man. These are a collection of miniature iron hammers discovered at Hilda, Innvik, Stryn, Sogn og Fjordane and now in Historisk Museum, Universitetet i Bergen (as B5766 (b)).

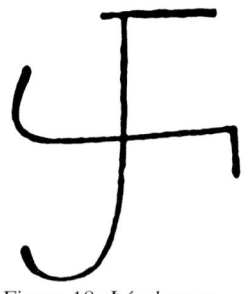

Figure 18: *Þórshamar*. (After Jón Árnason, 1862–1864, I, 446.)

---

[13] If Stig Jensen (1991, 50–51; cf. *OA*, 178; *VH*, 150, 276) is correct in assuming that the 'horned' head-gear of certain masks from Ribe and other places were intended to symbolise Odin's two ravens and the masks themselves to depict that god, then we would have an example of an attribute of another of the Norse gods being presented in heavily stylised form. Cf. Note 10 above; Figure 22 below.

# The Eyrarland image

Figure 19: Rune-stone from near Grästorp (Lärkegapet, Bjärby parish), Västergötland, Sweden (Vg 113).

Figure 20: Runic rock at Norra Åby, Södermanland, Sweden (Sö 86). (By permission of ATA, Stockholm; © Riksantikvarieämbetet.)

Figure 21: Rune-stone at Stenkvista church, Södermanland, Sweden (Sö 111).
(By permission of ATA, Stockholm; © Riksantikvarieämbetet.)

Figure 22: Lead alloy mask from Ribe (Jutland, Denmark) interpreted as representing Odin and his two ravens (Den antikvariske Samling, Ribe, ASR540x1).

# The Eyrarland image

The find is described by Haakon Schetelig (1904, 28–29, with illustration; cf. Figure 23 and Perkins, 1994, 660). It consists of a small, iron ring (about 2.5 centimetres in diameter) on which are hung nine objects with cruciform heads. The whole is very much corroded. As suggested, the nine objects have generally been identified as Thor's hammers (see, for example, Grieg, 1954, 193). And the hammers resemble the object held by EI in various ways. Each shaft extends beyond the head giving the end of the hammer a tripartite form (like the object held by EI). Each shaft, as well as being relatively short, is flat or rectangular in cross-section in much the same way as the 'shaft' of the object held by EI would be if it were solid rather than divided into two. As can be seen from illustrations, the faces of the heads of some of the hammers are somewhat rounded (although this may be due more to corrosion than original design). On the whole, then, it is reasonable to take the hammers from Hilda into account in the present context.

We return now to items (α) – (δ) set out on p. 107 above in the light of the three points (A) – (C) just made. How weighty are they as objections to the proposition that the object held by EI may be identified as a Thor's hammer? Point (B), the factor of stylisation, is of particular relevance in this context and should be especially borne in mind.

(δ) There is very little reason why two of Thor's important attributes, his beard and his hammer, should not be combined. As Gjærder has suggested (see (A) above), the combination of two signs or symbols is not uncommon in medieval and popular art. And the intention may well have been to represent Thor holding both his hammer and his beard.

(β) As noted, the faces of the hammers from Hilda may be somewhat rounded. It is not the case that all miniature Thor's hammers necessarily have square heads (cf., for example, the hammer from the Eketorp hoard mentioned in (B) above; cf. Figure 17, p. 110 above). Or the ends may have been rounded purely as an extra ornamentation. Certainly if the end of the object is intended also to represent the man's genitalia (see (A) above), then we have a very good reason why each of the three elements should be rounded.

(γ) It will be noted that the Thor's hammers from Hilda have quite considerable extensions to their shafts beyond their heads. And if the end of the object held by EI is intended to represent the man's genitalia (cf. (A) above), then the part of the object going down between the man's legs would again be readily explicable.

Figure 23: Nine iron Thor's hammers on a ring from Hilda, Innvik, Stryn, Sogn og Fjordane, Norway (HMB B5766(b)). (Photo: Ann-Mari Olsen; © Historisk Museum, Universitetet i Bergen.)

(α) Objections (β),(γ) and (δ) present, then, little difficulty. A perhaps somewhat greater problem, although by no means an insuperable one, is the fact that the object is twin-shafted. If it had a single shaft, identification with a Thor's hammer would be much more certain. On the assumption, however, that the object is a Thor's hammer (albeit attached to the figure's beard), the following possible explanations may be suggested for its twin shaft.

(i) It is not entirely impossible that full-sized double-shafted hammers did actually exist and were used for ritual and ceremonial purposes.

Certainly weapons used only for ceremonial purposes seem to have existed in pagan Scandinavia (cf., for example, Ellis Davidson, 1967, 195 and plate 19; Janson and Lundberg, 1987, 281–282). The fact that an officiant would be able to grasp such an object easily with both hands and lower it, head down, onto the object to be consecrated (e.g. a brides's lap; cf. *Þrymskviða*, stanza 30; Perkins, 1994; Sö 111 (Figure 21)) might have given such ceremonies more style.

(ii) We must remember that the object held is probably a combination of at least two things, beard and hammer (cf. point (A) above). The part of the object grasped by the man might be as much intended to represent his divided beard as the shaft of his hammer. And the part of the shaft just below the hands might be, at least in some degree, intended to represent an extension of his beard as well as the shaft of his hammer. This does not, of course, mean that the object resting on the figure's knees is not intended to represent the head of a hammer or that the two short vertical pieces leading down to it are not *to some extent* intended to give the impression of that hammer's shaft.

(iii) But the most likely single explanation for the double shaft of what we are assuming is a Thor's hammer is this. The modeller of EI appears to have been a person with a distinct liking for symmetry; the image of a man he has produced is probably as symmetrical as it could be. At the same time, competent though he was, he was also a person who was perfectly prepared to take at least some liberties in his representation of an object as well-known and commonplace as a Thor's hammer would have been, in short, a person who was prepared to stylise (cf. point (B) above). Now if he represented his figure clutching a single-shafted hammer (or an undivided beard), the symmetry of the object would have been disturbed; one arm would have had to be higher than the other. He could alternatively have represented the hands clasped together around a single shaft. But this might have been aesthetically less appropriate (the hands, which are rather broad with well-defined fingers, might have turned out to be a rather large, bloblike object), or it may have been technically more difficult (not least to represent the intertwined fingers) or both.

Explanation (i) would seem less probable than (ii) or (iii); and (iii) is the most probable. None of these three explanations necessarily precludes another and a combination of two or three of them is by no means impossible.

This rather lengthy discussion of Feature 10 has, it is hoped, shown that an identification of the object resting on EI's knees with a Thor's hammer is certainly possible. Those who reject such an identification on the grounds that the object in question is too dissimilar in form from a Thor's hammer may have seriously overlooked the factor of stylisation (cf. (B) above). On the other hand, we must guard against the circular argument here. The preceding discussion of Feature 10 has been based very much on the assumption that the figure holding the object is a representation of the god Thor. It would, then, be dangerous to deduce from the fact that the object held by EI might be a Thor's hammer that the man who holds it is intended to be Thor.

*Interim conclusions.* At this stage, with ten individual features of EI dealt with, some interim conclusions may be drawn. It may, at this point, reasonably and perhaps not unexpectedly be said that, by itself, any single one of the Features so far discussed will not suffice to demonstrate that EI is intended as a representation of Thor. Indeed two Features, Feature 3 and more especially Feature 9, are virtually insignificant in this context, the latter only marginally worth noting. Had it been possible at this stage of the argument to interpret the object in the man's hands unequivocally as a hammer, then that would, as noted, certainly have been suggestive of the god Thor. But such an identification has so far not been possible (although we shall return to the object in question below). What, on the other hand, can be said at this stage is that various *combinations* of the ten Features are rather more indicative. For example, EI has similar conical head-gear, beard and upturned moustaches to the figure from Lindby (quite possibly a representation of Odin) and those on the Ledberg stone (probably some of the Norse gods). And a particular likeness may be discerned with RI (which probably represents Frey; cf. Features 1, 4, 5, 6, and 8). In my view, then, enough information has been assembled so far to suggest that EI was intended to represent one of the Norse gods. There is, as far as I know, little or nothing touched on up to now which speaks against such a proposition. And if the object held by the figure is indeed a hammer (which it could be), then EI could well represent Thor. With this said, I now move on to draw attention to three further features of EI (Features 11, 12 and 13). The first of these has, I think, particular importance in the present context and consists not so much of a single feature of EI but rather of a combination of features, most, if not all of which (including Feature 10) have been discussed already (cf. also in this respect Feature 13). Feature 12 is of less importance to the overall argument.

*Feature 11.* Let us assume briefly that the object held by EI is, in fact, a hammer (cf. the discussion of Feature 10). We may then say that in broad outline, EI seen directly from the front represents the face of a man looking over the end of the shaft of a largish hammer. The man has piercing eyes (cf. Feature 2), a prominent nose (cf. Feature 3) and moustaches which (to repeat what has already been said) reach upwards across the cheekbones almost up to the corners of the eyes, where they have tightly curled terminals (cf. Feature 4). In addition, the face has a substantial beard which develops into the shaft of the hammer (cf. Feature 5). The faces of what we interpret as the hammer are parallel to the vertical line of the man's body.

Attention may now be given to four Viking-Age objects, two of which have been mentioned already (cf. Figures 24–27). The museum numbers of these are SHM 9822:810 (Skåne, unprovenanced; cf. *VH*, 190, 276), SHM 5671 (Erstorp (formerly called Erikstorp), Östergötland; cf. Ellis Davidson, 1967, 202 and plate 67; Bergenblad, 1972 and references), SHM 101 (Bredsätra, Öland; cf. *VArt*, 155–156) and DNM C1787 (Mandemarke, Møn; cf. Skovmand, 1942, 100–103). All four of these objects have generally been identified as Thor's hammers and this identification need scarcely be questioned. (The heads of all four have the traditional shape of Thor's hammers; cf. *DR*, col. 1007.) But they resemble each other and distinguish themselves from other Thor's hammers by the heads or faces at the ends of the shafts. It is true that a number of commentators have been inclined to regard these as zoomorphic. But others (most notably Stephens, 1878, 34–36) have discerned features which belong to representations of the face of the god Thor. Thus: (*a*) Turville-Petre (*MRN*, 83, caption to illustration 17) remarks on the piercing eyes of the hammer from Skåne and compares those of Thor (cf. Feature 2). Certainly the eyes of all four faces are particularly large or glaring or piercing. And those of the hammer from Mandemarke, picked out as they are in gold, give a particularly glaring effect. (*b*) What has often been interpreted as the large beak of a bird on the hammer from Skåne may be a

Figure 24: Silver Thor's hammer from Skåne, Sweden (otherwise unprovenanced; SHM 9822:810). (By permission of ATA, Stockholm; © Riksantikvarieämbetet.)

Figure 25: Thor's hammer from Er(ik)storp, Östergötland, Sweden (silver with filigree; SHM 5671). (By permission of ATA, Stockholm; © Riksantikvarieämbetet.)

## The Eyrarland image

Figure 26: Silver Thor's hammer from Bredsätra, Öland, Sweden (SHM 101). (By permission of ATA, Stockholm; © Riksantikvarieämbetet.)

Figure 27: Silver Thor's hammer from Mandemarke, Møn, Denmark (DNM C1787). (Photo: Kit Weiss; by permission of Nationalmuseet, Copenhagen.)

stylised representation of a large nose for Thor (cf. Feature 3). (*c*) As far as the Mandemarke-hammer is concerned, we should perhaps not entirely dismiss Stephens's interpretation (1878, 36) of the gold pieces inlaid in the forehead of the face as fragments of Hrungnir's whetstone still stuck in Thor's head (cf. *SnE*, 100–104). The man's face on this particular hammer also has heavy brows over the eyes (cf. Skovmand, 1942, 100: 'over Øjnene ses udstaaende Øjenbrynsbuer'); cf. *SnE*, 49: *Þórr lét síga brýnnar ofan fyrir augun*. (*d*) Ellis Davidson (1967, 202) remarks of the shafts of the hammers from Skåne and Er(ik)storp that they form 'a kind of beard below the face'. We may compare the way the beard of EI develops into or doubles as the shaft of what we posit is a hammer (cf. the discussion of Features 5 and 10 above).

If, then, we could say with certainty: (i) that the faces looking over the shafts of the four Thor's hammers in question are to be interpreted as those of Thor (and a critic like Ljungberg (1947, 123) could write, doubtless of these four hammers, 'med säkerhet är Tors ansikte avbildat på några Torshammare'); and (ii) that the face of EI represents that of one of the Norse gods (cf. the Interim conclusions above), then it would be reasonable to infer by analogy that the object held by EI is intended to represent a hammer, albeit it in stylised form; further that the god in question is Thor. But the reader might feel that these two points are still somewhat uncertain, particularly (i). No such uncertainty exists, however, in connection with a piece of evidence which is of central importance to the main issue of the present argument, the issue of what EI is intended to represent. The item in question has already been mentioned in passing (pp. 66, 102, 109). We may now consider it in greater detail.

The runic carving at Norra Åby, Södermanland (Sö 86; Figure 20 on p. 112) is situated not far north of Hjälmaresund in Lake Hjälmaren. It takes up practically the whole height of the rock (about 1.77 metres) and is about 1.55 metres broad. The actual runes are nearly all in a more or less circular band. The inscription, the details of which need not concern us here, is a memorial to a certain **herbiurn**. The top of the circle is broken by a moustached face. And beneath this face is an object which can only be interpreted as a hammer. It is true that this is to some extent represented in stylised form; as noted (pp. 109–110), the end of the shaft is wider than the faces of the head. But an attempt by Johannes Steenstrup (1929) to interpret it as a Christian cross has been rightly dismissed (by Helge Ljungberg, 1938, 240–243). Now it is doubtless to some extent because of the hammer that the face above it may be identified as that of Thor. But by no means entirely. There is independent evidence that we have here Thor's face: (a) the nose is accentuated (cf. Feature 3 above); (b) at the bottom of the face there is a 'peakt Beard' (so Stephens, 1878, 33; cf. Salin's reference (1913, 406) to the 'spetsiga hakskägg' of RI); (c) the eyes are particularly round and piercing (cf. the discussion of Feature 2 above and references); (d) but what is of particular interest in the present context is the face's moustache. As noted above, this has no small resemblance to the moustache of the Eyrarland man (cf. the discussion of Feature 4 above). In view of what precedes then, we can confidently say that here we have the face of Thor looking over his hammer. Or, as Ljungberg (1947, 119) unequivocally puts it, 'Torsansiktet framskymtar överst, omedelbart ovanför den tydligt ristade Torshammaren'. Now it should be noted that the hammer on Sö 86 has its head turned upwards. But here the rune-stone situated outside Stenkvista church just south of Eskilstuna (Sö 111) is of interest (cf. Figure 21 on p. 113). There seems to be general agreement that Sö 111 is the work of the same rune-master as Sö 86 (although the evidence need not be rehearsed here). And Sö 111 shows a Thor's hammer of very much the same shape as that on Sö 86, but with its head turned downwards; had the rune-master of both stones chosen to represent the hammer on Sö 86 in this way (which he easily could have done), then it would have had a pattern of even greater interest. It would have shown the face of Thor with large piercing eyes, a prominent nose, a beard and, most interestingly of all, an upturned moustache. This face would have stared at us over the end of the shaft of the hammer. We would have a combination of features which are paralleled *to some extent* amongst the four Thor's hammers just dealt with (SHM 101, 5671 and 9822:810; DNM C1787). Indeed, far from Sö 86 offering an 'utraditionell' picture of Thor (as suggested in H. Hellmuth Andersen, 1971, 8), I would suggest that it presents us with an almost entirely conventional representation of the god. And if we assume that the object the man of EI holds in his hands is a hammer, then the image would provide a striking parallel to Sö 86 which is definitely a representation of Thor. I hope that no further elaboration or amplification of the arguments is needed. It seems that the parallel evidence adduced here in the discussion of Feature 11 conclusively clinches the case for EI being a representation of the god Thor. And if it does not do that, then at any rate it confirms it so strongly that it renders Theory 1 considerably more probable that any other theory discussed so far.[14]

*Feature 12.* A very prominent feature of EI are the hands of the man, clutched around the object he is holding with fingers and knuckles conspicuous and to the front. It is worth noting that we hear of Thor's knuckles on another occasion in the literary sources. In the story of Thor's journey to Útgarða-Loki (*SnE*, 49–50), we are told how the god, when he discovered that one of his goats had been lamed, *herði hendrnar at hamarskaptinu, svá at hvítnuðu knúarnir*. If we assume that we have in EI Thor with his hammer represented in a conventional position, it would not be difficult to imagine the knuckles whitening

---

[14] It may be noted that the face of SHM 5671 (Er(ik)storp) is represented with open mouth and beneath it a stereotyped beard. Stephens (1878, 32–33) appears to have thought of the set of twelve silver pendants from Fölhagen, Gotland (SHM 3547) as representations of Thor and regarded them as having stylised beards. Certainly at least one of the objects has emphasised eye-brows (cf. *SnE*, 49 and p. 122 above) and nose, large eyes and moustache, and an open mouth (cf. *VArt*, 48; Features 2, 3 and 4 mentioned on pp. 101–103 above; *Vikingatid*, 26). As noted (pp. 119 and 122 above), I agree with Stephens that in the Thor's hammer SHM 9822:810 we have the stylised face of Thor looking over the end of the shaft of his hammer. But the face is also undoubtedly aquiline. Given the connection with wind-amulets suggested here, could its creator have introduced a feature of Hræsvelgr, the giant who took an eagle's form and flapped its wings to produce a wind? We note that the Lithuanian Vėjopatis (who in certain respects seems to resemble Thor and appears to produce a wind by blowing; cf. pp. 76–81 above), also had wings. And in later Icelandic poetry, Hræsvelgr is thought of as being able to produce a wind by blowing (cf. p. 44 above). Accepting, then, that the object held by EI is Thor's hammer, we may note its short shaft. Snorri (*SnE*, 122–125) gives the explanation with respect to Mjǫllnir that *forskeptit var heldr skammt* because of the malicious interruption by Loki in the form of a fly while it was being forged by the two dwarves, Eitri and Brokkr. Saxo (66) tells a different story according to which the handle of Thor's club was lopped off in battle by Høtherus and thus rendered useless. It is, of course, perfectly possible that the traditions represented by Snorri and Saxo's stories are secondary to the existence of short-shafted Thor's hammers of, for example, the type illustrated in Figure 17. Probably miniature Thor's hammers of this type served better as pendants. Cf. *MRN*, 85; Clunies Ross, 1994.

as the god clenches the shaft of his weapon in readiness for action (cf. Perkins, 1994, 662–663).[15]

*Feature 13.* One of the premises of the present investigation is, as stated, that the figurine from Rällinge (RI) is a representation, in miniature, of one of the Norse gods, most probably the god Frey. If this is correct (and the proposition is very widely accepted), then the general likeness between EI and RI is, of course, of considerable interest. We may particularly note that EI and RI are similar to each other in *height* and *weight*: EI is 6.7 cm. high and originally weighed about 115 gm.; RI is 6.9 cm. high and weighs 141.3 gm. And other likenesses have already been noted in the discussion of EI. For example, both objects are made of bronze; they have similar conical head-gear; the upper part of EI's moustache resembles the moustache of RI. The ears of the two figures are represented in a similar fashion. And here Adam of Bremen's description (470) of the idols in the temple in Uppsala is relevant. If RI is intended to be a miniature representation of Fricco (like the one in Uppsala and both *cum ingenti priapo*), and was found in Sweden where the cult of Frey appears to have been strong (cf. Note 7 in Chapter 1), then it would not be surprising to find in Iceland, where worship of Thor was predominant, a miniature representation of the god *cum sceptro*, or with some other emblem like the one resting on EI's knees (and which may, in fact, be intended to be a hammer), which could be interpreted as a *sceptrum*.

*Conclusions.* The preceding discussion may be said to have produced positive results in support of Theory 1. While, as noted, Features 3, 8 and 9 (for example) carry very little weight in this matter, they are, at the same time, by no means inconsistent with the proposition that EI was intended to represent Thor. And Features 1, 2, 4, 5, and 7 are

---

[15] According to Snorri Sturluson (*SnE*, 29; cf. *MRN*, 85), Thor had three especially valuable possessions: first, his hammer Mjǫllnir, second his *megingjarðar*, 'girdle of strength', and third a pair of iron gloves (*járnglófar*) of which Snorri says: *þeira má hann eigi missa við hamars skaptit*. One wonders, of course, whether these gloves mentioned by Snorri really had any place in tradition outside his writings or in the actual iconography of Thor (cf. Lorenz, 1984, 313; Stephens, 1878, 41–42). It seems possible that they did not. At all events, although the hands of EI are relatively large, there is no reason for thinking that they were intended to be regarded as gloved and there are no other suggestive signs, such as lines around the wrists.

much more indicative. Finally, Feature 11 (under which the less decisive Feature 10 is subsumed) is, in my view and taken together with the other evidence, conclusive. The whole discussion of Theory 1 has convincingly demonstrated, it may be argued, that in EI we have the face of the god Thor looking over the end of the shaft of his hammer. The likeness between the moustaches of EI and Sö 86 is of particular interest in this connection. And it is especially significant that Theory 1 explains most (if not all) of the idiosyncratic features of EI. This is an important factor in its favour. Here once more we draw attention to the remark by Carol Clover cited as a motto to this chapter and its implications. And in this context, we may give further attention to another feature of EI: Drescher and Hauck (1982, 263), who think EI is a playing-piece, characterise its head as 'überdimensioniert'. Probably few observers of EI would disagree with this description (even though it is found alongside the otherwise misguided contention that Theory 3 is correct; the very fact of EI's large head, which would tend to make the object top-heavy, militates against the proposition that it is a playing-piece; cf. p. 95 above). And EI's large head would be readily explicable in terms of Theory 1. The creator of EI, we may posit, sought to represent various of the traditional features of the god Thor, the large nose, the conical helmet, the beard, but most importantly the large eyes and extravagant moustaches. For this he needed, in relative terms, plenty of space, the space afforded by giving the figure a large head.[16] All in all, then, the evidence in favour of Theory 1 is considerably stronger than that in favour of the other Theories so far

[16] Bertelsen (1994, 61, 73), too, remarks on the disproportion in size between head and body as a feature of EI, that there is 'mikið misræmi í hlutfallinu milli stóra skeggjaða höfuðsins og líkamans, sem er lítill, mjór og kynlaus, með mjóa handleggi og læri og svo fótstuttur að fæturnar ná ekki til jarðar frá stólnum, sem virðist þó ekki hár. Mannsmyndin situr eins og barn í of háu sæti.' As the present argument shows, the apparently small size of the image's body cannot be used to argue (as Bertelsen goes on to do) that EI is not a representation of Thor. Nor can the fact that EI's feet do not reach the ground. This is to be explained by the fact that the back legs of the chair are relatively short, making the whole object lean backwards slightly (cf. Figure 10 on p. 86 above); were they somewhat longer, the toes would touch or nearly touch the ground and the impression noted by Bertelsen would not be present. One wonders whether the shorter back legs of the chair are to be regarded as an unintentional imperfection of EI. Or is it possible that its creator wished to ensure that if the

discussed. We shall return to this theory and further strong evidence in support of it below (pp. 132–134). We shall also pay attention to one further feature of EI which has not really been discussed so far (pp. 146–149 below). Lastly, in the discussion of Theory 9 below (pp. 128–131), a little further attention will be given to the object held by EI which, if Theory 1 is to be accepted, must be regarded as a Thor's hammer.

## Theory 2

The suggestion exists that EI might be a representation of the god Frey. This is explicit in Almgren, 1966, 144, and very possibly implicit in Barði Guðmundsson, 1943 (cf. *KH*, 362; KE1981, 77, footnote 5). It is true that the object resting on the man's knees may be intended to double as the man's genitalia (cf. p. 108 above) and that images of Frey were probably often conventionally fashioned emphasising this part of the god's anatomy (Adam of Bremen, 470–471; cf. RI). But Theory 1 is considerably more acceptable than Theory 2. The object held by the man of EI is probably primarily to be interpreted as his hammer; further, the man is seated as Thor was seated in the temple at Uppsala; and he may well be intended to have the staring eyes of Thor (cf. Features 11, 12, 7 and 2 in the discussion of Theory 1 above). And as also noted above, any theory that EI represents the god Frey would be precluded by a theory that EI represents the god Thor; the two theories are not really reconcilable, nor is a combination of the two acceptable. It is reasonable, then, to dismiss Theory 2 in favour of Theory 1.

## Theory 6

Lotte Motz (1992, 233) put forward the suggestion that not only EI but also BI (Figure 29 below) are statuettes which 'represent musicians, playing an instrument which shows close resemblance to a double flute'. She adduces examples of the double flute from a number of places, for example Anatolia, Greece and Sardinia. She draws attention

---

object fell from its upright position it would tend (as is the case) not to fall forward on its face? With respect to this last suggestion, cf. Note 11 above. And in connection with it, we note that the two feet of the figure from Lindby, Skåne (often identified as Odin; see pp. 100–101 above), are perforated for fixture to some other object, quite possibly in the upright position (cf. *VArt*, 154).

to the knob-like terminals of the object held by EI and compares 'the cuplike termination' of some of the musical instruments she refers to, for example, the *tibiae Phrygiae* of her figure 7, although she has to admit that she has not come across an example of the triplication of such bell-shaped cups. She also thinks (p. 237) that 'we might, in a more tenuous way, recognise the lower part of the moustache [of EI] as a stylised version of the *phorbeia*', a leather band tied around the head above the lips of the musician which 'helped to regulate the pressure in the cheeks so that they served as a kind of bellows'. And she goes on to argue that even RI is probably playing a flute and produces examples (and pictures) of other 'phallic flutists'. She has, however, to admit, at least in the case of BI, that the instrument 'does not clearly issue from the figure's mouth'. And all in all it may be said that the parallels Motz adduces are far-fetched and unconvincing. We must certainly regard her hypothesis as considerably less probable than Theory 1, namely, that EI is a representation of Thor. It is, however, not without interest that Motz suggests that EI represents a man playing some sort of musical instrument (see below).

## Theory 9

Even more recent than Motz's article on EI is that of Lise Gjedssø Bertelsen, published in 1994. Bertelsen's contribution deals with the development of the Mammen, Ringerike and Urnes styles of art in Iceland. Attention is given to EI as a representative of the Ringerike style (cf. pp. 91–92 above). As mentioned (Note 16 above), she notices the disproportionate size of the figure's head compared with its body and the fact that the toes do not touch the ground and feels she is able to state: 'Þessi litli mjói rindill með visna handleggi og lær, sem nær ekki til jarðar af lágum stól, getur varla verið þrumu- og stríðsguðinn Ásaþór, sterkastur goða og manna.' Bertelsen also rejects the proposition that the object held by EI is a Thor's hammer and contrasts the shape of the Thor's hammer from the boat-grave at Vatnsdalur in north-western Iceland (Þjms 1964:122; cf. Þór Magnússon, 1967, 18–19, 21; *VH*, 314). What, then, is EI, she asks? This question she is not able to answer; 'Sú gáta er enn óráðin', she writes. What she does contend, however, is that the object resting on EI's knees is, in all probability, a Christian cross held upside down. As parallels, she compares *inter alia* the pendant from Foss (Þjms 6077; cf. p. 91 above), which she is convinced is the Christian symbol (and not a Thor's hammer as some have thought), and perhaps more pertinently, what must be not only a cross but a pendant one found at Rauðnefsstaðir in southern Iceland and now in Þjóðminjasafn Íslands as Þjms 10919 (see Figure 28). At the same time, she thinks that EI is holding a bearded mask up to his face and argues that forked beards on masks are common within the Mammen and Ringerike styles. She gives various examples. Further, she finds the same constellation of motifs as she discerns in EI, mask above, cross below, on a rune-stone from Kolunda in Södermanland (Sö 112).

Some criticism of Bertelsen's arguments may be offered. Firstly, as already implied (cf. Note 16 above), her rejection of Theory 1 is not soundly based. EI's disproportionately large head and the fact that the feet do not reach the ground can be plausibly explained in terms of Theory 1. Moreover, Theory 1 accounts for more of the features of EI than Bertelsen's theory does. Indeed, apart from perhaps explaining the object resting on EI's knees, her theory, it should be stressed, leaves the question of what EI is in its entirety quite unsolved. And her interpretation of the object held by the figure of EI sorts ill with the other features of the object. It has little or no context. Bertelsen offers no explanation of what the figure is doing resting an inverted cross on its knees and at the same time holding a bearded mask against its face. While objects like the cross from Rauðnefsstaðir would, as Bertelsen reasonably suggests, have been held upright in use (in prayer) this is scarcely what the figure of EI is doing. And whatever the combination of motifs on Sö 112 was intended to represent, it explains little in connection with EI. It is, I suppose, something of a coincidence that Bertelsen should call Sö 112 in aid of her argument, while I use the nearby Sö 86 (together with Sö 111) as a key piece of evidence in mine (cf. pp. 122–124 above). But

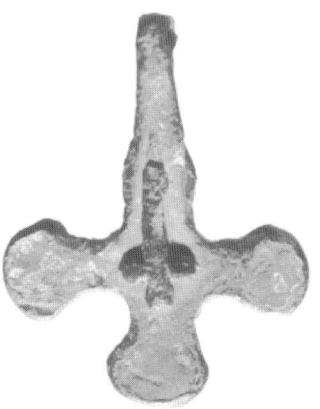

Figure 28: Cross (pendant) from Rauðnefsstaðir, Rangárvallasýsla, Iceland (Þjms 10919). (Photo: Ívar Brynjólfsson; © National Museum of Iceland, Reykjavík.)

that coincidence makes no difference to the issue. I am convinced that in Sö 86 we have the representation of a bearded Thor looking over his hammer. I am also convinced that the object held by EI can, without straining the evidence, be interpreted within the context of Theory 1, that is, as a Thor's hammer. Moreover, I am unable to accept Bertelsen's reasons for rejecting Theory 1.

With these things said, however, we may return to the cross from Rauðnefsstaðir (Þjms 10919) which Bertelsen produces as an important item of evidence in support of her arguments. At an early stage of the present investigation and before Bertelsen's article was published, I had noticed this item and its likeness to the object held by the figure of EI. Now here we approach the whole question of the similarity between representations of Thor's hammer on the one hand and Christ's cross on the other. The two symbols are, of course, representations of two originally quite different objects, the first a tool or weapon, the second, much larger, an instrument of execution. But in the Germanic world in general and in pagan Scandinavia in particular, they often became so similar that they were confused. Stylisation, imitation, emulation and perhaps even deceit were some of the factors which played a part in the process. That the two types of objects were made literally side by side is graphically illustrated by the well-known mould from Trendgården, Jutland (DNM C24451) which could be used to produce both Thor's hammers and Christian crosses. This object is sometimes taken as an indication of the relatively peaceful coexistence of Christianity and the cult of Thor (cf., for example, *VH*, 279); or perhaps of the two symbols being worn simultaneously (cf. Magnusson, 1976, 41); or perhaps of the cynicism of the creators of such religious objects (cf. Almgren, 1966, 142). In ch. 17 of *Hákonar saga góða* (*Hkr*, I, 171), Sigurðr jarl deceitfully, if diplomatically, interprets Hákon's *krossmark* to the heathen Kárr af Grýtingi as a *hamarsmark*. And doubtless devotees of Thor, wishing, say, to do business with Christians, found it politic to make the reverse misrepresentation. Against the background of these considerations, I offer some possible explanations for the similarity between the object held by EI (on the one hand) and the pendant from Rauðnefsstaðir (on the other). (*a*) That it is purely fortuitous or that some very slight degree of imitation (and then, of course, indirect) is involved (but that the object resting on EI's knees was intended solely as a representation of a hammer, the object from

Rauðnefsstaðir solely as one of a cross). (*b*) That some greater degree of imitation has taken place (but again that the object resting on EI's knees was intended solely as a representation of a hammer, the object from Rauðnefsstaðir solely as one of a cross). (*c*) That while EI was primarily intended to represent Thor, it was also intended that the object the figure holds could be construed as both a hammer and a cross. This may have been so that a pagan owner of the object could misrepresent the hammer as a cross when expedient. Or because it was intended for ownership by a person who genuinely had faith in both Thor and Christ. In this last connection we remember that EI was found in the *landnám* of Helgi magri who, we are told, basically believed in Christ but in certain circumstances put his trust in Thor. We might also note Vilhjálmur Ö. Vilhjálmsson's remark (*VH*, 314) concerning the pendant from Foss that it 'er ofte opfattet som en kombination af kors og thorshammer og som en særlig islandsk form fra trosskiftets tid'. Of these three alternatives, I favour (*a*) most and (*c*) least. With the two symbols, the cross and Thor's hammer, so common in medieval Scandinavia and so frequently stylised, it is not improbable that examples of each object which resembled the other quite closely would coincidentally be produced. But in my view, the object resting on the knees of EI was primarily intended to represent a Thor's hammer.[17]

---

[17] At this point and also in connection with Lise Gjedssø Bertelsen's theory that EI's face represents some sort of mask (see p. 129 above), it is perhaps worth noting that the Mexican god Quetzalcóatl had a manifestation as a wind-god in which role he assumed a special mask. Thus the *New Larousse encyclopedia of mythology* (1968, 433) has a picture of a statue with this in the caption: 'Quetzalcoatl in his manifestation as the wind god, when he is known as Ehecatl. This Aztec basalt statue shows him wearing the wind "mask" which always identified him surmounted by his own distinctive conical cap.' The figure in question appears to be blowing with his mouth. The same work (on p. 432) has another picture with this caption: 'Tlaloc, the rain god of pre-colombian Mexico, carved in relief on a slab of serpentine. This very ancient deity is always recognisable even in stylistic representations, always being shown with completely circular eyes.' Cf. p. 63 above. Taylor (1991) refers to Quetzalcóatl as 'the red-bearded god of agriculture'. He was also the god of travellers and merchants, with his staff as attribute and serving as an amulet (or the like; cf. H456).

## Summary

The preceding examination has shown that, of the theories as to what the Eyrarland image is intended to represent, Theory 1 (i.e the theory that the image was intended to represent the god Thor) must be deemed the most probable. Theory 1 explains more about the object than any of the other theories that have been considered. It seems that the oldest interpretation of the object, put forward as early as 1820, is very likely the correct one. And it is, of course, perfectly possible that this conclusion will come as no great surprise to many readers of this book; many will regard the conclusion arrived at so relatively laboriously in this chapter as having been obvious from the start. I would suggest, however, that the comparatively certain result produced by the present rather detailed investigation has been well worth while. And there is, of course, a feature of EI which has not really been dealt with so far, and has not received the necessary attention in the discussion of Theory 1 above, but which is of special interest. This is the circumstance that EI is represented not only clutching his beard but also with his mouth open. Now it will be abundantly clear at this stage of the argument that we must, as far as these features are concerned, interpret EI within the context of our discussion of the three objects to which special attention has been given in Chapter 3, i.e. the images from Lund (LI), Feddet (FI) and Chernigov (CI). First we must note that the conclusion arrived at in Chapter 3, that LI, FI and CI were intended to represent the god Thor, and the conclusion of the discussion of Theory 1 above in this chapter, that EI was meant to represent the same god, are results reached more or less independently of each other. Few direct comparisons between EI and the other three objects have so far been made (although it must be acknowledged that some, but only some, of the same evidence has been used in both arguments). Lindquist (1963) arrived at the conclusion that LI was intended to represent Thor without even mentioning EI; and the testimony of EI plays only a subsidiary part in Pushkina's similar conclusion (1984) with respect to CI. We can, then, say that any likenesses we discern between EI on the one hand and LI, FI and CI on the other will confirm the conclusion arrived at in the discussion of Theory 1 above. And likenesses there certainly are. What we have in EI is a figurine (like CI, made of bronze) of a man who is seated (like LI), who has round, staring eyes (like LI and

# The Eyrarland image

CI), who clutches his beard with both hands (like at least LI and FI) and who (like at least FI) appears to be blowing down into this beard.[18] The representation of the open mouth and the top part of the beard are perhaps particularly reminiscent of FI. It is true that, in the case of LI and FI, the man appears to clutch a single-stranded beard with one hand above the other, while in the case of EI, the man clasps a divided beard with hands at equal height; but this difference is probably due to a predilection for symmetry on the part of the creator of EI (cf. pp. 85 and 117 above). It is reasonable to conclude, then, that EI was not only intended to be a representation of the god Thor, but that the god is depicted involved in the same activity as I have posited that the Lund image, the image from Feddet and the Chernigov image are involved in, namely, blowing into his beard, *at þeyta skeggrǫddina* (or *skeggraustina* or *skeggbroddana*). And two features of EI (not really present in LI, FI and CI) are possibly of interest in this context.

(1) It has been noted (pp. 40–42) that the verb *at þeyta* was particularly used of the playing of wind-instruments. Any reader of this contribution looking at the picture of EI, particularly that taken from the side (Figure 10 above) must be reminded of a man playing some sort of wind-instrument. This is certainly, of course, an idea which occurred to Lotte Motz (cf. the discussion of Theory 6 above).

(2) The action of blowing a wind-instrument (cf. the immediately preceding) very often involves puffing out one's cheeks; and the process of blowing to produce a wind might very well involve much the same action. As noted above, one interpretation (although not necessarily the most probable one) of the words *blés Þórr fast í kampana* at *RRÓT* 328/20–21 is 'Thor buccas fortiter inflaret' (cf. pp. 40 and 44 above), suggesting that when Thor *þeytti skeggrǫddina*, he puffed out his cheeks. In view of these factors, it is not without interest that, when EI is seen from the front, we get the impression (cf. Frontispiece) that the god may well be puffing out his cheeks. It is true

---

[18] There can, of course, be little doubt that the staring or piercing eyes of various of the amulets representing Thor (effigies, Thor's hammers) dealt with in this study were intended as protection against the evil eye. Cf. pp. 54 and 57–58 above. A study of the differing ways in which the individual craftsmen produced the piercing or staring effect of Thor's eyes would probably be rewarding.

that this may be partly due to the figure's luxuriant whiskers. But not entirely. And at all events, the very definite impression given by the face of the Eyrarland image is, without doubt, that of a person blowing.

The main outcome of this chapter may now be summarised: it is that, just as it has been argued in Chapter 3 that LI, FI and CI represent the god Thor and that the god is blowing into his beard—he is *at þeyta skeggrǫddina* (or *skeggraustina* or *skeggbroddana*)—, so my conclusion here is that EI is intended to represent Thor and that he is portrayed engaged in the same action. It may further be concluded that EI served the same purpose as it has been argued in Chapter 3 that LI, FI and CI had. That purpose was to function as a wind-charm, thought capable of raising a wind at the wish of the person who owned or manipulated it (cf. pp. 74–76 above). EI differs, of course, from the other three objects in that the lower part of the beard doubles as a Thor's hammer (and is perhaps also intended to represent the god's genitalia). But otherwise all four objects have very much the same configuration. It is clear that we must interpret them in very much the same way.

With the main conclusions of this chapter arrived at in the preceding paragraph, we must here consider the testimony of two objects, the evidence of which might, at first sight, appear to militate against, or to be inconsistent with, those conclusions. Both these objects, RI (Figure 15 on p. 100) and BI (Figure 29 opposite), have been mentioned already.

(A) The bronze image from Rällinge, Södermanland (RI), holds his beard with his right hand (the left arm is missing) in very much the same way as, for example, CI. And yet RI is normally interpreted (and not least in what precedes in the present study) as a representation of the god Frey. If it is Thor who was represented by CI (and by LI, FI and EI) as able to raise a wind by blowing into his beard, why, it might perhaps be asked, should we find the god Frey involved in what might well be interpreted as the same operation? These answers may be given: (*i*) There is, of course, no reason why Frey, just as much as Thor, should not have been thought of as able to produce a wind by 'sounding the voice/bristles of his beard'. After all, the modern Icelandic evidence adduced above (pp. 48–50) suggests that other supernatural beings (e.g. Kári, Bárður Snæfellsás) were thought of as able to raise winds in this way. And there is certainly evidence that Frey was a god who might be invoked to get a favourable wind, and not least in Sweden where RI was found (cf. pp. 13–14, 17–18 above and Note 7 in Chapter 1). (*ii*) A second possibility presents itself. We have in what precedes (p. 127) dismissed the possibility that EI is a representation of Frey. Can we, on the other hand, equally confidently dismiss the possibility that RI is a representation of Thor? It is perhaps not entirely certain that we can. The identification of RI with Frey has, of course, been made on the basis of the figurine's erect penis (cf., for example, Adam of Bremen, 470–471). But Thor seems also to have been represented as an ithyphallic figure and EI itself may carry a representation of his genitalia (cf. p. 108 above). And certainly EI and RI are similar in a number of respects (cf. p. 125 above). If it is felt, then, that RI in some way presents difficulties for the conclusion just arrived at that LI, FI, CI and EI represent Thor blowing into his beard (to produce a wind), here are two possibilities, either of which disposes of those difficulties.

It should be noted, of course, that explanations (*i*) and (*ii*) preclude one another in this context and if one of them has to be given precedence, then it is (*i*) which must be preferred.

(B) The whalebone figure from a tenth-century grave at Baldursheimur, northern Iceland (BI; cf. Figure 29) has been described by, for example, Kristján Eldjárn (*KH*, 159–161, 357–361) and Graham-Campbell (*VArt*, 25). An argument that the existence of BI invalidates the conclusion arrived at above that EI is an image of Thor might conceivably be put forward along the following lines (cf., for example, KE1981; KE1983; *VArt*, 25):

Figure 29: Whalebone image from Baldursheimur, Suður-Þingeyjarsýsla (= BI; Þjms 6; height: 3.9 cm.). (Photo: Ívar Brynjólfsson; © National Museum of Iceland, Reykjavík.)

(1) BI is a playing-piece, the 'king' in a set of *hneftafl* (the view of both Kristján Eldjárn and Graham-Campbell);

(2) EI and BI are so similar that they must be regarded as having the same function (cf. p. 94 above);

(3) EI is therefore a playing-piece.

It should first be said that one cannot but agree with the second of these propositions. BI and EI are indeed so similar in the singular way the men are holding their beards that the same explanation must be given for both of them. But with that said, I, together with various others (e.g. Shetelig, 1937, 215–216), cannot agree that BI is a playing-piece. One of the main reasons for arguing that it is a playing-piece is that it was discovered alongside a set 'of twenty-four plain, turned pieces of cattle-bone ... together with an oblong carved die' (so *VArt*, 25); these pieces are regarded as the rest of the set. But it will be noted that while BI is made of whalebone, the twenty-four other pieces are of cattle-bone. (It must, however, be conceded that Icelandic playing-pieces are sometimes made of whalebone.) And where sets of playing-pieces have been discovered in Viking-Age graves, the 'king' does not normally seem to have differed from the other pieces in anything like the degree that BI differs from the twenty-four pieces of cattle-bone alongside which it was found; in this context, we may compare the set found in Grave 624 at Birka where the king is distinguished merely by a 'hemispherical cast mount of gilt-bronze' (cf. *VArt*, 24 and plate). And the mere fact that BI was found alongside playing-pieces of course by no means implies that it itself is a playing-piece; for example, CI was found together with both playing-pieces and dice but, as far as I know, the suggestion has never been made that it is itself a playing-piece. We may also note Grieg's remarks (1954, 184) on an object from Østre Alm, Hedmarken, itself probably an amulet but found alongside playing-pieces (cf. Note 8 above). And we have argued above (pp. 90–96), on considerations quite independent of the evidence of BI, that EI is most unlikely to have been a playing-piece. It is tempting, then, to turn around the argument described above, as follows:

(1) EI is not a playing-piece;

(2) EI and BI are so similar that they must be regarded as having the same function;

(3) BI can therefore not be a playing-piece.

And, of course, the thesis that BI is a playing-piece does nothing to explain the various idiosyncratic features of the object. For example,

Gjærder (1964, 100) refers to BI's rich growth of facial hair (cf. Features 4 and 5 of EI discussed on pp. 102–103 above). He also talks of the 'large, staring eyes' of BI, and we compare Graham-Campbell's description of the eyes of the Thor from Lund (*VArt*, 24) as 'large and round' and Pushkina's reference (1984, 86) to the 'round, somewhat staring eyes' (see p. 72 above) of the Thor from Chernigov (cf. the discussion of Feature 2 of EI on pp. 101–102 above). Shetelig (1937, 215–216) firmly and rightly argues that 'en så enkel tolkning [of BI as a 'king' in a board game] overbeviser ikke under sammenligning med . . . bronsefiguren [i.e. EI]'. And he continues: 'Så eiendommelige og overmåte sjeldne ting må ha sin selvstendige mening.' In other words, we return yet again to the proposition that 'the measure of a theory is what it explains'. We must interpret BI as the image of a god and then most reasonably as Thor. (It does not follow, of course, that because virtually all playing-pieces have flat bases or platforms (cf. p. 95 above), that all objects with flat bases or platforms will be playing-pieces.)

Doubts may, however, linger on the issue of whether BI is the image of a god or a playing-piece. Kristján Eldjárn (*KH*, 361; KE1981, 84; KE1983, 73) pointed to certain holes and incisions on the bottom of BI which he thought might indicate its being a playing-piece. But his more precise arguments are not clear to me. In this context, however, another possibility presents itself. Might it be possible to reconcile or combine the two theories as to what BI was intended to be? Kristján himself, although he concludes that BI is the *hnefi* in a set of playing-pieces, also concedes (*KH*, 361) that 'þrátt fyrir það gæti hún að stíl og handbragði verið í ætt við smágoð'. It is, then, perhaps not entirely inconceivable that BI was intended as a playing-piece but carved in imitation of miniature idols of Thor. Another possibility presents itself: In a short article in *OA* (186), for example, Else Roesdahl discusses primarily FI, but also BI, EI, RI and LI, under the heading 'Spil eller tro?'. She gives, in my view, unwarrantable support to the proposition that these objects (most unequivocally BI) are playing-pieces (though she has no explanation as to what the figures are doing with their beards). She does however concede that three of them (EI, LI, RI, though not BI) have often been interpreted as images of heathen gods and continues as follows: 'Men mon ikke disse figurer også er brugt til spil, ligesom formentlig den lille ravmand [i.e. FI]? Form og størrelse passer godt, og selv om nogle af dem måske gengiver de hedenske guder Thor og Frej, så var disse ikke fjerne og skræmmende. De indgik i dagliglivet. Og under alle omstændigheder stammer figurerne fra trosskiftets tid, hvor de religiøse forestillinger var i skred.' Here, then, we have the suggestion that at least some of the five figures under discussion served both as idols and as playing-pieces. But given this possibility with respect to BI, one can only speculate on the extent to which it was intended for, or used in, this second function. After all, all sorts of objects might be used as playing-pieces. One is reminded here, for example, of a scene from Guðný Halldórsdóttir's film *Kristnihald undir Jökli* (1989) where Séra Jón Prímus (played by

Figure 30: Séra Jón Prímus at his chess-board (from Guðný Halldórsdóttir's film *Kristnihald undir Jökli*). (By kind permission of Guðný Halldórsdóttir.)

Baldvin Halldórsson) plays chess with himself with a set made up partly of nuts and bolts, the valves of motor engines and even a key (see Figure 30; cf. Hávar Sigurjónsson, 1989, 15). And in this context we may note a small man's head made of bone to which Grieg (1954, 188–190) draws attention. Grieg thinks that this could well originally have been an amulet, and then a 'husgud', but that it was subsequently adapted to serve as a playing-piece by cutting away its lower part (the chin).[19] And the figure of Thor from Feddet (FI) may conceivably

---

[19] It should be noted that we are on slightly uncertain ground here. Grieg states that the object in question is in Nationalmuseet in Copenhagen. I have, however, not been able to establish its presence there.

The Eyrarland image 139

have been adapted in a similar way (although we should note Gjærder's statement (1964, 99) that it 'has never been longer'). Figurines of gods may, then, conceivably have doubled as playing-pieces or have been adapted to serve as them. And this might have been so of BI, which otherwise in all its essentials may have been intended to serve as an image of the god Thor. But, as noted above (under the discussion of Theory 3), the relatively much heavier Thor from Eyrarland, with its absence of a flat base, can certainly never have been intended to serve primarily as a playing-piece.

The evidence of RI and BI, then, scarcely detracts from the strength of argument in favour of the proposition that EI (and with it CI, LI and RI) are images of the god Thor and served as amulets to produce a favourable wind.

We may now return to a consideration of the provenance of EI.

EI came to light in Eyjafjörður in the north of Iceland, and all else being equal, we must, of course, assume that it was manufactured in that country. And in favour of this proposition is the fact that it was found no more than seventy kilometres from Baldursheimur in Mývatnssveit where the analogous BI was found, which itself could very well be of Icelandic origin. Moreover, between Mývatnssveit and Eyjafjörður, about 12 km. east of Akureyri, lies Fnjóskadalur, probably the area where the production of iron from bog-ore was more intensively practised than anywhere else in medieval Iceland (cf. *KL*, XII, cols 97–98, map and references). If the techniques of casting an object in bronze like the Eyrarland image by the lost-wax process were practised in medieval Iceland, then it is precisely in Fnjóskadalur that one might expect this to have happened. There is, as far as I know, very little tangible evidence for bronze-casting in Viking-Age Iceland of the sort found, to take a random example, in Viking-Age Ribe (cf. Jensen, 1991, 30–35; see also Lundström, 1981, 85–89; Mattusch, 1988, 219–240; *VABC*, s.v. *Gjuterifynd*). But we are perhaps here in danger of placing too much trust in an *argumentum ex silentio*. And we should also note that itinerant craftsmen like the one who may have owned the tool-chest from Mästermyr in Gotland (cf. Note 1 in Chapter 2) was probably capable of bronze-casting (cf. *VABC*, 180), and such craftsmen might well have been active in Iceland. On the other hand, we must remember that amulets are portable objects (not least the sort we here have in mind, intended for use by seamen). They are more or less as portable as coins, and no one would suggest, for example, that the many and various coins which are found in Viking-Age graves in Iceland were minted in that country. It is tempting, therefore, and perhaps even necessary to consider a provenance for EI in a place other than in Iceland.

In this context, then, we may give attention to the places outside Iceland where the parallels and analogues to EI alluded to on pp. 97–100 are found. On one point of comparison with objects found outside Iceland, namely, the shape of the head of the hammer held by the Eyrarland Thor, the closest parallel comes from Sogn, western Norway, i.e. in the iron Thor's hammers from Hilda (cf. pp. 110 and 115–116 above). But otherwise it is in a rather different area, in central Sweden, Södermanland, Östergötland, Öland, Skåne and Sjælland, where we find most parallels. A near parallel to EI, the bronze image taken to represent Frey (cf. p. 125 above) is from Rällinge in Lunda parish, Södermanland, not far from present-day Nyköping. And perhaps the most important piece of evidence in the identification of EI as Thor, the runic rock at Norra Åby, Södermanland (Sö 86; cf. pp. 122–124 above), is found, as noted, a short distance from the northern shore of Lake Hjälmaren. (From here, there was, of course, easy access by land and boat to Lake Mälaren, most easily along Eskilstunaån and via what is now Torshälla, older Thorshargh(er), a centre for trade, as well as for the cult of Thor, on the eastern part of Lake Mälaren and in Rekarne; cf. *NK*, XVI, 252.) In Östergötland we find the rune-stone at Ledberg which, as noted (cf. pp. 97–99 above), provides various parallels. Also in Östergötland, at Er(ik)storp (close to the monumental Rök stone, with its mention of Thor), one of the four Thor's hammers of special interest in connection with EI (SHM 5671) was found; the other three come from Møn, Skåne and Öland (on this last locality, cf. also p. 80 above). The small bronze figure from Lindby which may represent Odin (cf. p. 100 above) comes from a place very close to Skåne's southernmost tip. Meanwhile two further beard-clutching figures, LI and FI, come from Skåne and Sjælland respectively.

In his article in *Viking* (1937), Haakon Shetelig drew attention to a number of artefacts in heathen Icelandic graves which have connections with the areas of Scandinavia just referred to (and with the Viking colonies south and east of the Baltic). These objects include bronze-work, e.g. parts of harnesses and scabbard-chapes of a type practically unknown in Norway but found in relatively high proportion in Iceland. For example, a scabbard-chape (Þjms 5251) from a grave at Lundur in the Fnjóskadalur just mentioned is almost certainly an import into Iceland, probably from the area around the Baltic (cf. *KH*, 273–276). Another from Hafurbjarnarstaðir (Gullbringusýsla; Þjms 559; cf. *KH*, 73–78, 271–272) is also of a type commonest around the Baltic and occurring as far east as the lower Volga region (cf. *VArt*, 75). And comparable scabbard-chapes have been found in Skåne, Gotland, Södermanland, Västergötland and Birka (where, according to Shetelig (1937, 213), a matching mould has also been found).

It is to this last place, Birka, or perhaps more broadly the area around it, that we must turn our attention as a possible place for the manufacture of EI. In the Viking Age, Lake Mälaren, not least its eastern end, lay at the centre of an area of great cultural and historical importance. Helgö, Birka, Adelsö, Sigtuna, Uppsala and Södertälje were places which all played their different roles over different periods. And since Shetelig was writing, excavations at both Birka and nearby Helgö have shown these places to have been centres of commerce and various industries, not least metal-working including bronze-casting. And such products were widely disseminated throughout the Baltic and Scandinavian area and probably not least to Iceland (cf., for example, Holmqvist, 1979, 27–35 and *passim*; *KH*, 438). And it was close to Birka (as Adam of Bremen stresses) that the temple at Uppsala was situated, with its idols, including Thor, seated and holding a *sceptrum* (quite possibly a hammer, or a hammer in the form of a sceptre; cf. *MRN*, 93). As Adam of Bremen states, Thor was thought to have control of wind and weather. The temple was visited on a regular basis, not only by people from the surrounding provinces, some willingly, some perhaps less so, but doubtless also from further afield. For example, the rune-master of Sö 86 could well have been there and the iconography of its idol of Thor might well have influenced him when he worked further off in Rekarne (not far from the religious and trading centre at Torshälla). The modeller of RI (an object found in Södermanland less than 80 km. from Södertälje) could also have been there and seen the idol of Fricco with its huge phallus. The proposition therefore presents itself that, just as RI could well be a conscious replica of the idol of Fricco in the temple at Uppsala, so EI might be a similar model of the idol of Thor in that same place.[20] Whether EI could actually have been made

---

[20] In Perkins, 1994, I suggest that Thor could well have been *conventionally* represented sitting (as he is by EI) with his hammer resting on his knees and

Figure 31: Two Danish Thor's hammers: (left) from Vålse, Falster (DNM 3538); (right) from Sejerby, Sejerø (off western Sjælland; DNM 18196). (By permission of Nationalmuseet, Copenhagen.)

in Uppsala is a different matter. The idea is not necessarily to be dismissed. But here one's thoughts turn rather to the two centres further south, Birka and Helgö, both, as noted, well known for their work in bronze and both important trading centres with connections in all directions (cf., for example, Adam of Bremen, 470–474). In its prime, Birka was the larger and more important of the two places. And here there is ample evidence for the cult of Thor in the various miniature Thor's hammers in the graves there, for example. Chronological objections might possibly be raised. Some scholars (e.g. Kristján Eldjárn) date the object to the eleventh century, even as late as about 1050 (cf. pp. 91–92 above); on the other hand, Birka is thought to have been in decline by the 970s. But this dating of EI is very uncertain, and

---

the idol in Uppsala might well have so represented him. If I am right on this point, that would, in turn, help to explain the rather idiosyncratic shape of the heads of certain miniature Thor's hammers, one from Vålse, Falster (DNM 3538), a second from Sejerby, Sejerø (DNM 18196), a third from Fønskov, Fyn and a fourth from Othem, Gotland (cf. Mackeprang, 1938, 171; Skovmand, 1942, 82, 95–99, 103–107; Trotzig, 1983, 366; *VH*, 200, 263; Figure 31). The outer side of the heads of all four hammers has the form of two concave arcs of equal length; in the appropriate size they would thus rest very comfortably on a sitting man's knees. In general, the conventionally pointed head of many portrayals of Thor's hammer (cf. *DR*, col. 1007; Mackeprang, 1938, 171, for examples) might well be a stereotyped representation of the male member (cf. p. 108 above).

there is evidence for at least some presence on Birka in the last two decades of the century (cf. Holmqvist, 1979, 136–140; Clarke and Ambrosiani, 1995, 75). On the other hand, Helgö is perhaps of greater interest in this context. It had, of course, a longer history than Birka, stretching over some 800 years. And while Birka probably took over some of Helgö's functions in the Viking Age, Helgö may well have survived it well into the eleventh century (cf. Holmqvist, 1979, 136–140). It was pre-eminent as a centre for metal-working, not least in bronze. In addition, it seems, as its name might suggest, to have been something of a cult-centre. Not only have Thor's hammers been found here as at Birka, but also 26 or so gold foils (Swedish: *guldgubbar*), which probably also have cultic significance and were probably manufactured locally. But even if EI was not produced in any of the various places mentioned so far (Uppsala, Birka, Helgö, or perhaps even Torshälla), it could have been cast somewhere in the Mälaren area. Adam of Bremen's account of the temple at Uppsala shows that paganism and the cult of Thor were thriving in the area in the second part of the eleventh century; and the techniques necessary to produce a bronze object like EI were doubtless also actively practised. In this connection it should be noted that knowledge of, and probably respect or reverence for two places in the area, Uppsala and Sigtuna, are demonstrated by the names of two adjacent Icelandic farms, *Uppsalir* and *Sigtún(ir)*, less than 20 km. south of where EI was found (*HTB*, II, 123; cf. Holtsmark, 1956, 46).[21] Indeed, it is not impossible that EI was first brought to Iceland by a heathen who had obtained it at or near the cult-centre at Uppsala as a sort of pilgrim's souvenir. At all events, if EI was made and/or acquired in the area around Uppsala or, for example, on Helgö, then its associations with these famous, far-off and holy places could well have given it special value as an amulet in Iceland, thought of as having particular efficacy (cf. p. 57 above).

The possibility exists, then, that EI was manufactured in Birka or Helgö or the surrounding area. But with that said, the point already made above must be reiterated: the existence of BI possibly speaks somewhat against the proposition that EI was produced outside Iceland.

---

[21] Less than another 20 km. more or less southwards from Uppsalir lies the farm of Hleið(r)argarður (cf. *ÍF*, I, 270–271; XII, 271, 302; *HTB*, II, 116). This name, of course, calls to mind Lejre in Denmark with its cult-festivals, quite possibly to some extent associated with Thor (cf. Mansikka, 1922, 324).

As noted, this object, made of whalebone (a material one associates less with the Baltic than with the Atlantic) is in certain respects a particularly close analogue to EI; and there is no very compelling reason for doubting that it was produced in Iceland. And if BI was produced in Iceland, it could be argued, it is likely that EI was produced there also. These indeed would be reasonable arguments. On the other hand, the circumstances might have been different. For example, EI (or an image like it) might have been produced outside Iceland but imitated in Iceland by the craftsman of BI (or a predecessor); indeed, there appears to be evidence for various forms of imitation of Swedish and Baltic bronze-work by Icelandic craftsmen. Various possibilities present themselves, then, and we should probably keep an open mind on the question of where EI was originally produced. But if the object was not made in Iceland (as it is not entirely certain that it was), then we should perhaps give serious consideration to the area around Lake Mälaren as its place of origin.

In concluding this chapter and at this stage accepting that EI is a representation of Thor, I now offer a considerably more speculative suggestion as to a possible model or possible models for EI which might help to explain certain features of it. This is to some extent linked (although not inextricably) to the suggestion made above that EI was manufactured in the area of Sweden around Birka and Helgö. We must first, however, digress briefly to consider certain features of CI, BI and especially RI.

Kristján Eldjárn (KE1981, 82) wrote of BI that the figure sits 'almost in a Buddha position on a round platform'. As noted, Samokvasov (1908, 199) thought the heavily oxidised CI might possibly have been a Buddha. And Salin (1913, 407–408) was somewhat puzzled by the fact that RI is sitting 'på österländskt sätt'. He did, however, un-equivocally identify the figure with the Norse god Frey. Salin died in 1931, but, had he lived to witness the excavations which began in the 1950s at Helgö not more than 90 km. north-east of Rällinge, he might not have been so surprised. These brought to light a bronze Buddha (SHM 25514:2200; 8.4 cm. high; *VH*, 257; Figure 32), sitting, of course, in a very oriental position. And when we look more closely at RI we find that the god is not only sitting cross-legged like a Buddha, but that the figure's left hand is resting on its left knee just as a Buddha's (admittedly right hand on right knee; cf. the Buddha's *mudrā*s) so frequently does. And I wonder, much more tentatively, whether we

The Eyrarland image

Figure 32: Buddha found on Helgö, Uppland (SHM 25514: 2200; height: 8.4 cm.). (By permission of ATA, Stockholm; © Riksantikvarieämbetet.)

might take the knob on RI's conical helmet as perhaps a stylised representation of the Buddha's *uṣṇīṣa* (the protuberance on the top of the cranium). (This feature of RI seems also to have somewhat puzzled Salin (1913, 406); it is absent from the Norse gods' helmets as depicted on the Ledberg stone (Ög 181) and, of course, EI.) Finally, it is not without interest to compare the double platform on which BI sits with the not dissimilar two-zone lotus-throne of the Buddha from Helgö.

My suggestion, then (and this is scarcely inconsistent with various of Salin's remarks on RI), is that while RI, BI and CI are certainly essentially intended to represent Norse gods (RI: Frey; BI and CI: Thor), all three (with the possible exception of CI) have features taken over from representations of the Buddha. And while RI itself could well have been manufactured at Helgö or Birka, it is, of course, not necessary to assume that it had the Helgö Buddha as its direct model (although the proposition need not be dismissed). The Norse of the Viking Age could have encountered images of the Buddha in numerous other contexts, both inside and outside Scandinavia. And an image like BI would, I suggest, hardly have had a Buddha as its direct model but rather older images of Thor with the same relevant characteristics. On the other hand, the first images of Norse gods with the characteristics of Buddhas could well have been produced at Helgö or in its immediate surroundings.[22]

We turn to EI. The figure we now take to be the god Thor is represented here in a very different way, sitting upright on a chair with arms held up to clasp a hammer which rests on his knees. Now in this context (and not least in connection with the possible interpretation or representation of the seated god's hammer as a sceptre (*sceptrum*) in Adam of Bremen's description of the temple at Uppsala; cf. *MRN*, 93), it is of interest to compare certain ancient Egyptian amulets representing deities (or similar beings) seated on thrones and holding sceptres or other objects, often symbolic. Examples of such amulets are pictured in Figure 33 (AES 64620; cf. Andrews, 1994, 19); Figure 34 (AES 64586; cf. Andrews, 1994, 33–34); and Figure 35 (AES 71027; cf. Andrews, 1994, 47). Andrews dates AES 64620 and AES 64586 to the Third Intermediate Period (c. 1069–702 BC), and AES 71027 to the Late Period (c. 702 BC–AD 323).

Comparisons (and sometimes contrasts) between EI on the one hand and these three Egyptian amulets on the other may be itemised as follows:

---

[22] Holmqvist (1979, 41) writes as follows on the find of the Helgö-Buddha: 'Ett av de vackraste bevisen för detta [i.e. Helgö's trading connections eastwards] är väl den lilla bronsstatyetten av en indisk Buddha, som hittades på Helgö vid tredje årets grävningar. Det är en utsökt liten figur med kastmärke av guld i pannan samt målade läppar och ögonbryn. En tvillingbroder till vår Buddha finns i Kashmir, Indien, och de tillhör båda en sällsynt grupp av bronser, vilka är daterbara till 500- och 600-talen e Kr. Hur Buddhabilden hamnat på Helgö är ännu en olöst gåta, men vid fyndtillfället hade den ett band av läder

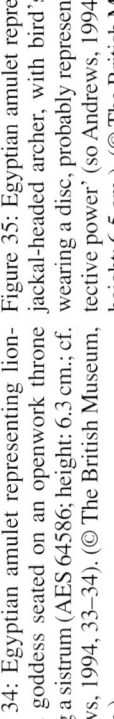

Figure 33: Egyptian amulet representing the god Shu clasping a *was*-sceptre under his chin (AES 64620; height: 6.2 cm.; cf. Andrews, 1994, 19). (© The British Museum, London.)

Figure 34: Egyptian amulet representing lion-headed goddess seated on an openwork throne holding a sistrum (AES 64586; height: 6.3 cm.; cf. Andrews, 1994, 33–34). (© The British Museum, London.)

Figure 35: Egyptian amulet representing a 'seated jackal-headed archer, with bird's wings and tail, wearing a disc, probably representing a divine protective power' (so Andrews, 1994, 47; AES 71027; height: 6.5 cm.). (© The British Museum, London.)

(1) The virtually perfect symmetry of EI, which has already been remarked on in what precedes (cf. pp. 85 and 117) and which is such a striking feature of the figure, seems to find a parallel in the symmetry of ancient Egyptian sculpture in general and the three Egyption amulets discussed here in particular.

(2) Although the Egyptian amulets tend to be lighter than EI in weight, simply because they are often made of lighter material than bronze, they are of comparable height. AES 64620 is 6.2 cm. high, AES 64586 is 6.3 cm. high and AES 71027 is 6.5 cm. high. EI is, as noted, 6.7 cm. high.

(3) The chair on which EI is seated is, of course, far less elaborate than those of the Egyptian amulets. Even so, it has the same proportions to the rest of the object as the thrones of the Egyptian amulets in question have to their figures. It is, like them, both armless and low-backed.

(4) The object held by the figure of EI is connected to his beard and rests on his knees. In a similar way, one of the Egyptian amulets of the type in question (i.e. AES 64620) represents the god Shu with a so-called *was*-sceptre (on which cf. Andrews, 1994, 80) which he holds with raised hands under his chin and which appears to go down between his knees. And another common type, represented by AES 64586,

---

kring halsen och ena armen [i.e. the figure's left arm; cf. *VH*, 257]. Det är därför sannolikt att den burits som ett slags amulett. Därvid blir situationen genast något påtagligare. Man ser för sin inre syn den köpman från Helgö, som på vidsträckta östliga vägar funnit inte blott sin märkliga amulett utan även andra dyrbara ting. De många tidiga arabiska mynten vittnar ju därom. Med allt detta som stöd kan vi våga påståendet, att vi haft en väl dokumenterad östhandel redan långt före vikingatiden. Och vänder vi så våra blickar något mera söderut, finner vi den flödande guldströmmen, som vi redan talat om, samt importen av glas och andra lyxartiklar.' This is an interesting picture Holmqvist paints of a merchant from Helgö carrying the Buddha as an amulet. If he did this, he would probably have done so from the belt, for the object, 8.4 cm. high, is a relatively large one. In connection with the leather thong around the Buddha's neck and left arm and the Buddha being possibly suspended from this as an amulet, we note that RI, BI and SHM 13701 (the figure from Skåne often thought to represent Odin; cf. pp. 100–101 above) have all lost their left arms. Readers here should not be confused by back-to-front pictures (in e.g. Trotzig, 1995, 36; *VH*, 147) which suggest that Odin (Lindby) and Frey (Rällinge) have lost their *right* arms; cf. Notes 9 and 10 above). Could the lost arms have been used to hang the objects by (e.g. around the neck or from the belt)?

has a lion-headed goddess holding a sistrum, which was an attribute of the goddess Bastet, but which might be understood as some sort of sceptre by an uninitiated observer. This is connected to the figure's beard but also rests on its knees. We note also AES 71027, a jackal-headed archer with his weapon at the ready (cf. Thor's hammer) and connecting the chin and knees.

(5) The head and head-gear of the Egyptian amulets and of EI appear to be of special significance. In the case of EI, the figure wears a helmet of a type probably thought to be characteristic of the Norse gods and its face carries features peculiar to Thor; in the case of the Egyptian amulets, we find either animal heads/masks and/or symbolic head-gear (wigs, crowns, etc.).

My very tentative suggestion, then, is that just as images of the Buddha may have partly provided models for the type of Norse god-amulet represented by RI, BI and perhaps CI, so Egyptian god-amulets (or imitations of them) may, to some extent, have provided models for statuettes like EI. And there is no reason why, say, a craftsman of the area around Lake Mälaren should not have seen, perhaps even owned, an Egyptian amulet of this type. It is true that, as far as I know, no example has come to light in Scandinavia. But articles from Egypt have been found. The glass gaming-pieces from Grave 750 at Birka (found, perhaps not without significance in the present context, alongside a silver Thor's hammer) are thought by, for example, Holmqvist (1979, 134) to be probably of Egyptian manufacture. Coptic bronze found its way all over Europe and the bronze ladle discovered at Helgö is reckoned to be from the eastern Mediterranean, quite possibly Coptic work from Alexandria. Threading holes and suspension loops (like the ones we find on all three objects under discussion) were common on Egyptian amulets and would have made for added portability and thus wider dissemination. And other very portable objects from the same part of the world, Arabic coins, found their way in great quantities to Sweden and some even to Iceland. Finally we note that various Egyptian objects have been discovered in Poland, an area which had commercial contacts with central Sweden (cf. Śliwa, 1994). These include an amulet apparently representing a minor divinity (*pataikos*). This is of a type which, according to Śliwa (463), 'enjoyed particular popularity towards the end of the Third Intermediate Period'. Just, then, as at least one Buddha was known in Scandinavia, so Egyptian amulets of the kind in question may also have been.

CHAPTER FIVE
## CONCLUSIONS. CONTEXTS

> Der Handel und Wandel zur See vermittelst der Winde in esse kompt.
> MATTHÄUS PRAETORIUS

> Fiǫlð um viðrir     á fimm dǫgum,
> enn meira á mánaði.
> HÁVAMÁL

WE MAY NOW REVIEW the main arguments of the present study. In Chapter 1, it is suggested that the impressive expansion of Scandinavians in the Viking Age depended to no small extent on a genius for exploiting available means of transport. Over water, this would have involved not only rowing but also, of course, as much utilisation of wind-power as possible. The wind, however, not least for sailing-vessels of the type used by the Vikings, is relatively unreliable as a locomotive force. In the attempt to control or raise favourable winds, magic was resorted to and deities (both heathen and Christian) were invoked. Of the Norse pantheon, quite possibly Odin, Frey and Njǫrðr were called upon in this connection. But it was most usually Thor who was thought of as the god most likely to be helpful, particularly amongst those crossing the North Atlantic to Iceland. Evidence is produced from various sources (amongst others, *Flóamanna saga*, Dudo of St Quentin, Adam of Bremen, *Landnámabók*) that Thor was perceived as having special power in this respect. One may wonder how Thor was thought of as controlling the wind. A passage from *Rǫgnvalds þáttr ok Rauðs* (which exists independently and is also incorporated in *Óláfs saga Tryggvasonar in mesta*) represents Thor as able to raise a wind by 'blowing into his beard' (*at þeyta skeggbroddana*) or 'sounding the voice of his beard' (*at þeyta skeggrǫddina/skeggraustina*). An examination of the passage and its vocabulary shows that it probably reflects a belief or tradition which actually existed; the evidence is based to some extent on comparative considerations and also on accounts in post-Reformation Icelandic traditions of Thor, as well as other wind-figures (Kári, Bárður Snæfellsás), being able to produce a wind by the same means. The first part of

Chapter 3 discusses amulets in general and wind-amulets in particular. On the basis of the conclusions of Chapter 2 and also of a more general discussion, the hypothesis is proposed that small images of the god Thor existed in Norse Scandinavia which represented the god blowing into his beard; and that these were thought to be able to raise a favourable wind for those who owned or manipulated them. The remaining part of the chapter discusses three objects representing men clutching their beards which could indeed be such images of Thor. These are: (a) a walrus-ivory figure seated on a chair discovered in Lund, Skåne, now part of Sweden (LI); (b) an amber figure found on Feddet, Roholte parish, Sjælland, Denmark (FI); (c) a bronze figure from the burial mound of Chernaia Mogila, Chernigov, Ukraine (CI). The conclusion of the chapter is that these three objects are indeed representations of Thor (as certain previous scholars have thought, at least in the cases of LI and CI); and that in holding their beards, they are represented as blowing into them. They may, then, be interpreted as wind-amulets. And in respect of this interpretation, some parallel may be found in an object described by Matthäus Praetorius in the seventeenth century and observed by him near Klaipėda (formerly Memel, in present-day Lithuania). This a local fisherman had placed at the stern of his ship, and it took the form of an effigy of a human figure made of bark which the fisherman called *Vėjopatis*, 'Lord of the winds'. This had two faces with open mouths and was apparently thought by the fisherman to be able to raise a wind by blowing. In Chapter 4, attention is given to the bronze figure from the farm of Eyrarland in Eyjafjörður in northern Iceland (EI). I firmly dismiss any notion that this could, as some have suggested, be a playing-piece. Indeed, a detailed investigation of various 'features' of EI has shown, conclusively I think, that in EI we have a representation of none other than Thor (cf. pp. 96–127 above). Useful comparative pieces of evidence are, for example, the rune-stone from Ledberg church in Östergötland (Ög 181) which seems to depict the Norse gods at Ragnarǫk, the very similar image from Rällinge, Lunda parish, Södermanland (RI) which most regard as a representation of Frey, and four Thor's hammers (SHM 101, 5671 and 9822:810; DNM C1787) which in certain ways resemble EI. But a key piece of evidence is the carving on the runic rock at Norra Åby, Södermanland (Sö 86) which depicts Thor's face looking over his hammer. After the identification of EI as an image of Thor has been established, it is in turn compared with the three beard-clutching figures treated in Chapter 3. Like them, EI holds his beard with both hands and appears perhaps to be blowing. EI is, then, like those three, LI, FI and CI, interpreted as a wind-amulet. The small whalebone image found in a grave at Baldursheimur in north-eastern Iceland is then discussed and it is concluded that it too represents Thor. Next I attempt to answer the question of where EI was made. There is, as far as I know, no reason why it should not have been made in Iceland. But if it was not made there, it is not improbable that it comes originally from the Mälaren area of central Sweden, perhaps Uppsala, perhaps Birka, perhaps Helgö. Finally in Chapter 4, I very tentatively suggest that, while CI, BI and RI ultimately derive some of their features from images of the Buddha, so EI may in some way be indebted to a certain type of Egyptian amulet, which represents gods and other figures sitting upright on small thrones and holding sceptres or other objects, which sometimes rest on their knees and/or are connected to their chins or beards. In Chapter 2 and in the Appendix (pp. 159–164 below), information is given about *Rǫgnvalds þáttr ok Rauðs* (in which we find the key passage about Thor blowing into his beard) and also about a somewhat related story, 'Rauðs þáttr ins ramma', which appears in Snorri Sturluson's *Óláfs saga Tryggvasonar* in *Heimskringla*.

The thesis of this study is, then, that LI, FI, CI, EI and probably also BI are images of the god Thor which served as wind-amulets. Given this result and in concluding the investigation, I now feel the temptation to give imagination free rein and attempt to visualise the broader circumstances in which the objects may have been used as wind-amulets. I intend to yield to this temptation with respect to two of the objects, CI and EI.[1] What follows, then, is a reconstruction of the en-

---

[1] FI was found very close to Præstø Fjord in Sjælland, doubtless as much a resort for sailing-vessels in the medieval period as it is today. The place where LI was discovered, Lund in Skåne, is less than 10 km. from Lommabukten, which must have provided harbours for the relevant area. We think, for example, of places like Löddeköpinge (and, incidentally of the find there of a whetstone incised with a sketch of a man with 'pointed head-gear' (so *VArt*) at the helm of a sailing-boat with, however, lowered sails; cf. *VArt*, 79, 255). Place-names suggest that the cult of Thor was widespread in Sjælland and Skåne and there was probably a cult-centre at Lejre (cf. *AR*, II, 116–117; cf. Note 21 in Chapter 4). On the other hand, if, as is not inconceivable, LI was made in Trøndelag (cf. Note 8 in Chapter 3), we may perhaps think of its use at a place like Agdenes (cf. Perkins 1999, 193 and note 2).

vironments in which CI and EI might have been used. It may to some extent appear over-fanciful; it may well, on certain points, be repetitive of what has already been said. Nevertheless, we shall first consider the figurine of Thor found in Chernaia Mogila at Chernigov (cf. pp. 3 and 70–73 above). Here we might, for example, imagine a Scandinavian merchant of Chernigov in, say, about the year 940. He could well, like one of the merchants mentioned in the Russo-Byzantine treaty of 944, have been called Þorsteinn (or Þórðr or Þorbjǫrn; cf. p. 73 above and references) and like a namesake out in far-off Iceland (Þorsteinn, son of Þórólfr Mostrarskegg; cf. pp. 24–25 above) have thought of himself as having some special relationship with Thor (cf. *Eyrbyggja saga*, chs 3–7 (*ÍF*, IV, 6–13)). Such a person might have taken part in the Rus ventures which penetrated down the Dnieper to the Black Sea and then to Constantinople to trade (cf. *RPC*, 73). The existence of these ventures is demonstrated, for example, by finds of Byzantine coins in Chernigov and its surroundings, by *The Russian primary chronicle*, but first and foremost by Constantine Porphyrogenitus's circumstantial account in the ninth chapter of his *De administrando imperio* (*DAI*; on the necessity for them, cf. *ER*, 112–138). At an early stage of the journey, along the Desna, just downstream from Chernigov, the settlement of Shestovitsa would have been passed where Thor's hammers have been found (cf. p. 73 above). In Kiev the merchant would have joined the rest of the flotilla in their *monoxyla*. And here also in Kiev largish idols and effigies of Thor (quite probably under the name *Perun*) were to be found, some of them perhaps adorned with impressive moustaches (cf. pp. 102–103 above). And miniatures of such idols could well also have existed. In June the flotilla would move off from Kiev down the Dnieper (cf. *RGA²*, s.v. *Dnjepr*) and quite probably, whenever a following wind blew, sails were hoisted to assist progress. (How much more welcome such a wind would have been, how much more of an *óskabyrr* (cf. *Edda*, 157), on the return journey upstream!) The first serious obstacle presented itself in the form of the formidable Dnieper Rapids, although success in negotiating these, a process described as 'at best perilous, at worst, suicidal' (*ER*, 92) had of course little to do with the wind. The danger was, however, considerably aggravated by the threat of stalking Pechenegs and many must have perished here, amongst them the pagan prince Sviatoslav in 972. (We note that between the sixth and seventh rapid lay a 'Perun Island', quite possibly with connections with Perun/Thor; cf. *RGA²*,

V, 534 and references.) And when past the rapids the flotilla put in at the Island of St Gregory (Khortitsa) to perform pagan rites, it was presumably to express 'thankfulness and relief at having completed the most dangerous part of the journey and their hopes of a safe passage from Khortitsa to Constantinople' (so Obolensky in *DAI*, II, 55). As noted, Mansikka has connected these rites with Scandinavian Thor worship. And the 'gigantic oak-tree' mentioned by Constantine on the island could well have connection with Thor worship; it might well be one of a series of such oaks along the Desna-Dnieper river-route which marked cult-places where travellers put ashore to make offerings after completing difficult stages of their journeys (cf. R. Rolle in *RGA²*, V, 533, who refers to 'Perun-Eiche'; *RGA²*, VI, 533–534). At the mouth of the Dnieper our merchant would have put in at the Island of St Aitherios (Russian *Berezan'*; cf. Swedish *Björkö* (see Arbman, 1955, 153)). Norse presence here is confirmed not least by the find of a memorial runic inscription for one of the many Norsemen who must have died on this route (cf. *VH*, 309 and references).[2] In these parts favourable winds were of particular importance for navigation and Rolle (*RGA²*, V, 536) talks of the winds from four different directions needed by nineteenth-century shipping for entering and leaving the Dnieper (cf. also *ER*, 113). And the clause in the Russo-Byzantine treaty of about 944 prohibiting the Rus from wintering on their return journey from Constantinople in these rather inhospitable parts implies that at least before that date they sometimes did so and then quite probably partly because of unfavourable winds. Nor did the disadvantage of such winds diminish as the flotilla began skirting the western coast of the Black Sea. Here again, at least initially, were stalking Pechenegs; with a perverse, onshore wind, the flotilla could be forced ashore and our merchant's skull and those of his comrades (*félagar*) might end up as drinking goblets in Pecheneg hands (cf. *DAI*, I, 62–63; *RPC*, 90). And even when this threat had passed and on the last leg of the journey, the normal dangers of seafaring and the

---

[2] It is interesting to note that there is some evidence for bronze-casting on Berezan' (cf. *RGA²*, V, 537). Rus merchants quite probably had another material necessary for the production of an image like EI, namely wax (cf. *ER*, 88, 90, 134, 145). One wonders if they might have produced amulets like EI and CI actually on the island. After all, a rune-stone seems to have been carved there, relatively simple though it is (cf. *VH*, 309).

necessity of reliance on the wind persisted (cf. *RPC*, 60); there was still the frustrating business of waiting for a wind (*at bíða byrjar*) at resting-places along the coast. However peaceful the intentions of the travellers, there was probably still the threat of harassment from an understandably suspicious Byzantine navy, armed with its Greek fire. It is true that the Byzantines may have supplied the Rus with sails and other equipment while they were in the capital (cf. *RPC*, 65; *ER*, 104), but 'vem kan segla förutan vind?' And certainly if the merchant had bad luck with the wind in these parts, Christian observers might well attribute this to his pagan beliefs (cf. *RPC*, 60; Liudprand of Cremona, 186). And there was, of course, the prospect of an even more arduous return journey, with its long, exhausting slog of more than 1,000 km. up the rivers, a distance further than from Iceland to Norway (cf. p. 5 above). For our merchant, then, sailing to Byzantium would have been an enterprise 'fraught with such travail and terror, such difficulty and danger' (as Constantine puts it) that it would not be surprising if he sought the aid of his deity for its successful conclusion. And if he thought he could get the fair winds so advantageous to his venture by the use of a wind-amulet such as I posit CI to be, then he would, of course, have made full use of it. Certainly the god (quite possibly identifiable with Perun/Thor) worshipped by the Rus merchant whose funeral Ibn Fadlan witnessed on the Volga in about 922 was believed to have control of the wind (see Birkeland, 1954, 23). And members of the same group of merchants, in praying for success in trading, prostrated themselves before a tall wooden figure with a human face, around which were placed a number of 'small figures' (cf. Birkeland, 1954, 20; *VAch*, 399; also Almgren, 1966, 138–139, for an imaginative modern reconstruction, in which, incidentally, LI plays a part; on the other hand, the 'small figures' in Ibn Fadlan's account are said to represent the wife and children of the larger god rather than miniatures of him). Finally we remember that CI itself, and also BI, were found in pagan graves. The pagan Norse often saw death as a sea-journey to the realm of the dead; and it is often thought that the many ships under full sail and clearly with following winds to be found on Gotlandic picture-stones represent vessels bearing the dead on such journeys (cf. *MRN*, 269–274 and plates 24–27). If, then, CI and BI are, as has been argued, wind-amulets, it is hardly surprising if such objects were placed in the graves of the dead to give a fair wind to speed them on their last voyages.

And second, in the same vein, we may consider the Eyrarland image. This was, as noted, found in Eyjafjörður, probably within the bounds of what is now Akureyri. There is ample evidence that Eyjafjörður in early times was not only something of a trading centre but also a resort for ocean-going shipping. For example, a short distance from Stóra-Eyrarland there could well have been some sort of market at the place called *Kaupangur*. And place-names like *Knar(r)arnes* on the eastern side of the fjord are indicative of ocean-going *knerrir* (cf. *ÍF*, X, 172, note 2; XIV, 270, note 1; *HTB*, II, 133). While the use of Akureyri as a port was a later development, largish ships could well have found harbour there as early as the Viking period. And the place-name *Naust* just to the south of Eyrarland suggests, of course, the presence of ships and boats there. But probably most interesting in this connection was the harbour and trading-place called *Gásir* on the western side of the fjord which could be reached from Eyrarland by a short, well-frequented road (cf. *Sturlunga saga*, 1906–1911, I, 479).[3] Both literary and archaeological evidence indicates that Gásir was one of the primary harbours (if not the most important) in Iceland in the medieval period. From here numerous Icelanders travelled to Norway and further afield. And to Gásir came various foreign merchants, mainly from Norway but perhaps also from other places. On the other hand, Gásir in particular and Eyjafjörður in general are not necessarily well blessed with favourable winds. For example, Jón Hjaltason (1990, 14), thinking probably primarily of the eighteenth or nineteenth century, writes:

> Eyjafjörðurinn, langur og þröngur, varð aldrei óska-siglingaleið seglskipa. Ósjaldan þurfti að bíða byrs til að komast út úr firðinum, jafnvel dögum saman. Þegar ekki hreyfði vind var stundum gripið til þess að manna skipsbátinn og beita hásetum fyrir skipið í bókstaflegum skilningi þess orðs.

Certainly a favourable wind would have been regarded, here as elsewhere, as an enormous benefit, and an unfavourable one could mean disaster. Men had both good and bad luck in this respect. Mention has already been made of the story of Oddr Ófeigsson, able to make the round trip from Iceland to Orkney in just a few weeks to get malt for his wedding. Meanwhile the Norwegians he encounters in the

---

[3] On Gásir (there are other forms of the place-name which need not concern us here), see Margrét Hermannsdóttir, 1987, and references.

nearby Þorgeirsfjörður ('víst komnir úr Eyjafirði'; so Helgi Þorláksson, 1989) have to wait there for most of the summer. And we may note the case of the outlawed Þorleifr jarlsskáld Ásgeirsson, who took ship one summer at Gásir in Eyjafjörður, was driven back by contrary winds (*varð aptrreka*) and had to spend the following winter in hiding in Iceland before he finally got away to Norway (*ÍF*, IX, 216). Or we may recall the story of the people becalmed on a ship off Hrísey, so desperate for a wind that they were ready to kill the man eventually exposed as responsible for their plight (cf. Note 10 in Chapter 1). In general, wind conditions often made it impossible to get to Norway and back to Iceland in a single summer and there was often a need to winter abroad (cf. *KL*, s.v. *Vinterliggare*). It must, then, have been the ambition of many captains of Icelandic ocean-going ships *at fara tvívegis*, 'to get abroad and back in one summer' (cf., for example, *Grágás*, 1992, 67, 95, 269). And those sailing out of Eyjafjörður, whether from Gásir or elsewhere, would have been no exception. As noted, in need or desperation men often have recourse to the supernatural. In Christian Iceland we hear of merchants calling, for example, on Bishop Þorlákr for a fair wind (cf. p. 14 above); and God, Christ or Mary were probably also often invoked. In pagan times it was doubtless often Thor. In this connection, we note, for example, that there was probably a recognised sailing-route between Gásir and Agdenes in Norway (cf. *ÍF*, IX, 264–265) and it is at Agdenes that we hear of offerings made to Thor (amongst other gods) for a favourable wind (cf. above, pp. 13–14 and Note 6 in Chapter 1). We note the place-name *Þórsnes* just north of Akureyri and Turville-Petre's remark (*MRN*, 86–87) that precisely such names as this suggest that Thor must in early Iceland have been regarded as the god of seafarers. Third, we note that both Gásir and Eyrarland lay within the larger *landnám* of Helgi inn magri Eyvindarson, who is said to have lived at Kristnes, about 10 km. south of Akureyri (cf. p. 24 above). Of Helgi we remember that though he believed in Christ, he put his trust in Thor while on sea-voyages. Helgi also allowed Thor to guide him to a place to settle in Iceland. If, then, the Eyrarland image is what I have suggested it is, a wind-amulet representing the god Thor, it is just in the area of Iceland now discussed that one could expect it to have been owned and used. It, like CI, could well have belonged to a merchant, this time trading out of Eyjafjörður, say, at the end of the tenth century or the beginning of the eleventh. It may have been cast in Eyjafjörður itself, or perhaps in Fnjóskadalur just the other side of Vaðlaheiði. Alternatively it could have been made somewhere around the eastern end of Lake Mälaren, perhaps not far from the heathen temple at Uppsala. Our merchant might even have been in these foreign parts himself and acquired it there. And while he may have traded mainly out of Gásir, he may have laid up his ship for the winter at, say, Naust, hard by Eyrarland. The introduction of Christianity into Iceland in whatever form would have made little difference to his use of the amulet. Even in the decades after the formal conversion, he would have continued to use it—and to invoke Thor himself—to help him get a fair wind when he wanted one. Perhaps when ashore in Iceland he would have been more discreet in his use of it. But while at sea or in places where heathendom still survived, he would have felt no such inhibitions. When he gave up seafaring, he may have passed it on to a son or other, younger, man. Time passed, however, and as the Church got a firmer grip on men's beliefs and practices, the use of such objects became less acceptable. The Eyrarland image might then have been forgotten or hidden or lost. It might have been deliberately buried in the ground. We do not know. But whatever its fate in the Middle Ages, it came to light again early in the nineteenth century. Wind-power took it to Denmark where it was housed for more than a hundred years. In 1930 it was returned to Iceland, doubtless by more modern methods of locomotion. And now (I submit) Thor is found ensconced in the Þjóðminjasafn in Reykjavík, his hammer at the ready on his knees. Miniature though he is, he may still appear to some to huff or to puff, *skegg at hrista*. Some may think he glares as fiercely as when he struck fear into the heart of Þjálfi's father. Many will concur in the suggestion that he has a 'noble' and 'dignified' demeanour (cf. KE1981, 84). Many might feel they are indeed in the presence of Ása-Þórr, defender both of Miðgarðr and of Ásgarðr. But even those who cannot concede these things will probably agree that the Eyrarland image is an object of interest, even of fascination. Its idiosyncratic features pose problems, demand explanations. It raises questions which cannot be lightly ignored. The present study seeks to provide some solutions to these problems, to offer some answers. And if these are not accepted, then others must be provided.

APPENDIX

# *RǪGNVALDS ÞÁTTR OK RAUÐS* AND 'RAUÐS ÞÁTTR INS RAMMA'

THE CENTRAL ARGUMENT of the present study relies to a very great extent on a passage in the Old Icelandic *Rǫgnvalds þáttr ok Rauðs* (*RR*). It also alludes, albeit in passing, to the passage in Snorri Sturluson's *Heimskringla* known as 'Rauðs þáttr ins ramma' which has certain elements in common with *RR*. Because of this and because there has not infrequently been confusion about the nature and status of the two texts involved, it seems appropriate to assemble certain basic facts about them in this appendix. The two items are treated in rather different ways as appropriate and for some information the reader is simply referred to the body of the book or to other works. (Neither *Rǫgnvalds þáttr ok Rauðs* nor 'Rauðs þáttr ins ramma' should, as has occasionally happened, be confused with *Rauðúlfs þáttr*, which has sometimes been called *Rauðs þáttr ok sona hans* (*ÓH*, 655–682). This last is a totally unrelated story connected with King Óláfr inn helgi Haraldsson. On *Rauðúlfs þáttr* in general, see *KL*, XIII, 678–679 and references; and on its preservation, cf. *ONP*, 359–360.)

(I) *Rǫgnvalds þáttr ok Rauðs*

**(1) Preservation:** Eight manuscripts with independent value contain a text or part of a text of *Rǫgnvalds þáttr ok Rauðs* (cf. *ONP*, 383; facsimile editions of individual manuscripts and/or references to places where further discussion of them can be found are noted in square brackets).

(i) AM 557, 4to (Skálholtsbók) (written c. 1420–1450; now in Reykjavík). This is the only manuscript in which *RR* appears as a continuous whole (ff. 35v–38r) [Strömbäck, 1940; Stefán Karlsson, 1970, 137–138; *Hallfr*, xlix–lix].

*RR* is found incorporated as four separate passages (corresponding to *ÓT*, I, 313/8–322/21 (*Þessi – ritat*), 325/12–327/4 (*Óláfr – gæzlu*), 328/9–332/17 (*En – trú*) (but cf. Note 3 in Chapter 2), 349/13–351/7 (*Óláfr – brennuna*)) into *Óláfs saga Tryggvasonar in mesta* (*ÓT*) in these manuscripts:

(ii) AM 61, fol., ff. 32va–33va, 33vb–34ra, 34ra–34va, 36rb–36va (probably written in the third quarter of the fourteenth century; now in Copenhagen) [Ólafur Halldórsson, 1982; ÓT, III, xxiii–xl].

(iii) Perg. fol. nr 1 (Bergsbók), ff. 45va–47rb, 47va–47vb, 48ra–48vb, 51va–51vb (written c. 1400 or in the first decades of the fifteenth century; now in Stockholm) [Lindblad, 1963; ÓT, III, clxiv–cxcvii].

(iv) AM 325, IX 1 b, 4to, ff. 3vb–6ra, 6vb–7ra, 7rb–8va, 12ra–12va (written c. 1650–1700; now in Copenhagen) [ÓT, III, ccxxviii–ccxxix].

(v) Papp. fol. nr 22 (Húsafellsbók), ff. 52v–54r, 54r–54v, 54v–55v, 58r (written shortly before 1650; now in Stockholm) [Ólafur Halldórsson, 1976; ÓT, III, ccvi–ccxxviii].

(vi) AM 62, fol., ff. 15va–16vb, 17rb–17va, 17va–18rb, 18rb–18va (written c. 1350–1400; now in Copenhagen) [Ólafur Halldórsson, 1993; ÓT, III, lxxxvi–cxii].

(vii) Gl. kgl. sml. 1005, fol. (Flateyjarbók), cols 146–149, 150, 151–152, 152 (written c. 1387–1395; now in Reykjavík) [Finnur Jónsson, 1930b; MS, 197–198; ÓT, III, cxii–cxxvii].

And one section of RR (corresponding to ÓT, I, 349/13–351/7) is found incorporated into ÓT in:

(viii) AM 53, fol., f. 27va–27vb (written in the second half of the fourteenth century; now in Copenhagen) [ÓT, III, xl–lxix].

**(2) Redactions, relationships of manuscripts, etc.:** The two main redactions of RR are represented by AM 557, 4to on the one hand (i.e. RR557) and the remaining manuscripts on the other (i.e. RRÓT). For some discussion of the differences and relationship between these two redactions, see pp. 28–29 above. Amongst the texts of RRÓT, those of AM 62, fol. and Flateyjarbók form a sub-group over against the others. AM 53, fol. is obviously less satisfactory as a witness to the text of RR by virtue of its limited extent. On the relationship of the manuscripts of ÓT (and with it RR) to each other, see ÓT, III, cclxviii–cccxxiii (stemma, p. cccix).

**(3) Editions:** Editions of RR are as follows (cf. ONP, 383):

Fms, I, 288/9–297/13, 299/23–301/11, 302/17–306/19 (but cf. Note 3 in Chapter 2); II, 17/26–19/17 (based on AM 61, fol. with a few variants from other manuscripts; normalised).

Flat, I, 288/18–293/13, 294/22–295/17, 296/9–298/14 (but cf. Note 3 in Chapter 2), 298/21–299/16 (unnormalised).

$Flat^2$, I, 319/14–324/33, 326/14–327/13, 328/6–330/21 (but cf. Note 3 in Chapter 2), 330/29–331/28 (normalised).

*ÓT*, I, 313/8–322/21, 325/12–327/4, 328/9–332/17 (but cf. Note 3 in Chapter 2), 349/13–351/7 (based on AM 61, fol. with variants from other manuscripts with independent value apart from Papp. fol. nr 22 and AM 557, 4to; unnormalised).

*ÓT*, III, ccxviii–ccxxi (variants from Papp. fol. nr 22).

*ÓT*, III, 95/24–102/32 (a text of the version in AM 557, 4to; unnormalised).

A normalised text of *RR* based on the edition in *Flat* (although with the beginning omitted) is to be found in Gardiner, 1949, 50–64. Other 'popular' editions of the *þáttr* may exist.

**(4) Translations:** (Danish) Rafn, 1826–1837, I, 260–268, 270–271, 272–276; II, 16–18; (Latin) Sveinbjörn Egilsson, 1828–1829, I, 311–320, 322–323, 324–328; II, 17–18; (English) Sephton, 1895, 196–203, 204–205, 207–209, 221–222. These translations are based on the edition in *Fms* (see (3) above).

**(5) Discussion, commentary, etc.:** Finnur Jónsson, 1920–1924, III, 85–86; Finnur Jónsson, 1930a, 123, 131; Bjarni Aðalbjarnarson, 1937, 117; Ljungberg, 1938, 123–124; Strömbäck, 1940, 15–18; Harris, 1980; Ólafur Halldórsson, 1990, 53; Würth, 1991, 34, 43, 48, 54, 97, 125–126.

**(6) Summary:** see pp. 29–33 above.

**(7) Sources, analogues and parallels:** see pp. 33–35 above.

**(8) Date, authorship:** see pp. 35–36 above.

(II) 'Rauðs þáttr ins ramma'

**(1) Preservation:** The text sometimes referred to as 'Rauðs þáttr ins ramma' only exists as a passage in *Óláfs saga Tryggvasonar* in Snorri Sturluson's *Heimskringla* (chs 78–80) and, where it is presumably borrowed from *Heimskringla*, in *Óláfs saga Tryggvasonar in mesta*. It is edited in *HkrFJ*, I, 396–402 and *Hkr*, I, 324–328 (and the borrowing in *Óláfs saga Tryggvasonar in mesta* in *ÓT*, II, 127–132). On the preservation of *Heimskringla* and also on editions, translations, etc., see Whaley, 1991, 41–62 and references.

**(2) Content:** (ch. 78) Rauðr inn rammi is represented as a rich and powerful chieftain on the island (or islands) Goðey (or Goðeyjar) in the fjord Sálpti in Hálogaland (modern Godøy in Saltfjorden, near Bodø). Rauðr is described as *blótmaðr mikill ok mjǫk fjǫlkunnigr*. He has many Lapps (*Finnar*) in his following. When Rauðr and his friend, Þórir hjǫrtr, learn that the proselytising Óláfr Tryggvason is in Hálogaland with a large force, they assemble a fleet and sail south to meet the king. Rauðr has a particularly splendid ship, adorned with gold. The two sides meet in a major battle; in this the Háleygir are put to flight. Of Rauðr's escape, it is said: *røri Rauðr með dreka sinn út til hafs, ok því næst lét hann draga segl sitt. Rauðr hafði jafnan byr, hvert er hann vildi sigla, ok var þat af fjǫlkynngi hans* (cf. *ÓT*, II, 128, which has the words *því næst lét hann vinda á segl sitt* (cf. also variants) instead of *því næst lét hann draga segl sitt*). He then sails home to Goðey. Þórir hjǫrtr puts ashore, but is pursued by Óláfr and his dog Vígi. Óláfr kills Þórir himself. The dog Vígi is wounded.

(Ch. 79) Óláfr sails slowly northwards, making conversions as he goes. *En er hann kom norðr at Sálpti, ætlaði hann at fara inn í fjǫrðinn ok finna Rauð, en hregg veðrs ok stakastormr lá innan eptir firðinum, ok lá konungr þar til viku, ok helzk it sama hreggviðri innan eptir firði, en it ýtra var blásandi byrr at sigla norðr með landi.* Óláfr makes use of this last-mentioned wind to take him north to Ǫmð (Andøy) where he makes further converts. He then turn south again, *en er hann kom norðan at Sálpti, þá var hregg út eptir firði ok sjádrif.* This wind lasts several nights and Óláfr asks his bishop, Sigurðr, if he knows of any expedient against it. *Byskup segir, at hann myndi freista, ef guð vill sinn styrk til leggja, at sigra þenna fjándakrapt.*

(Ch. 80) The bishop puts on his full vestments and has Óláfr's ship, Tranan (Traninn), sprinkled with holy water and a crucifix attached to its prow. The Scriptures are read, prayers offered, candles lit and incense burnt. Then, at the head of the fleet in line, Tranan is rowed up the fjord towards Goðey. The rowers now feel no wind against them. The path along which they row is calm, but the waves around them are so high that they cannot see the mountains along the fjord. One ship follows the other through this channel of calm water. After a day and a night's rowing they arrive at Goðey and surprise a sleeping Rauðr. Rauðr is brought before the king who orders him to accept baptism. Rauðr refuses outright and blasphemes God. The king becomes angry and promises him the worst of deaths:

> Þá lét konungr taka hann ok binda opinn á slá eina, lét setja kefli á millum tanna honum ok lúka svá upp munninn. Þá lét konungr taka lyngorm einn ok bera at munni honum, en ormrinn vildi eigi í munninn ok hrøkkðisk frá í brot, því at Rauðr blés í móti honum. Þá lét konungr taka hvannnjóla-

trumbu ok setja í munn Rauð—en sumir menn segja, at konungr léti lúðr sinn setja í munn honum—ok lét þar í orminn, lét bera útan at slájárn glóanda. Hrøkkðisk þá ormrinn í munn Rauð ok síðan í hálsinn ok skar út um síðuna. Lét Rauðr þar líf sitt.

Óláfr takes possession of much of Rauðr's property and has his followers either forced to accept Christianity or killed or tortured. He also takes possession of Rauðr's ship which is more splendid than his own; he calls it *Ormrinn* because of its likeness to a dragon (later in *Hkr* (*ÍF*, XXVI, 336) it is called *Ormr inn skammi* in contradistinction to *Ormr inn langi*). He makes further converts in the area of Rauðr's old home and then heads southwards along the coast of Norway; *ok varð í þeiri ferð mart þat, er í frásǫgn er fœrt, er trǫll ok illar véttir glettusk við menn hans ok stundum við hann sjálfan. En* (the author of *Heimskringla* continues) *vér viljum heldr rita um þá atburði, er Óláfr konungr kristnaði Nóreg eða ǫnnur þau lǫnd, er hann kom kristni á.* Óláfr prepares to spend the winter in Niðaróss.

**(3) Sources:** These may be dealt with under three headings.

(a) It is clear that Snorri had Oddr Snorrason's *Saga Óláfs Tryggvasonar* (*ÓTOdd*) as a direct source for much of these three chapters (cf., for example, *ÍF*, XXVI, cxxiii–cxxiv). Sometimes there are verbal likenesses between the texts in question. The following passages from *ÓTOdd* must have influenced Snorri to a greater or lesser extent.

(i) *ÓTOdd*, 137–143: Óláfr's encounter with Þórir hundr on an expedition to Hálogaland, the story of the latter's death and the wounding of the dog Vígi.

(ii) *ÓTOdd*, 117–119: The story of Hróaldr of Goðey who calls on the gods for a wind to prevent the approach of Óláfr Tryggvason. Óláfr's bishop throws hallowed water against the contrary wind and waves and they subside. The king is able to reach Hróaldr's island. When Hróaldr refuses to accept baptism, Óláfr has him hanged.

(iii) *ÓTOdd*, 165–166: The story of Hróaldr of Moldafjǫrðr. He is a heathen and by magic produces large breakers to prevent the approach of Óláfr to his home. Óláfr simply sails into these waves in his ship and they subside. The king preaches Christianity to Hróaldr, but he refuses to accept the faith and is executed.

(iv) *ÓTOdd*, 166–167: The account of the treatment meted out to an unnamed man in the same district as Hróaldr of Moldafjǫrðr. He speaks against the king at an assembly where the king is preaching Christianity. The saga continues (the text of AM 310, 4to from *KS*, I, 136):

Þá lét konungr taka hann ok bauð, at einn yrmling léti þeir skríða í munn honum, ok svá var gert. Tóku þeir orminn ok luku upp munn mannsins, ok blæss hann í móti orminum, en ormrinn hröktist frá munninum ok vildi allt heldr en skríða í munn honum. Þá lét konungr taka heitt járn ok binda við orminn, en þá er hann kenndi hitans, þá skreið hann í munn honum ok hröktist þegar niðr í kviðinn ok þar út, ok þá hafði hann í munni sér hjarta þessa manns.

(v) *ÓTOdd*, 173–179: Encounters with Thor and with trolls. These must, at least partly, account for the passing mention by Snorri of *trǫll ok illar véttir*.

(b) Bjarni Aðalbjarnarson (1937, 129) argued on the basis of a passage in *ÓT* (II, 135) that Snorri must have taken the story of Óláfr Tryggvason's appropriation of Rauðr's ship from the lost saga of Óláfr Tryggvason by Gunnlaugr Leifsson (cf. *Hkr*, I, 327, note 5). (He did not, it is clear, have it from Oddr Snorrason's saga.) If Gunnlaugr's lost saga told of that event, it might very well also have contained the whole story of the events leading up to Rauðr's death and then in quite some detail. And this wording from Snorri's 'Rauðs þáttr ins ramma' suggests that Snorri may have had more than one source about the death of Rauðr: *Þá lét konungr taka hvannnjólatrumbu ok setja í munn Rauð*—en sumir menn segja, *at konungr léti lúðr sinn setja í munn honum*—*ok lét þar í orminn* (my emphases). One of these sources may well have been Gunnlaugr's lost saga.

(c) It is quite possible that the story of the approach of Óláfr's fleet to Rauðr's farm has been influenced by the account of the Israelites led by Moses crossing the Red Sea in Exodus 14; cf. *Stjorn*, 1862, 285–289; *Veraldar saga*, 1944, 25–26. (For the possible influence of the same biblical story elsewhere in saga-literature, cf. Bjarni Guðnason, 1993, 136–138; cf. also p. 33 above.)

**(4) Authorship, date:** On the attribution of *Heimskringla* to Snorri Sturluson (1178/9–1241), see Whaley, 1991, 13–19 and references. As suggested on p. 35 above, it is usual to date *Heimskringla* to around the year 1230.

# BIBLIOGRAPHY AND ABBREVIATIONS

Icelanders with patronymics are listed under their first names. S and Ś are treated as one letter, as are d and ð, ö and ǫ; accents are disregarded. Þ, æ and ö follow z, and Aa = Å comes at the end. Quotations from unnormalised texts are sometimes given in normalised form without signal.

Adam of Bremen = 'Adami Bremensis Gesta Hammaburgensis ecclesiae pontificum', *Fontes saeculorum noni et undecimi historiam ecclesiae Hammaburgensis necnon imperii illustrantes*, ed. and trans. Werner Trillmich and Rudolf Buchner, 1961, 135–499.

Aeneas Sylvius = 'Aeneas Sylvius Preussen betreffende Schriften', Theodor Hirsch *et al.* (eds), *Scriptores rerum Prussicarum*, IV, 1870, 212–253.

AES = Department of Ancient Egypt and Sudan, British Museum, London.

*AEW* = Jan de Vries, *Altnordisches etymologisches Wörterbuch*, 1977.

Albrectsen, Erling (trans.), *Dudo. Normandiets historie under de første hertuger*, 1979.

*Alexanders saga,* ed. Finnur Jónsson, 1925.

Almgren, Bertil, 'Vikingatågens höjdpunkt och slut', *Tor*, 9, 1963, 215–250.

Almgren, Bertil *et al.*, *The Viking*, 1966.

Andersen, H. C., 'Aldingarðurinn Eden', *Iðunn. Tímarit til skemmtunar og fróðleiks*, 5, 1887, 46–64.

*H. C. Andersens Eventyr og Historier,* Jubilæumsudgave . . . udvalget ved Sophus Bauditz, I, 1905.

Andrews, Carol, *Amulets of ancient Egypt*, 1994.

*AR* = Jan de Vries, *Altgermanische Religionsgeschichte*, 2 vols, 1956–1957.

Arbman, Holger, *Svear i österviking*, 1955.

Árdal, Páll J., *Ljóðmæli og leikrit*, 1951.

Arne, T. J., 'Några i Sverige funna bronsstatyetter af barbarisk tillverkning', *Fornvännen*, 4, 1909, 175–187.

Arrhenius, Birgit, 'Vikingatida miniatyrer', *Tor*, 7, 1961, 139–164.

*AS* = Hjalmar Falk, 'Altnordisches Seewesen', *Wörter und Sachen*, 4, 1912, 1–122.

ATA = Antikvarisk-topografiska arkivet, Riksantikvarieämbetet, Stockholm.

*BA* = *Bibliotheca Arnamagnæana*, 1941– .

*Bandamanna saga*: in *ÍF* VII.
Barði Guðmundsson, 'Uppruni íslenzkrar skáldmenntar', *Helgafell*, 2, 1943, 155–167.
Bergenblad, Harry, 'Guldskatten från Erikstorp', *Strövtåg i Lysingsbygden*, 1972, 185–189.
Bertelsen, Lise Gjedssø, 'Yngri víkingaaldarstílar á Íslandi', *Árbók Hins íslenzka fornleifafélags 1993*, 1994, 51–73.
BI = the whalebone figure from Baldursheimur, Suður-Þingeyjarsýsla, Iceland (Þjms 6; cf. Figure 29).
Birkeland, Harris, *Nordens historie i middelalderen etter arabiske kilder*, 1954.
Bjarni Aðalbjarnarson, *Om de norske kongers sagaer*, 1937.
Bjarni Guðnason, *Túlkun Heiðarvígasögu*, 1993.
Blindheim, Martin, 'The gilded Viking ship vanes. Their use and technique', *The Vikings*, ed. R. T. Farrell, 1982, 116–127.
Blöndal, Sigfús, *Islandsk-dansk Ordbog*, 1920–1924.
*Bósa saga* = *Die Bósa-Saga in zwei Fassungen*, ed. Otto Luitpold Jiriczek, 1893.
Bridge, Adrian, 'Gaddafi's blow for solitude', *The Independent*, 8th April, 1989, 42.
Briem, Ólafur, *Heiðinn siður á Íslandi*, 1945.
Brown, Andrew, 'The little miracle in Lady Margaret Road', *The Independent*, 23rd September, 1995, 1.
*Byskupa sǫgur*, ed. Jón Helgason, 1938–1978.
Bæksted, Anders, *Goð og hetjur í heiðnum sið. Alþýðlegt fræðirit um goðafræði og hetjusögur*, trans. Eysteinn Þorvaldsson, 1986.
Cameron, Morag, 'Highland fisher-folk and their superstitions', *Folklore*, 14, 1903, 300–306.
CI = the bronze figure from Chernaia Mogila, Chernigov, Ukraine (GIM 76990/1539/77; cf. Figure 7).
Clarke, Helen, and Björn Ambrosiani, *Towns in the Viking age*, 1995.
Clover, Carol J., 'The long prose form', *Arkiv för nordisk filologi*, 101, 1986, 10–39.
Clunies Ross, Margaret, 'Þórr's honour', *Studien zum Altgermanischen. Festschrift für Heinrich Beck*, ed. Heiko Uecker, 1994, 48–76.
*Collegial-Tidende*, No. 7 and 8. 10th February, 1821.
C–V = Richard Cleasby and Gudbrand Vigfusson, *An Icelandic-English dictionary* (2nd ed. by William A. Craigie), 1957.
Daggfeldt, Bertil, 'Vikingen—roddaren', *Fornvännen*, 78, 1983, 92–94.

*DAI* = Constantine Porphyrogenitus, *De administrando imperio* I, ed. Gy. Moravcsik, trans. R. J. H. Jenkins, 1967. II, Commentary, ed. R. J. H. Jenkins (with contributions by, among others, D. Obolensky), 1962.

Dalin, A. F., *Ordbok öfver svenska språket*, 1850–1853.

*DMA* = *Dictionary of the Middle Ages*, ed. Joseph R. Strayer, 13 vols, 1982–1989.

DNM = Nationalmuseet, Copenhagen.

*DR* = *Danmarks runeindskrifter . . . Text*, ed. Lis Jacobsen and Erik Moltke, 1942.

Drescher, Hans, and Karl Hauck, 'Götterthrone des heidnischen Nordens', *Frühmittelalterliche Studien*, 16, 1982, 237–301.

Dudo 1865 = *De moribus et actis primorum Normanniæ ducum auctore Dudone Sancti Quintini decano*, ed. Jules Lair, 1865.

Dudo 1998 = Dudo of St Quentin, *History of the Normans*, trans. Eric Christiansen, 1998.

*Edda* = *Edda. Die lieder des Codex Regius nebst verwandten denkmälern*, ed. Gustav Neckel, revised by Hans Kuhn, 1962.

EI = the (figure represented by the) Eyrarland image from Eyjafjarðarsýsla, Iceland (Þjms 10880; cf. Frontispiece and Figures 9–11).

Ekbo, Sven, 'Die Etymologie des finnischen *Ruotsi* "Schweden"', *Jahrbücher für Geschichte Osteuropas*, 34, 1986, 354–356.

Ekelund, Gunnar, 'Silverskatten från Eketorp', *Från bergslag och bondebygd. Örebro Läns Hembygdsförbunds årsbok*, 11, 1956, 143–175.

Ellis Davidson, H. R., *Gods and myths of northern Europe*, 1964.

Ellis Davidson, H. R., 'Thor's hammer', *Folklore*, 76, 1965, 1–15.

Ellis Davidson, H. R., *Pagan Scandinavia*, 1967.

*ER* = Simon Franklin and Jonathan Shepard, *The Emergence of Rus: 750–1200*, 1996.

Falk, Hjalmar, 'De nordiske hovedguders utviklingshistorie', *Arkiv för nordisk filologi*, 43, 1927, 34–44.

FI = the amber figure from Feddet, Roholte parish, Sjælland, Denmark (DNM C24292; cf. cover picture and Figure 6)

Finnur Jónsson, *Den oldnorske og oldislandske litteraturs historie*, 2nd ed., 3 vols, 1920–1924.

Finnur Jónsson, 'Óláfs saga Tryggvasonar (hin meiri)', *Aarbøger for nordisk Oldkyndighed og Historie*,1930a, 119–138.

Finnur Jónsson (ed.), *Flateyjarbók (Codex Flateyensis). MS. No. 1005 fol. in The Old Royal Collection in the Royal Library of Copenhagen*, 1930b.

*Flat* = *Flateyjarbok. En Samling af norske Konge-Sagaer*, ed. Guðbrandr Vigfusson and C. R. Unger, 3 vols, 1860–1868.

*Flat²* = *Flateyjarbók*, ed. Sigurður Nordal, 4 vols, 1944–1945.

*Fms* = *Fornmanna sögur eptir gömlum handritum*, 12 vols, 1825–1837.

*FN* = *Fornaldar sögur Norðurlanda*, ed. Guðni Jónsson, 4 vols, 1954.

Frazer, J. G., *The magic art and the evolution of kings*, 2 vols, 1911.

Frazer, James George, *The Golden Bough. A Study in Magic and Religion*, abridged edition, 1963.

Fritzner = Johan Fritzner, *Ordbog over det gamle norske Sprog*, vols I–III, 1883–1896; reprint: 1954. Vol. IV: Finn Hødnebø, *Ordbog over det gamle norske Sprog af Dr. Johan Fritzner. Rettelser og tillegg*, 1972.

Fuglesang, Signe Horn, 'Viking and medieval amulets in Scandinavia', *Fornvännen*, 84, 1989, 15–27.

Gardiner, Edwin (ed.), *Fornar smásögur úr Noregskonunga sögum*, 1949.

GIM = Gosudarstvennyi Istorichechii Muzei, Moscow.

Gjærder, Per, 'The beard as an iconographical feature in the Viking Period and the early Middle Ages', *Acta archaeologica*, 35, 1964, 95–114.

Gomme, Alice Bertha, *The traditional games of England, Scotland, and Ireland*, 2 vols, 1894–1898.

*Grágás. Lagasafn íslenska þjóðveldisins*, ed. Gunnar Karlsson, Kristján Sveinsson and Mörður Árnason, 1992.

Grieg, Sigurd, 'Amuletter og gudebilder', *Viking*, 18, 1954, 157–209.

Grimm, Jacob, *Deutsche mythologie*. Vierte ausgabe besorgt von Elard Hugo Meyer, 3 vols, 1875.

*Guta lag och Guta saga*, ed. Hugo Pipping, 2 vols, 1905–1907.

H = an article by various authors entitled 'Charms and amulets', *Encyclopædia of religion and ethics*, ed. James Hastings, vol. III, 1910, 392–472. (Numerals refer to the page numbers of this volume.)

Hagen, B, *Unter den Papua's*, 1899.

Hallberg, Göran, *Ortnamn på Öland*, 1985.

*Hallfr* = *Hallfreðar saga*, ed. Bjarni Einarsson, 1977.

Harris, Joseph, 'Folktale and thattr: the case of Rognvald and Raud', *Folklore forum*, 13: 2–3, 1980, 158–197.

Hávar Sigurjónsson, 'Filming a novel fascination', *Iceland review*, 27: 1, 1989, 10–16.

Helgi Guðmundsson, 'Hreytispeldi', *Gripla*, 3, 1979, 224–226.

Helgi Þorláksson, 'Sólundir og Sólskel', *Orðlokarr sendur Svavari Sigmundssyni fimmtugum*, ed. Eiríkur Rögnvaldsson and Sigurgeir Steingrímsson, 1989, 27–30.
Hellmuth Andersen, H., 'Tordenguden', *Skalk*, 3, 1971, 4–8.
Hkr = Snorri Sturluson, *Heimskringla*, ed. Bjarni Aðalbjarnarson, 3 vols, 1941–51.
HkrFJ = *Heimskringla. Nóregs konunga sǫgur af Snorri Sturluson*, ed. Finnur Jónsson, 4 vols, 1893–1901.
HMB = Historisk Museum, Bergen.
Holm, Gösta, 'Tre bidrag till norrön etymologi', *Eyvindarbók. Festskrift til Eyvind Fjeld Halvorsen*, ed. Finn Hødnebø et al., 1992, 118–122.
Holmqvist, Wilhelm, *Vikingar på Helgö och Birka*, 1979.
Holtsmark, Anne, *Studier i norrøn diktning*, 1956.
Holtsmark, Anne, *Norrøn mytologi. Tru og mytar i vikingtida*, 1970.
Howitt, A.W., 'On some Australian beliefs', *The journal of The Anthropological Institute of Great Britain and Ireland*, 13, 1884a, 185–198.
Howitt, A.W., 'On some Australian ceremonies of initiation', *The journal of The Anthropological Institute of Great Britain and Ireland*, 13, 1884b, 432–459.
HTB = P. E. Kristian Kålund, *Bidrag til en historisk-topografisk beskrivelse af Island*, 2 vols, 1877–1882.
HWDA = Hanns Bächtold-Stäubli (ed.), *Handwörterbuch des deutschen Aberglaubens*, 10 vols, 1927–1942.
*Iceland 1986*, ed. Jóhannes Nordal and Valdimar Kristinsson, 1987.
ÍF = *Íslenzk fornrit*, 1933– (references to vol. III and vol. IV are to the editions of 1972 and 1985 respectively).
ÍO = Ásgeir Blöndal Magnússon, *Íslensk orðsifjabók*, 1989.
Jansson, Sven B. F., *Runes in Sweden*, trans. Peter Foote, 1987.
Janson, Sverker and Erik B. Lundberg (eds), *Med arkeologen Sverige runt*, 1987.
Jensen, Stig, *Ribes vikinger*, 1991.
*Jómsvíkinga saga*, ed. Ólafur Halldórsson, 1969.
Jón Árnason, *Íslenzkar þjóðsögur og ævintyri*, 2 vols, 1862–1864.
Jón Hjaltason, *Saga Akureyrar*, I, 1990.
*Jónsbók*, ed. Ólafur Halldórsson, 1970.
*Karlamagnus saga ok kappa hans*, ed. C. R. Unger, 1860.

KE1981 = Kristján Eldjárn, 'The bronze image from Eyrarland', *Speculum norroenum. Norse studies in memory of Gabriel Turville-Petre*, ed. Ursula Dronke et al., 1981, 73–84.

KE1983 = Kristján Eldjárn, 'Þórslíkneski svonefnt frá Eyrarlandi', *Árbók Hins íslenzka fornleifafélags 1982*, 1983, 62–75. (Icelandic version of KE1981 with revisions.)

*KH* = Kristján Eldjárn, *Kuml og haugfé úr heiðnum sið á Íslandi*, 1956.

*KL* = *Kulturhistoriskt lexikon för nordisk medeltid*, 22 vols, 1956–1978.

Klemens Jónsson, *Saga Akureyrar*, 1958.

KM = Kulturen, Lund.

*Konungs skuggsjá*, ed. Finnur Jónsson, 1920.

*Konungs skuggsjá*, ed. Magnús Már Lárusson, [1955].

*Kristni saga*: in *Hauksbók*, ed. Eiríkur Jónsson and Finnur Jónsson, 1892–1896, 126–149.

*KS* = *Konunga sögur*, ed. Guðni Jónsson, 3 vols, 1957.

Kuhn, Hans, *Kleine Schriften*, 4 vols, 1969–1978. (Vol. II includes 'Das nordgermanische Heidentum in den ersten christlichen Jahrhunderten', 296–326; and 'Das Fortleben des germanischen Heidentums nach der Christianiserung', 378–386.)

*Kvæði Eggerts Ólafssonar, útgefin eptir þeim beztu handritum er feingizt gátu*, 1832.

Kålund, Kr., 'Islands fortidslævninger', *Aarboger før nordisk Oldkyndighed og Historie*, 1882, 57–124.

Laxness, Halldór, *Þjóðhátíðarrolla*, 1974.

LI = the (man represented by the) walrus-ivory figure from Lund, Sweden (KM 38.252; cf. Figures 3–5).

Liljegren, J. G., 'Utdrag af twänne bref till Hans Excellence Stats-Ministern för Utrikes Ärenderne, m.m. Herr Grefwe L. v. Engeström från Professorn Magister J. G. Liljegren. (Af den 28 Februari och 23 April 1820)', *Iduna*, 8, 1820, 135–157 and Tab. 2, Fig. 3.

Lind, E. H., *Norsk-isländska dopnamn ock fingerade namn från medeltiden*, 1905–1915.

Lind, E. H., *Norsk-isländska personbinamn från medeltiden*, 1920–1921.

Lind, E.H., *Norsk-isländska dopnamn ock fingerade namn från medeltiden. Supplementband*, 1931.

Lindblad, Gustaf (ed.), *Bergsbók. Perg. fol. nr. 1 in The Royal Library, Stockholm*, 1963.

Lindquist, Ivar, 'Två vikingatida gudabeläten', *Kulturen 1962*, 1963, 70–78.
Liudprand of Cremona = *The works of Liudprand of Cremona*, trans. F. A. Wright, 1930.
Ljungberg, Helge, *Den nordiska religionen och kristendomen*, 1938.
Ljungberg, Helge, *Tor. Undersökningar i indoeuropeisk och nordisk religionshistoria*, 1947.
Longfellow = *The Poetical Works of Longfellow*, 1904.
Lorenz, Gottfried (ed. and trans.), Snorri Sturluson, *Gylfaginning*, 1984.
*LP* = Finnur Jónsson, *Lexicon poeticum antiquæ linguæ septentrionalis. Ordbog over det norsk-islandske skjaldesprog oprindelig forfattet af Sveinbjörn Egilsson*, 2nd ed., 1931.
Lundström, Per, *De kommo vida . . . Vikingars hamn vid Paviken på Gotland*, 1981.
Mackeprang, Mogens B., 'Thors Hammer', *Tilskueren*, 55, September, 1938, 170–181.
Magnusson, Magnus, *Hammer of the North*, 1976.
Mannhardt, Wilhelm, *Letto-Preussische Götterlehre*, 1936.
Mansikka, V. J., *Die Religion der Ostslaven*, 1922.
Margrét Hermannsdóttir, 'Fornleifarannsóknir að Gásum og víðar í Eyjafirði árið 1986', *Súlur. Norðlenskt tímarit*. XIV. árg., 27 hefti, 1987, 3–39.
Matthías Jochumsson, *Ljóðmæli*, 5 vols, 1902–1906.
Matthías Þórðarson, *Þjóðminjasafn Íslands. Safnskrá 1930*. 1930. (Unpublished inventory of certain items in Þjóðminjasafn Íslands.)
Mattusch, Carol C., *Greek bronze statuary*, 1988.
Meaney, Audrey L., *Anglo-Saxon amulets and curing stones*, 1981.
Meulengracht Sørensen, Preben, *The unmanly man. Concepts of sexual defamation in early Northern society*, trans. Joan Turville-Petre, 1983.
Meyer, Elard Hugo, *Germanische Mythologie*, 1891.
Mjólkursamsalan, 1994 = one-litre milk-carton issued by Mjólkursamsalan í Reykjavík in 1994.
Modéer, Ivar, 'Vindholm och Väderö', *Germanska namnstudier tillägnade Evald Lidén*, 1932, 138–146.
Mogk, E., 'Die Menschenopfer bei den Germanen', *Abhandlungen der philologisch-historischen Klasse Der königlich sächsischen Gesellschaft der Wissenschaften*, 27, 1909, 601–644.

Moltke, Erik, *Runerne i Danmark og deres oprindelse*, 1976.
Montelius, Oscar, 'Solgudens yxa och Tors hammare', *Svenska Fornminnesföreningens tidskrift*, 10, 1900, 277–296.
Motz, Lotte, 'New thoughts on an archaic artifact', *The mankind quarterly*, 32:3, Spring, 1992, 231–240.
*MRN* = E. O. G. Turville-Petre, *Myth and religion of the North. The religion of ancient Scandinavia*, 1964.
*MS* = *Medieval Scandinavia. An encyclopedia*, ed. Phillip Pulsiano, 1993.
Müllenhoff, Karl, *Die Germania des Tacitus*, 1900.
Munch, 1922 = *Norrøne gude- og heltesagn* ordnet og fremstillet av P. A. Munch; tredje utgave . . . ved Magnus Olsen, 1922.
Nerman, Birger, *Sveriges första storhetstid*, 1942.
*New Larousse encyclopedia of mythology*, new ed., 1968.
*NG* = Axel Olrik and Hans Ellekilde, *Nordens gudeverden*, 2 vols, 1926–1951.
*Nihongi. Chronicles of Japan from the earliest times to A.D. 697*, 2 vols, trans. W. G. Aston, 1896, reprint: 1956.
Nilsson, Bruce E., 'The runic 'fish-amulet' from Öland: a solution', *Medieval Scandinavia*, 9, 1976, 236–245.
*NK* = *Nordisk kultur*, 32 vols, 1931–1956.
*NO* = Leiv Heggstad, Finn Hødnebø, Erik Simensen, *Norrøn ordbok*, 1975.
*Norðanfari*, 10th February, 1870.
Norlén, Gunnar, '"Blås Kajsa." Kring en svensk sjömanstradition', *Skrifter utgivna av Religionshistoriska Institutionen i Uppsala*, 10, 1972, 61– 83.
Novikova, Galina L., 'Iron neck-rings with Thor's hammers found in Eastern Europe', *Fornvännen*, 87, 1992, 73–89.
*NS* = Jørn Sandnes and Ola Stemshaug (eds), *Norsk stadnamnleksikon*, 1976.
*Nynorskordboka. Definisjons- og rettskrivingsordbok*, ed. Magne Rommetveit *et al.*, 2nd ed., 1986.
*OA* = *Oldtidens Ansigt. Faces of the past. Til Hendes Majestæt Dronning Margrethe II, 16. april 1990*, ed. Poul Kjærum and Rikke Agnete Olsen, 1990.
Obolensky, Dimitri, *The Byzantine Commonwealth*, 1974.
*ÓH* = *Saga Óláfs konungs hins helga. Den store saga om Olav den hellige efter pergamenthåndskrift i Kungliga Biblioteket i Stockholm nr. 2 4$^{to}$*, ed. Oscar Albert Johnsen and Jón Helgason, 1941.

*ÓHLeg = Ólafs saga hins helga. Efter pergamenthaandskrift i Uppsala Universitetsbibliotek, Delagardieske samling nr. 8^{II}*, ed. Oscar Albert Johnsen, 1922.

Ólafur Halldórsson, 'Um Húsafellsbók', *Minjar og menntir. Afmælisrit helgað Kristjáni Eldjárn*, ed. Guðni Kolbeinsson, 1976, 391–406.

Ólafur Halldórsson (ed.), *The great sagas of Olaf Tryggvason and Olaf the Saint. AM 61, fol.*, 1982.

Ólafur Halldórsson, 'Lidt om kilderne til Den store saga om Olav Tryggvason', *Selskab for Nordisk Filologi, København. Årsberetning 1987–1989*, 1990, 46–57.

Ólafur Halldórsson (ed.), *The saga of King Olaf Tryggvason. AM 62 fol.*, 1993.

OM = Olaus Magnus, *Historia om de nordiska folken*, 1982.

*ONP = Ordbog over det norrøne prosasprog. Registre.* 1989.

*ÓT = Óláfs saga Tryggvasonar en mesta*, ed. Ólafur Halldórsson, 3 vols, 1958–2000.

*ÓTOdd = Saga Óláfs Tryggvasonar af Oddr Snorrason munk*, ed. Finnur Jónsson, 1932.

Page, R. I., *Norse myths*, 1990.

Perkins, Richard, 'Rowing chants and the origins of *dróttkvæðr háttr*', *Saga-Book*, 21:3–4, 1984–1985, 155–221.

Perkins, Richard, 'The Eyrarland image. Þrymskviða, *stanzas 30–31*', *Sagnaþing helgað Jónasi Kristjánssyni sjötugum 10. apríl 1994*, ed. Gísli Sigurðsson et al. 1994, 653–664.

Perkins, Richard, 'The gateway to Trondheim: Two Icelanders at Agdenes', *Saga-Book*, 25:2, 1999, 179–213.

Perkins, Richard, '*Potenti murmure verborum grandia cete maris in littora trahunt*', *Studien zur Isländersaga. Festschrift für Rolf Heller*, ed. Heinrich Beck and Else Ebel, 2000, 223–230.

Pierson, William (ed.), *Matthäus Prätorius' Delicae Prussicae oder Preußische Schaubühne*, 1871.

*PL = Patrologiæ cursus completus, Series latina*, ed. J.-P. Migne, 221 vols, 1844–1864.

Pushkina, 1984 = Т. А. Пушкина, Бронзовый идол из Черной Могилы, «Вестник Московского Университета. Серия 8: История», 3, May–June, 1984, 86–87.

Rafn, Carl Christian (trans.), *Kong Olaf Tryggvesøns Saga* in vols I– III (1826–1827) of *Oldnordiske Sagaer udgivne i Oversættelse af Det nordiske Oldskrift-Selskab*, 12 vols, 1826–1837.

Ramskou, Thorkild, 'Lindholm Høje', *Acta archaeologica*, 26, 1955 (1956), 177–185.
Reuterswärd, Patrik, 'Windows of divine light', *Konsthistorisk tidskrift*, 51, 1982, 95–102.
$RGA^1$ = *Reallexikon der germanischen Altertumskunde*, ed. Johannes Hoops, 4 vols, 1911–1919.
$RGA^2$ = *Reallexikon der germanischen Altertumskunde von Johannes Hoops*. Zweite, völlig neu bearbeitete und stark erweitete Auflage, ed. Heinrich Beck et al., 1973– .
RI = the bronze figure from Rällinge, Södermanland, Sweden (SHM 14232; cf. Figure 15).
RPC = *The Russian primary chronicle. Laurentian text*, trans. Samuel Hazzard Cross and Olgerd P. Sherbowitz-Wetzor, 1973.
RR = *Rǫgnvalds þáttr ok Rauðs* (see Appendix (I) and references there).
RR557 = The version of *Rǫgnvalds þáttr ok Rauðs* preserved in AM 557, 4to (see Appendix; references are to *ÓT*, III)
RRÓT = The version of *Rǫgnvalds þáttr ok Rauðs* preserved in *ÓT* (see Appendix; references are to *ÓT*, I).
Rybakov, 1949 = Б. А. Рыбаков, Древности Чернигова, «Материалы и исследования ло археологии СССР», 11, 1949, 7–93.
*Saga boutique. Tax free. Summer, 1994*. Issued by Icelandair/Flugleiðir, 1994.
Salin, Bernhard, 'Några ord om en Fröbild', *Opuscula archæologica Oscari Montelio septuagenario dicata*, 1913, 405–411.
Samokvasov, 1908 = Д. Самоквасовъ, Могилы Русской земли, 1908.
Saxo = *Saxonis Gesta Danorum*, ed. J. Olrik and H. Ræder, 1931.
Schach = Roswin Finkenzeller, Wilhelm Ziehr and Emil M. Bührer, *Schach. 2000 Jahre Spiel-Geschichte*, 1989.
Schetelig, Haakon, 'Fortegnelse over de til Bergens Museum i 1902 indkomne sager ældre end reformationen', *Bergens Museums aarbog 1903. Afhandlinger og aarsberetning*, 1904, 3, 1–39.
Schnall, Uwe, *Navigation der Wikinger*, 1975.
Schomerus, Rudolf, *Die Religion der Nordgermanen im Spiegel christlicher Darstellung*, 1936.
Sephton, J. (trans.), *The saga of King Olaf Tryggwason*, 1895.

Shetelig, Haakon, 'Islands graver og oldsaker fra vikingetiden', *Viking*, I, 1937, 205–219.
SHM = Statens Historiska Museum, Stockholm.
*Skj* = Finnur Jónsson (ed.), *Den norsk-islandske skjaldedigtning*, 4 vols, 1912–1915.
Skjølsvold, Arne, 'Et eiendommelig smedgravfunn fra Mysen', *Universitetets Oldsaksamling. Årbok 1949–1950*, 1951, 34–48.
Skovmand, Roar, 'De danske Skattefund fra Vikingetiden og den ældste Middelalder indtil omkring 1150', *Aarbøger for nordisk Oldkyndighed og Historie*, 1942, 1–275.
Śliwa, Joachim, 'Some remarks on the aegyptiaca found in Poland', *Hommages à Jean Leclant*. Volume 3: *Études isiaques*, ed. Catherine Berger *et al.*, 1994, 461–468.
*SnE* = *Edda Snorra Sturlusonar*, ed. Finnur Jónsson, 1931.
*SnE* 1998 = Snorri Sturluson, *Edda. Skáldskaparmál*, ed. Anthony Faulkes, 1998.
Solheim, Svale, *Nemningsfordomar ved fiske*, 1940.
Spence, Lewis, *Myth and ritual in dance, game, and rhyme*, 1947.
*Stakar rímur frá 16., 17., 18. og 19. öld*, ed. Finnur Sigmundsson, 1960.
Steenstrup, Johannes, *Normandiets Historie under de syv første Hertuger 911–1066*, 1925.
Steenstrup, Johannes, 'Hammer og Kors', *Arkiv för nordisk filologi. Tilläggsband till band XL, ny följd. Studier tillägnade Axel Kock*, 1929, 44–61.
Stefán Karlsson, 'Ritun Reykjarfjarðarbókar. Excursus: Bókagerð bænda', *BA*, 30, 1970, 120–140.
Stephens, George, *Thunor the Thunderer, carved on a Scandinavian font of about the year 1000*, 1878.
Stephensen, Björn, 'Ljóðabréf', *Sunnanfari*, 13:9, September, 1914, 66–67.
*Stjorn. Gammelnorsk Bibelhistorie fra Verdens Skabelse til det babyloniske Fangenskab*, ed. C. R. Unger, 1862.
Ström, Krister, 'Thorshammerringe und andere Gegenstände des heidnischen Kults', *Birka II:1. Systematische Analysen der Gräberfunde*, ed. Greta Arwidsson, 1984, 127–140.
Strömbäck, Dag, *Sejd*, 1935.

Strömbäck, Dag (ed.), *The Arna-Magnæan manuscript 557 4to*, 1940.
Strömbäck, Dag, 'Att helga land', *Folklore och filologi*, 1970, 135–165.
*Sturlunga saga*, ed. Kr. Kålund, 2 vols, 1906–1911.
Sveinbjörn Egilsson (Egilssonius) (trans.), *Historia Olavi Tryggvii filii* in vols I–III (1828–1829) of *Scripta historica islandorum de rebus gestis veterum borealium latine reddita*, 12 vols, 1828–1846.
*Sverris saga etter Cod. AM 327 4º*, ed. Gustav Indrebø, 1920.
Sö = *Södermanlands runinskrifter*, ed. Erik Brate and Elias Wessén, 1924–1936. (References are to the number of the inscription.)
Sö 86 = runic carving on a rock at Norra Åby, Södermanland, Sweden (cf. Figure 20 and Note 6 in Chapter 3).
Sö 111 = rune-stone at Stenkvista church, Södermanland, Sweden (cf. Figure 21).
Söderwall, K. F., *Ordbok öfver svenska medeltids-språket*, 3 vols, 1884–1918.
Tacitus, Cornelius, *Germania*, ed. and trans. Alf Önnerfors, 1961.
Tacitus, *The Agricola and the Germania*, trans. H. Mattingly, revised by S. A. Handford, 1970.
Taylor, Paul Beekman, 'Quetzalcóatl and the Norse gods', *The International Saga Society newsletter*, 5, 1991, 1–3.
*Thómas saga erkibyskups. A life of Archbishop Thomas Becket, in Icelandic with English translation, notes and glossary*, ed. Eiríkr Magnússon, 2 vols, 1875–1883.
Thomsen, Vilhelm, *The relations between ancient Russia and Scandinavia and the origin of the Russian state*, 1877.
Thorlacius, [B.] and C. J. Thomsen, 'Fortegnelse paa de Oldsager, som fra 1816 til 1820 ved Gave eller Kiøb ere komne til Museet', *Antiqvariske Annaler*, 3, 1820, 352–410.
Thoroddsen, Theodora, *Ritsafn*, ed. Sigurður Nordal, 1960.
Trotzig, Gustaf, 'Den gamla och den nya religionen', *Gutar och vikingar*, ed. Ingmar Jansson, 1983, 357–394.
Trotzig, Gustaf, *Vikingar*, 1995.
Turville-Petre, G., 'Thurstable', *English and medieval studies presented to J. R. R. Tolkien on the occasion of his seventieth birthday*, ed. Norman Davis and C. L. Wrenn, 1962, 241–249.
Turville-Petre, E. O. G., *Scaldic poetry*, 1976.
U = *Upplands runinskrifter*, ed. Elias Wessén and Sven B. F. Jansson, 4 vols, 1940–1958. (References are to the number of the inscription.)
U 1161 = rune-stone at Altuna church, Uppland, Sweden.

Usener, H., 'Zwillingsbildung', *Strena Helbigiana sexagenario obtulerunt amici*, 1900, 315–33.
*VABC* = Carin Orrling (ed.), *Vikingatidens ABC*, 2nd ed., 1995.
*VAch* = Peter Foote and David M. Wilson, *The Viking achievement*, 1970.
van Houts, Elisabeth M. C., 'Scandinavian influence in Norman literature of the eleventh century', *Anglo-Norman studies VI. Proceedings of the Battle Conference 1983*, ed. R. Allen Brown, 1984, 107–121.
*VArt* = James Graham-Campbell, *Viking artefacts*, 1980.
*Veraldar saga*, ed. Jakob Benediktsson, 1944.
Vg = *Västergötlands runinskrifter*, ed. Hugo Jungner and Elisabeth Svärdström, 1940–1970. (References are to the number of the inscription.)
Vg 113 = rune-stone near Grästorp (Lärkegapet), Bjärby parish, Västergötland, Sweden (cf. Figure 19).
*VH* = *Viking og Hvidekrist. Norden og Europa 800–1200, Den 22. Europarådudstilling*, ed. Else Roesdahl, 1992.
*Vikingatid* = Maj Odelberg, Lena Thålin-Bergman and Inger Zachrisson, *Vikingatid*, 1982.
Watson, Lyall, *Heaven's breath. A natural history of the wind*, 1984.
Wessén, Elias (ed.), *Fornsvenska texter*, 1959.
Whaley, Diana, *Heimskringla. An introduction*, 1991.
*WM* = *Wörterbuch der Mythologie* herausgegeben von H. W. Haussig. Erste Abteilung: *Die alten Kulturvölker*. Band II: *Götter und Mythen im alten Europa*, 1973.
Würth, Stefanie, *Elemente des Erzählens. Die þættir der Flateyjarbók*, 1991.
Þjms = Þjóðminjasafn Íslands, Reykjavík.
Þór Magnússon, 'Bátkumlið í Vatnsdal í Patreksfirði', *Árbók Hins íslenzka fornleifafélags 1966*, 1967, 5–32.
Þorlákur Þórarinsson, 1780 = *Nockur Liood-mæle . . . Þorlaaks Þorarens Sonar*, 1780.
Ög = *Östergötlands runinskrifter*, ed. Erik Brate, 1911–1918. (References are to the number of the inscription.)
Ög 181 = rune-stone at Ledberg church, Östergötland, Sweden (cf. Figures 13 and 14).
ÖLM = Örebro Läns Museum.
*Qrvar-Odds saga*, ed. R. C. Boer, 1888.
Aasen, Ivar, *Norsk Ordbog*, 2nd ed., 3rd printing, 1918.